Because It Is Right

Because It Is Right

INTEGRATION IN HOUSING

James L. Hecht

Little, Brown and Company

Boston • Toronto

LIBRARY OF CONGRESS CATALOG CARD NO. 74–121436

01366 W0511 T10/70

Second Printing

"Incident" from *On These I Stand* by Countee Cullen copyright,
1925, by Harper & Brothers; renewed 1953 by Ida M. Cullen. Reprinted by permission of Harper & Row, Publishers, Inc.

Published simultaneously in Canada
by Little, Brown & Company (Canada) Limited

PRINTED IN THE UNITED STATES OF AMERICA

To Amy . . . for so much.

Acknowledgments

Hundreds of people who believed in the purpose of this book voluntarily assisted the author. It is only possible to mention here those who devoted many, many hours, or made unique and indispensable contributions.

The Right Reverend Harold B. Robinson and the Right Reverend Lauriston L. Scaife, Bishops of the Episcopal Diocese of Western New York, introduced the author to the publisher. Their indispensable support of the proposed project was aided by several others: the late Charles A. Pearce of Tarrytown, New York, and Daniel R. Acker, Dr. Ralph W. Loew and Marian North of Buffalo.

This book could never have been written had not the author's employer, E. I. du Pont de Nemours and Company, been the sort of company it is. Also, many of the author's associates at Du Pont assisted with the book. Two deserve special mention: John J. Burchenal and Dr. Robert E. Naylor, Jr., both of Wilmington, Delaware. Their support of the project was augmented by substantial assistance in obtaining material and in reviewing the manuscript.

The author was greatly aided by Mary Constance McCarthy, now of the University of Chicago, and Mary Lee

Xanco of the State University of New York at Buffalo — two professional librarians who volunteered their talents as research assistants.

A small group of dedicated people carefully read and skillfully criticized the entire manuscript: Dr. Charles H. Blatchford III, University of Hawaii; Edward W. Blatchford of New York; Dr. Arthur D. Butler, State University of New York at Buffalo; Nancy DeRoin of Chicago; Marian Nichol of Buffalo; and LeRoy E. Smith, Buffalo *Evening News*.

The following reviewed parts of the manuscript, and most of them helped in gathering material for the book: Anthony Bannon, Buffalo *Evening News*; Lucie Buchbinder of San Francisco; Patrick J. Cea, New York State Department of State; Donna Cervini of Oak Park, Illinois; Robert W. Chandler, the Ford Foundation; Monsignor John J. Conniff of Buffalo; Eugene P. Conser, National Association of Real Estate Boards; Dr. Thomas J. Dougherty of Buffalo; Anthony L. Dutton of Buffalo; Dr. William C. Fischer, State University of New York at Buffalo; Dr. L. Saxon Graham, State University of New York at Buffalo; John P. Guttenberg, Jr., Xerox Corporation; James Harvey, formerly of the American Friends Service Committee; Betty Hoeber of New York; Edward L. Holmgren of Chicago; Dr. John F. Kain, Harvard University; Reverend Robinson G. Lapp of Denver; Reverend George Laurent of Baltimore; Howard W. Lewis, Jr. of Palo Alto, California; Samuel H. Liberman II of St. Louis; T. Forrester Lord of Houston; Michael Mazer, formerly with OEO in Washington; Davis McEntire, University of California at Berkeley; Margy Meyerson of Buffalo; Morris Milgram of Philadelphia; Reverend Robert B. Moore, formerly of Buffalo; William R. Morris, NAACP; Dr. Richard C. Pearce, State University College at Buffalo; Laurence D. Pearl, HUD, Washington; Sol Rabkin, Anti-Defamation

League of B'nai B'rith; Thomas V. Rafferty, OEO, Atlanta; Sol Robinson, the Urban Coalition; William J. Salman of Houston; Carol Schiller of Los Angeles; Reverend Howard Smith, formerly of Chicago; James E. Wallace, formerly of Buffalo; Dr. Richard B. Warnecke, State University of New York at Buffalo; Ellee Workman of Philadelphia; and George E. Wyatt, Jr. of Buffalo. All of these, and many others not mentioned, made important contributions to the book. However, any errors of fact or judgment are the sole responsibility of the author.

The author would be remiss if he did not acknowledge the efficiency and cooperation of his secretary, Kathleen M. Evers.

A good editor is expected to influence every page of a manuscript for which he is responsible. However, this was only part of the contribution of Charles B. Everitt of Little, Brown. It was he who caused the author to frame the book in terms of the entire nation rather than to write primarily about Buffalo.

Since it is almost perfunctory for a married author to thank his wife, I hope I do justice here to mine. More than anyone else, Amy B. Hecht made this book possible — not merely by her encouragement, assistance and advice but, above all else, by motivating me to do what I have done because it was right.

J.L.H.

Introduction

To deplore is far easier than to change. Many books describe and analyze the problems of the Negro in America, but few give much detail on the focal point of this book: methods that have succeeded in achieving change.

Because It Is Right is about discrimination in housing, how it can be ended, and what is needed to achieve integration. As we shall see, America's race problem will never be solved until we have integration in housing. Thus the relevance of this book is even greater today than before voices were raised for black separatism and benign neglect.

Special emphasis is given to the Buffalo area and a fair housing group there called HOME (Housing Opportunities Made Equal). There are two reasons. Buffalo is where the author lives and the area about which he can write most knowledgeably. Equally important, people in Buffalo have brought about changes that few believed could happen.

This book deals only with the problems of ending discrimination in housing and achieving racial integration. But anyone who seeks to alter our society should find the book helpful in the formulation of strategy and tactics, and a source of hope that great changes are possible within the framework of law and with respect for the rights of all.

Contents

ACKNOWLEDGMENTS   *vii*

INTRODUCTION   *xi*

1/*Discrimination*   3

2/*The Myths and the Truths*   23

3/*The Villains and the Mavericks*   49

4/*The Law and Its Enforcement*   70

5/*The Fair Housing Group —*
   Its Strategy and Tactics   107

6/*The Church*   128

7/*A Promise Kept*   158

8/*The Employer*   173

9/*The Black Side*   198

10/*The Activists*   219

11/*The Hopes and the Challenges*   253

NOTES   *281*

Because It Is Right

1 / Discrimination

"IF YOU HAVE NOT gone through it yourself you cannot know what it is like."

The audience listened intently to the fashionably dressed, sepia-skinned woman standing before them. Joanne Champion told how she and her husband had spent seven months finding a house in 1963, before there was an effective anti-discrimination law in New York State. Because the Champions were aware that they would have problems, they had made their requirements very flexible — so flexible that every real estate broker they telephoned immediately said he could surely find something for them. But then, before going through with an appointment which might prove embarrassing, Mrs. Champion would add, "We are a Negro family."

Six brokers were contacted in this way. Through a multiple listing system, each had access to the listings of over 150 other firms. Yet five made no appointments; the sixth called once — to offer a house in an area adjacent to the ghetto.

Mrs. Champion tried answering ads placed by people who were selling their homes themselves. The "We are a Negro family," however, was all that seemed to matter. The typical response was "We have to think about it" or "I'll have to speak to my husband — and then I'll call you back." But the promised calls never came. One woman said she would show her house provided Mrs. Champion got most of the neighbors to sign a petition stating they would not object. When Mrs. Champion said she did not think it necessary that the neighbors approve her seeing the house, the woman — her annoyance clearly evident — terminated negotiations by saying, "I didn't expect you to be the type who cared about the neighbors."

What type of woman was Joanne Champion? A graduate of Wellesley College, with a master's degree in zoology from the University of Michigan, she was married to a doctor, had three children between the ages of three and eight, taught science at a private girls' school, and served on the women's committee of the Albright-Knox Art Gallery.

On one occasion Dr. and Mrs. Champion answered an ad placed by a real estate broker and went to see the house without mentioning in advance they were Negro. The broker, after showing them the house, expressed surprise that they did not want to buy it. The Champions explained that this house did not appeal to them, but they would like to see others. None was offered.

Fortunately, they did see some other houses. Hard work by several Negro real estate brokers uncovered four possibilities. Three more came through the personal efforts of fair housing activists. In seven months the Champions saw eight houses before they bought one in an all-white area.

Mrs. Champion recalled the difficulties her father, a Harvard-trained physician, had encountered when he tried to buy a house in an all-white area in Jersey City twenty years earlier. "I remember how frustrated he was and how mad we all were. But there is nothing like having it happen to you. . . . I had encountered prejudice in the South, but there you expected it and were ready to take it. The subtlety here hurts more."

As Joanne Champion continued her talk she spoke more slowly, groping for the right words. "It is something that hurts very deeply . . . it was the first time I became really aware of what it was like . . . it hurts in another way also. Negroes work hard for their money. To find that they cannot get the same for their dollar as a white person — that is one of the toughest things they have to take. If you are white, you don't need to have anything but money. Your future neighbors don't investigate you before they let you buy a house. But if you are a Negro you face discrimination no matter who you are, no matter what type of standards you have, no matter what you have achieved."

If Joanne Champion's story is not typical of what has happened to countless Negro families throughout the nation, that is only because the Champions had the patience, the skill and the connections to succeed. Discrimination in the Buffalo area in the early 1960's was relatively typical of that in the nation. Also typical was the pattern of segregation which resulted. According to 1960 census data, 52,000 Negroes were crowded into seven of Erie County's 162 census tracts, yet over 75 percent of the census tracts were "all-white" — a vast area of 800,000 people of whom fewer than one tenth of one percent were Negroes. Moreover, many of the Negroes in these all-white areas were servants and caretakers, who have always been welcome to live among whites. The rest consisted of about 70 "pioneer" families — families who had been the first to move into white areas.

In these all-white areas only one or two percent of the housing was available to Negroes, and for a family to locate this housing was generally impossible. Very few are willing to endure the strain of constant rejection.

No exceptions were made to the practice of discrimination, not even for a celebrity such as Ernie Warlick. Now a sports commentator for WGR in Buffalo, Warlick was the star end of the Buffalo Bills when he looked for nonghetto housing in 1963. Although he was the sort of person who commanded attention wherever he went, a popular after-dinner speaker, and the idol of many young people, when Warlick decided to buy a home in the town of Amherst, an "exclusive" suburb with some 80,000 middle-income white residents, the first real estate broker he asked to help him said, "Ernie, you wouldn't be happy here." Others refused to cooperate and gave no explanation.

More typical of the Negro who sought housing outside the ghetto is Henry Wilson, a foreman at a steel plant. He and his wife Marcella started looking soon after New York State's antidiscrimination law went into effect. When they found a house which they liked in South Buffalo, they offered the asking price of $13,900. However, the real estate broker informed them they also would have to assume the mortgage, which would necessitate a down payment of $8,800, far in excess of the $1,000 they were prepared for. Shortly thereafter the house was sold to a white for $13,000 and a down payment of $500.

Harold Amos, a postal clerk, had even greater difficulties. He started looking for a house outside the ghetto in 1959. Although he was assisted by many people, it was not until four years later, with the help of New York's antidiscrimination law, that he moved into his new home. Despite the law, the builder almost managed to avoid the sale because specifications which the builder submitted to the Federal Housing Administration as part of the required procedure for a mortgage approval contained an "error." Although the house was a standard design used by the builder, one of the dimensions in the specifications was five feet too long. This delayed approval of the mortgage application until two days before the deadline for the sales contract. The builder was immediately notified, but he claimed that he did not receive notification until after he had sold the house to another buyer on the day the conditional sales contract expired. Fortunately, the other buyer immediately relinquished any claim when informed by the Amoses' lawyer that legal action was planned to void the sale.

Charles Broadus grew up on a sharecropper farm in Georgia. Life on the farm was hard; he was twelve before he first used an indoor toilet. When he was fifteen he came to Buffalo and, while finishing high school, lived with an older brother and worked part time as a busboy at the Hotel Stat ler. Eventually he found a job as an automation tender on the production line at the Ford plant. He practiced thrift. When he married in 1958 at the age of twenty-seven, he had enough money for a down payment on a house.

In the South, Charles Broadus had heard that everyone in the North was treated equally. Consequently, when he saw an advertisement for a house which met his requirements and was located near his job, he went to the large Buffalo real estate company that had placed the ad. The man who waited on him made a telephone call. Upon returning he told Broadus that the house was sold and added, "You shouldn't look at these houses. Here's a book with the listings you should look at."

Broadus looked at the book. The houses were all in the Negro area. "Do any of these houses have a garage?" he asked.

"No, but a couple have driveways."

7

Some of Charles Broadus's friends had told him that a Negro could not buy in most places. He had found it hard to believe. . . . Now he knew.

There is nothing unique about what happened in Buffalo. The story has been the same everywhere. Fame and fortune seldom have made much difference. Willie Mays could not buy a house he wanted in San Francisco. Another star out-fielder, Curt Flood of the Cardinals, faced a white landlord who was armed with a gun when he tried to move into a California home. Mike Garrett, who received $300,000 to sign a pro football contract, could not rent an apartment in a white Kansas City neighborhood.[1]

When Dr. Percy L. Julian bought an expensive fifteen-room house in Oak Park in 1950, the color of his skin was more important to many people in that Chicago suburb than the fact that he was one of the nation's leading chemists. The water commissioner refused to turn on the water until the Julians threatened to go to court. There were threats by anonymous telephone callers, and an attempt was made to burn the house down. But Dr. Julian — then the chief of soy bean research for the Glidden Company and now the director of his own research institute, a man known throughout the scientific world for his synthesis of hormones and development of processes for their manufacture — hired private guards and moved into the house.[2] He still lives there.

Like most Negroes, Ralph Bunche, the Under-Secretary-General of the United Nations has not been immune from discrimination. Yet none of the unhappy experiences in his adult life remains as vivid as one which occurred when he was a boy in Los Angeles. He lived then with an uncle whose fair complexion made him not readily recognized as a Negro. As a result, the uncle was able to rent a house in a white area, but when the landlord became aware of his racial identity he had the locks changed on the doors while the family was away. Finding himself locked out, Bunche's uncle, a mild-tempered but physically strong man, broke the door open, refused to vacate the house for several months, and deducted the cost of repairing the door and changing the locks from the following month's rent.

Many cases of housing discrimination are disguised in such a way that the Negro family does not realize it is being deceived. This is particularly true for rental housing, which is in short supply in most cities. Because desirable apartments are quickly taken, an unsuspecting Negro family may never know the truth if, when they ask to rent an empty apartment, they are told, "I'm sorry, the apartment already has been rented, but please let me have your name and telephone number so that we can contact you if something else comes up soon."

Other subtle deceptions are used. A misrepresentation that in addition to the advertised rent the tenant will pay the utility bills, and that these run as high as $50 per month, may be enough to save the landlord from the problem of parrying an offer to rent. Sellers can falsely represent the price of a house. Another tactic is to claim that someone has bought the house or has an option to buy it, but the advertisements are continuing because of a contract with the newspaper.

But most Negro families seeking housing outside the ghetto have been quickly confronted with ugly realities. For example, in Buffalo, Dr. Frank Cole, a cancer research scientist, was directed to a low-income public housing project in a Negro area by a rental agent who had told him the $150 per month apartment he wished to rent was not available. Countless Negroes seeking to purchase a home have heard a real estate broker ask, "Do you really want to live here?" Usually the question was accompanied by an offer to see a "nice" house on a street in the ghetto.

There were many other obvious brush-offs. A homeowner who had just advertised his house for sale claimed he was not sure he was going to sell it. Another said, "I have a son who may want to buy it." Some homeowners even took their houses off the market to avoid selling. Details varied, but to Negroes looking for a place to live they all conveyed the message, "We don't want any niggers here."

Another tactic was stalling. Real estate brokers and rental agents frequently were unable to find the keys to houses and apartments which they were advertising. On one occasion an advertised apartment was not shown because it was claimed there were no light bulbs in it. It was common to break appointments, often without notification. In Buffalo a real estate broker apologized to a white civil rights worker for a week's delay in letting him see an advertised house. The broker explained the delay had been purposely caused; the civil rights worker had been mistaken for a Negro when he telephoned because he lived in the ghetto and had a Southern accent and an Anglo-Saxon name.

Some incidents had a touch of humor. One builder allowed a Negro family to look at a lot — at night. Another Negro family, getting out of their car to keep an appointment, saw a well-dressed woman with a frightened look scurry from the porch into the house. Within a few seconds all the lights went out. The Negro family rang the bell off and on for ten minutes, but no one came to the door. Each time they rang, the bell was clearly audible in the inhabited silence within.

Finding a new place to live, often an arduous task for whites, can become a nightmare for a Negro family. The many trips and appointments which are a necessary part of the normal homeseeking process become agonizing when combined with frustration and rejection. The normal difficulty of deciding when to give notice or to sell one's present house is compounded by the terrible uncertainties that result from discrimination in housing.

No white can fully comprehend the degradation and humiliation experienced by black families who encounter discrimination. At best, whites can remember how they felt when they were rejected: the emptiness a girl feels when the boy she likes stops calling; the anxiety a man experiences when he is not consulted or informed about something which concerns him at work; the sting and hurt which go with any snub. But even then it is difficult to project what it must mean to a family to be denied a home they want and can afford. They are not only deprived of a home; they are deprived of something to which they believe they have a right.

Shakespeare attempted to describe the agony of discrimination when Shylock said:[3]

> Hath not a Jew eyes? hath not a Jew hand organs, dimensions, senses, affections, passions? fed with the same food, hurt with the same weapons, subject to the same diseases, healed by the same means, warmed and cooled by the same winter and summer. . . . If you prick us, do we not bleed? if you tickle us, do we not laugh? if you poison us, do we not die? and if you wrong us, shall we not revenge?

Some Negroes fight discrimination. But the great majority avoid such a debilitating experience. Instead they pay a different price. They live in the ghetto.

The law of supply and demand dictates that rents in the ghetto will be higher than those charged for equivalent quarters in more desirable neighborhoods. For example, in Buffalo the Negro population of about 85,000 is increasing by about 2,000 per year. Thus even though the ghetto area slowly spreads out, the housing demand continually exceeds the supply. As a result the average Negro family in Buffalo spends about $15 per month more for rent than white families with equivalent quarters. In fact, the 1960 census data show that the median rental paid by Negro families in Buffalo was $74 per month, only one dollar less than that paid by whites, but that the Negroes were living in dwellings which had less space and were of poorer quality.

The same is true in every other large urban area in the United States. It has been estimated that Chicago's nearly one million Negroes pay an average of $20 per month more rent than do whites with similar housing.[4] In certain census tracts in Chicago, both whites and Negroes paid a median rental of $88 in 1960, but the average number of rooms for non-whites was 3.35 compared to 3.95 for whites, and 31 percent of the black families lived in units which were deteriorated or dilapidated compared with only 12 percent of the whites.[5]

It is indeed ironic that Negroes, whose incomes average so much less than whites', must pay more for housing. It is this "color tax," as well as poverty, which accounts for the appalling housing in which so many Negroes live. In Cleveland, Dallas, Detroit, Kansas City and St. Louis over one-third of Negro families pay more than 35 percent of their income for rent.[5] Yet many of these families live in inadequate housing. In America's cities, 15 percent of black families have no hot water, 15 percent share bathrooms with other families, and 21 percent have no bathtub or shower available. [6]

The Negro living in the ghetto is usually limited in the types of housing available to him. New houses and houses on lots of reasonable size are at best scarce. In Buffalo there probably is not a single private home in the ghetto with a backyard as large as those found in relatively inexpensive housing in nearby suburbs. Also, in Buffalo's ghetto area there are fewer than a hundred private homes less than twenty-five years old and, except for public housing projects, most rental units in the area are over forty years old. One exception is a new moderate-income development of 230 units financed by a federal government program. Currently there is a waiting list of over 300 families for these apartments, which rent between $90 and $123 per month.

The greatest hardship of all is the ghetto itself. It is not merely that the houses are old, there are no spacious lawns, and the area is overcrowded. Most of all, it is a place where Negroes know they must live and whites know it also.

Robberies are everyday occurrences. It is the inevitable result of close proximity with those who have no hope for the future. Yet the police, who should be viewed as protectors, are viewed as enemies. Police insensitivity is part of the heavy cross the ghetto dweller must bear. It is not only the sensational incidents of brutality which make the newspapers; it is the everyday harassments: a shove, the needless use of a nightstick, the insulting "get a move on, boy."

There is no escape from danger. Fire spreads death and destruction with terrifying speed. Rats bite people in their beds, carrying diseases such as leptospirosis, Haverhill fever and relapsing fever. The 15,000 cases of rat-bite reported annually in the United States occur mostly in ghetto slums, and many cases of rat-bite never are reported. In Cleveland rats were found in 7,000 of the 30,000 structures inspected.[7]

The children in the ghetto play amid the garbage in the streets because there are not enough playgrounds or youth programs. They go to old, overcrowded schools where almost all the children are black. Their teachers, many of whom are not fully certified and most of whom have little experience, further cripple their educational attainment by low expectations. The result: more than three times as many black students drop out of high school as whites; of those who make it, their performance on standard achievement tests averages 3.3 years below that of whites.[5]

Most of the women shop in drab neighborhood stores where the prices usually are higher than in other parts of the city, or where poorer quality is marketed at the same price. Those who understand this and who are able to do so, shop outside of the ghetto.

The great majority of ghetto residents dislike the street gangs, the prostitutes and the loiterers. But they regard these people with far less resentment than the white men who cruise the area and proposition respectable women on the streets.

To live in the ghetto is not pleasant. Yet for many the worst part of all is that there is no choice. As James Baldwin wrote in *Nobody Knows My Name*: "The people in [the ghetto] know they are living there because white people do not think they are good enough to live anywhere else. No amount of 'improvement' can sweeten this fact."

The problems of black Americans have mistakenly become associated in the minds of many people only with the ghettos in the cities. This is because in the cities there has been rebellion and the problems of the Negro have become those of the entire community. But almost ten million blacks, nearly half of those in the nation, do not live in the hundred largest cities. Many are still in small Southern communities; the remainder live in the North and the West in places where usually they are a minority of less than 10 percent.

These millions of black Americans who do not live in big city ghettos are often forgotten.

There is not much to say about open housing in small Southern communities. A dual housing market still is accepted by most blacks as a way of life. It was summarized by one white Southerner when he said, "We don't talk about that here."

While small Southern communities practice segregation, those outside the South practice hypocrisy. There is an inexcusable sophistry in the statement so often made by otherwise responsible citizens in small Northern communities that, "We haven't got any racial problem here. The colored people and the white people get along very well together . . . The colored do tend to live together, but they live on a number of different streets and white people live on the same blocks."

The reality is that white people think things are satisfactory because the blacks have no effective means by which they can do something about their grievances. While blacks go to school with whites, and some whites live in the same neighborhoods as Negroes, most housing is not available to blacks. As a result, in small communities where Negroes are a small minority, black families usually have a rough time finding places to live.

Circleville, Ohio, is such a town. It is as American as apple pie. Most of the thirteen thousand people who live in Circleville have pride in their community, the center of a rich agricultural area whose economy has been strengthened by new industry. But what has been good for the white people has not been as good for the blacks. The best evidence is in the statistics. Although the total population increased over 50 percent in the past twenty years, the black population decreased.

Most of those who left were young people looking for

better opportunities. However, Mr. and Mrs. James Bailey figured they would stay in Circleville, where they had grown up and their families still lived. In high school James had been the most valuable player on the football team and Carolyn, the daughter of a businessman, was a majorette in the band. But when they returned to Circleville, after Bailey had spent four years in the Marines, they could not find anyone who would rent them a suitable apartment, There were several available, but not to them. After much agony they finally got something through a friend of Mrs. Bailey's mother. Four years later, with Bailey a salesman for a lumber company and Mrs. Bailey holding a good office job at the GE plant, they were ready to buy a house. They could have afforded one in the good section of town, but because of discrimination they bought a house from a school friend of Mrs. Bailey's "around our neighborhood."

Another young Negro woman from Circleville also was frustrated by discrimination when she returned to live near her relatives. Finally, with the help of people from outside of the community, she found an apartment for herself and her children. The officers from the Lockbourne air base who assisted her had a special reason — her husband had died in Vietnam.

Housing discrimination is not, of course, directed only at Negroes. Puerto Ricans, Mexican-Americans, American Indians, Orientals and Jews continue to experience such discrimination and, on occasion, other minorities encounter problems. That such injustices persist increases the importance of ending discrimination against blacks. Progress made in reducing discrimination against Negroes helps eliminate the consequences of prejudice against others.

Less than a decade ago real estate brokers in Grosse Point, Michigan, hired private detectives to rate prospective home purchasers' "swarthiness," accent, dress, employment and education. A person of Polish descent needed fifty points to qualify; an Italian needed sixty-five; a Jew needed eighty-five; Negroes and Orientals were always excluded.

Today in New York City discrimination against Puerto Ricans almost equals that practiced against blacks. Mexican-Americans encounter serious discrimination in Texas and California. Although Orientals now face fewer barriers than five years ago, they still encounter some, particularly in California. The problems for Jews also are far fewer today than in the past, but there remain some upper middle-class and upper-class areas where Jews still are likely to be rebuffed when they attempt to buy a house.

Discrimination in housing is part of a cruel cycle which perpetuates the problems of the Negro.

The high rentals Negroes must pay often necessitate overcrowding. In the United States in 1960, 11 percent of nonwhite families, compared to 2 percent of white families, had 1.51 or more persons per room.[5] The resultant deterioration of living conditions and personal relationships greatly influences the families who live under these conditions. People who live in substandard, overcrowded housing tend to suffer poor health and to be passive and pessimistic.[8]

In addition, the Negro is profoundly affected as a person by the low self-image discrimination creates. John Howard Griffin, a white writer who posed as a Negro by undergoing a series of medical treatments which temporarily changed the color of his skin to black, wrote in *Black Like Me*, "The Negro sees and reacts differently not because he is Negro, but because he is suppressed. . . ." The adverse effects of segregated schools on the learning of Negro children have become well recognized. When the army was segregated, Negro soldiers committed four times more crimes than

17

whites; in the integrated army there has been very little difference in crime rates.[9] Similarly, all-black army units often performed poorly in combat; Negro soldiers in integrated units have given excellent performance. The message is unmistakable: discrimination not only denies equality, but causes America's blacks to be poorly prepared for equality.

Discrimination in housing also prevents what otherwise would be an effective way of breaking down traditional prejudices. Well-known psychologists such as Gordon Allport, Kenneth Clark, Morton Deutsch and Thomas Pettigrew have shown that while prejudices are caused in many ways, more favorable attitudes between whites and blacks usually result when there is equal-status interracial contact in a noncompetitive situation.[10]

People are prejudiced against the unfamiliar. White people avoid not only Negroes, but strange foods and those who dress differently from themselves. But if they live near Negroes, they see schoolchildren struggling with their homework, fathers worrying about the local baseball team, expectant mothers going through the problems of pregnancy, tenants complaining about landlords. As a result of this exposure, they recognize how much these "other" people are like themselves.

Another important factor is the relation between attitudes and behavior. Behavior is not the result of attitudes. Rather the two are closely interrelated, and attitudes often are altered as the result of behavior.[11] The phenomenon has been termed "cognitive dissonance." In simple terms, if someone behaves contrary to his attitudes, he tends to adjust his attitudes in the direction of his behavior. Thus a person may be moderately positive about a proposed purchase, such as a house or a car, but once the contract is signed his moderate attitude becomes stronger. Obviously the effect of cognitive dissonance will be to decrease unfavorable prejudices in in-

DISCRIMINATION

terracial housing situations in order that the attitude be
more consistent with the pattern of behavior. Conversely,
when people discriminate they will need to increase their
prejudicial attitudes to justify their behavior.

Group conformity is another source of prejudice. Conformity can affect some people so strongly that in a test situation they will designate the shorter of two lines as the longer
if several others already have made this choice. In an interracial housing situation, where most whites decrease their
prejudices, the effect of conformity will be to develop more
favorable attitudes. In all-white communities, however, conformity influences people to have unfavorable prejudices.

Unfortunate learning situations often cause prejudices. A
child who is told by his father that Negroes are dirty and
immoral has that prejudice until something changes it. Although prejudice rarely originates in personal experience, it
can happen: a woman who has had little contact with Negroes and has her purse snatched by a Negro youth may gen-
eralize that all Negroes are thieves. Obviously the contacts
afforded by close proximity in housing provide opportunities
for new perspectives.

Individual personalities are important. The insecure use
prejudice as a defense mechanism; they feel more important
when they can look down on someone else. This is somewhat
akin to the "scapegoat theory" which holds that prejudice is
the result of the redirected aggressions of those who experience frustrations from a source against which it is not
practical to retaliate. Prejudices also arise when there is
conflict caused by competition between blacks and whites.

There is, of course, no simple model which explains why
prejudices are formed or destroyed. Under some circumstances close interracial proximity causes negative attitudes
because of differences in status or conflicts in goals. But the
effect of interracial contact almost always is to decrease pre-

19

judices and improve attitudes. A man living in an interracial area in Illinois wisely noted, "Our prejudices are deeper than we know. We get over them only by living in the midst of experiences which contradict them."[12]

White Americans pay enormous penalties for the discrimination they practice.

Two-thirds of the people on the earth are not white. The relationship of the United States to governments representing this world majority ranges from uneasy acceptance to open hostility. But always this diplomatic relationship suffers because of our domestic racial problem. The leaders of non-white nations cannot help feeling that if Americans unfairly treat their own colored countrymen, they will certainly exploit foreigners who are colored. It is, of course, impossible to estimate how much our internal racial situation harms America's efforts to provide leadership towards world peace, but there is little doubt that it erodes our position. And it will continue to do so until discrimination disappears in housing and in other aspects of American life. In the meantime racial incidents in the United States will continue as top news stories abroad, particularly in Africa, and foreign nationals who have visited or studied in the United States will continue to return to their countries smarting from the discriminatory treatment they encountered.

The economic costs of the ghetto, a severe tax burden on the white community, are to a large extent chargeable to discrimination and the feelings of hopelessness it creates. Juvenile delinquency and adult crime in the ghetto are more than double that in the rest of the city. Police protection, although inadequate, costs far more than in other areas. Destruction of public property by vandalism is high and the cost of public assistance is disproportionately large.

Future costs may be even greater. A vicious cycle of decay

has started in our cities. As the Negro population builds up in the ghetto and fringe areas, middle-income whites move to suburban areas. The city's tax base is decreased, the public school system in the city becomes less academically competitive, and city services decline. As a result, more whites leave the city and the cycle is continued. If left unchecked, the cities will continue to decrease in population, municipal services will further deteriorate, and only the poor and the black will remain.

A different danger is that preoccupation with racial issues will so exhaust the energies of top public administrators that other problems, such as education, housing, transportation and pollution, will receive inadequate attention. Racial considerations also may lead to public actions contrary to the public interest. Atlanta's Mayor Ivan Allen, Jr. has noted, "We have not made a logical decision in Atlanta which has not been perverted by the race issue."

There also is a danger of more serious civil insurrections than in the past. History clearly demonstrates that logic is often the victim of emotion, and that the denial of basic rights breeds desperation and violence.

However, the most compelling reason of all to end discrimination was eloquently phrased by President John F. Kennedy when he urged Congress to pass a civil rights act, "not merely for reasons of economic efficiency, world diplomacy and domestic tranquility—but, above all, because it is right."

Discriminatory practices collide sharply with other values in our culture. Consequently, many people have feelings of guilt about the treatment that Negroes receive.[13] Even the worst bigots usually cannot condone their actions and therefore dress up racist movements with symbols of righteousness. The inner conflicts experienced by most of those who have prejudices have been termed "prejudice with compunction" by psychologist Gordon Allport. Swedish economist Gunnar Myrdal termed it "An American Dilemma."

Because discrimination is wrong, when we practice it we hurt ourselves. We deny our children the chance to witness the ideals of integrity, fair play and equality that we try to teach them. As a result of this duplicity, there is a conflict of values which increases the confusion of perplexed adolescents. For acts of commission by some and acts of omission by others, everyone pays a price.

Equally important is the opportunity which is lost. We deny ourselves a chance to be what we want to be, what we could be, what we ought to be, and what we would relish being.

2 / *The Myths and the Truths*

On December 29, 1963, most people in the Buffalo area were preoccupied with the holidays. But, with sudden swiftness, festivities were almost forgotten by the residents of Cindy Drive in the suburb of Amherst. On the day after Christmas one of their neighbors, Jack Watson, had sold his house to the Reverend Paul Smith, the associate director of the Buffalo Urban League and a Negro.

Cindy Drive is in the kind of area known as a "nice neighborhood." The $20,000-$25,000 homes were relatively new. Because people were friendly with their neighbors and often did things together, the immediate response of several people was that a meeting should be held to discuss the situation. About a dozen of the families living closest to the house which was sold were invited by the organizing group to a meeting on December 29.

Tension mounted. One of the neighbors telephoned the real estate broker who had sold the Watsons' house and demanded that a "sold" sign be placed in front so that if someone were going to bomb the house there would be no mistaking which was the right one. When the broker refused to put up a sign, the neighbor took a "sold" sign from the front of another home recently sold by the same real estate firm and placed it in front of the Watsons' house.

But at 174 Cindy Drive, Warren and Priscilla Hammond were thinking very differently. As the night of December 29 approached, their responsibility became clear. They were not civil rights people; in fact, they had never participated in any activity aimed at creating equal opportunities. However, to judge a person by the color of his skin was a violation of their religious beliefs and, as the time of the meeting approached, the Hammonds began to feel that no matter what the outcome, they had to support the Smiths. To do less would abrogate their profession of faith.

At the meeting there was at least one representative of each of the families hurriedly called together. Although not without fear, the Hammonds never faltered in their support of the right of the Smiths to buy on Cindy Drive and in their intention to make the Smiths feel welcome. Some of the others were noncommittal; most were strongly opposed. Some of the comments about the Paul Smiths coming to Cindy Drive indicated the undercurrents of prejudice:

"They may be charming, but some of their charm will rub off on their black friends who will want to join them."

"I can't understand how a man can want to do so much harm to a neighborhood."

"Why do they want to move where they aren't wanted?"

"The people who sponsored this wouldn't want one moving into their neighborhood and ruining their property values."

"Why don't they build separate housing?"

"If he is in the Urban League he must be either a radical or a martyr."

"If we ignore them maybe they'll move away."

Throughout the evening, concern was expressed that "more will come." Intermarriage was discussed at length.

One man said, "It's all Kennedy's fault. He put them up to it. But did he have any living next door to him?"

There was talk about possible measures to keep the Smiths out. The desire was there, but no acceptable plan emerged. In part this resulted from reminders by the Hammonds that the purchase of the house by the Smiths was not only their right, but was protected by law; in part the confused response was the result of the absence of any reasonable way to thwart the sale. By the time the meeting broke up a wait-and-see attitude was beginning to emerge, although it did appear that another meeting aimed at "action" would be held.

It never was held. There was plenty of talk, both in and out of the neighborhood. Several days later Priscilla Hammond received a telephone call from a friend who lived several miles away asking her if she had heard that a Negro family had bought a house somewhere on Cindy Drive. But with time, reason began to replace emotion. Some of the neighbors who at first had been noncommittal were now saying that the Smiths should be welcomed to the neighborhood. Some who previously had called for "action" now were saying that things weren't too bad, that Negro families were going to be moving to many suburban neighborhoods and at least they were getting a good family.

When the Smiths moved in about a month later, the excitement had died down. Several people helped welcome them. Others kept away. But the Smiths already had more friends and social life than they could handle. They had bought their home as a place to live, not as a means of meeting white people. They appreciated the friendly gestures of those who welcomed them; they did not care that there were some who ignored them, as long as they let them live in peace.

25

In Pittsburgh the cast was different, but the story was similar when an economics professor, moving to another city, sold his Hastings Street home to the Fosters, a Negro family. Dr. Lewis Foster was a physician whose family included three children and an attractive wife whose father was a basketball coach at a local university. When the news broke in the neighborhood, people who had hardly talked to each other for years were in frequent communication. Some typical remarks were:[1]

"They're moving in the school janitor and his ten children."

"They made a fortune selling to them."

"They'll throw garbage in the street and turn this into another Hill District."

"The NAACP placed them here."

"It's a big Negro numbers writer who'll set up here."

"How can I sit on my front porch and look at those black faces?"

Three people in the neighborhood attempted to have the economics professor fired from his new job. Another tried to buy the house. Several visited Mayor Lawrence, who refused to see them, and four or five threatened to sell immediately. However, as a result of the diligent efforts of a staff worker for Pittsburgh's Commission on Human Relations and active support of the Negro family by a couple who lived across the street, the neighborhood simmered down. When the Fosters moved in there were many friendly gestures and very few noticeably hostile ones. Because the Fosters' yard was the best suited for play in the neighborhood, it quickly became the congregating place for most of the children. However, one of the next-door neighbors remained antagonistic and eventually moved away.

There are too many variables to allow any example to be typical of what occurs when a Negro moves to a previously all-white neighborhood. But some generalization is possible. The events on Cindy Drive and Hastings Street demonstrate the emotional impact of initial Negro entry into a white area, the myths that people have come to believe, and the strong influence that individuals can have on what happens.

The intensity of the emotional response by whites to the entry of blacks into their neighborhood can be very strong. When a Negro family attempted to move to Cicero, Illinois, in 1951, thousands rioted for several days and martial law was necessary to restore order.[2] Less than a year later a mob estimated at four thousand attempted to burn a house in Chicago after they heard Negroes planned to move into the building.[2] Mob violence exploded in Levittown, Pennsylvania, in 1957 after William Meyers, a refrigeration technician, and his family became the first Negroes in that all-white community of sixty thousand.[3] In the Detroit suburb of Dearborn in 1966 a crowd, which at times reached three hundred, stoned a house into which they thought Negroes were going to move because the white man to whom the flat had been rented hired Negroes to move his furniture.[4] Later that year four hundred policemen were required to restore order in the Kensington area of Philadelphia after a young Negro family rented an apartment.[5]

A different type of mob action was used to keep Negroes out of Deerfield, Illinois, in 1959. With 95 percent of the eligible voters casting ballots, the residents of this middle class suburb of Chicago voted by more than two to one to condemn for parks two pieces of land which were being used for small developments of one-family houses planned for racially integrated occupancy.[6] A similar but less well-known case occurred in the all-white St. Louis suburb of Creve

Coeur in 1956 when the local board of aldermen condemned for a public park a two-acre site on which a Negro surgeon was building a $55,000 home.[7] Recently in Lackawanna, New York, the city council zoned for recreational use a thirty-acre site the development of which would have brought blacks into an all-white neighborhood.

Terror has been a standard procedure to preserve the racial homogeneity of neighborhoods in the South. Studies reporting on Negro housing in Atlanta and New Orleans not only document frequent incidents of arson and bombing, but also make clear that these often were done in collusion with the police.[8] Moreover, acts of terrorism have not been confined to the South. In 1953 attempts at Negro entry into white neighborhoods encountered arson, bombings or other forms of violence in Kansas City, East St. Louis, Cleveland, Indianapolis, Long Island and Los Angeles.[2] In the 1960's violence decreased, but did not end.[9]

Often combinations of such techniques were used to keep Negroes out. When a prominent philanthropist in an upstate New York city made available thirty acres of land in a nearby suburb for a housing development free of racial discrimination, there was no problem getting either a builder or financing. Although Negro occupancy in the development was forecast at less than 10 percent, when the plans were presented to the town council a councilman asked, "Is this the nigger project we have been hearing about?" The council deferred approval. At a public meeting shortly thereafter, a wealthy businessman opposing the project declared that he knew all people were equal and that Negroes had given their lives in the war, but that did not give them the right to rape white men's daughters. Rumors circulated that shacks on forty-foot lots would be built for eight hundred Negro families. Violent threats were made to the backers of the project. In the face of this opposition, the landowner withdrew his offer.[10]

Instances of mob action, condemnation proceedings, rezoning and terrorism do not occur often and their frequency is decreasing.[11] The most frequent tactic used to prevent a Negro from buying in a white area has been to bring pressure on the seller. Another method has been for people in a neighborhood to buy a house which otherwise might be sold to a Negro family. Thus when a Negro family in Buffalo attempted to purchase a house on Berryman Drive in suburban Snyder in 1963, a group of neighbors outbid the black family. The group took a loss of several thousand dollars so that they could prevent having as their neighbor the assistant dean of the School of Social Work at the State University of New York at Buffalo. In suburban Philadelphia a real estate broker earned commissions by persuading a neighborhood group to buy a house for later resale because the house initially had been listed with a nondiscriminatory broker. And in Oak Park, Illinois, a real estate broker bought a house himself rather than sell it to a Negro physics professor.[12]

A variety of factors determine what happens in a neighborhood about to experience initial Negro entry. One of the most significant is the location of the neighborhood relative to where Negroes live. Often there is little reaction when Negro entry takes place very near an existing Negro neighborhood, because people expect there will be racial transition and accept it when it comes. Exceptions to this occur, but usually only when there is some distinct physical boundary, such as railroad tracks or a main thoroughfare, between the Caucasian and Negro areas. Reactions are also usually moderate in neighborhoods far from large concentrations of blacks, but in an area where a number of Negro families already have pioneered nearby neighborhoods. The most violent reactions are likely to occur in all-white neighborhoods a short distance from large black areas.

The emotional responses generated on Cindy Drive were influenced by geography. While the nearest Negro neighborhoods were more than six miles away, there were only three Negro families within a radius of two miles, and most of the people on Cindy Drive were not aware of their presence.

The socioeconomic status of the Negro family and the neighborhood significantly affect neighborhood reaction. Acceptance is more rapid if the black family has higher socioeconomic status than the average in the neighborhood. And integration usually proceeds best in areas where the residents are well-educated and have high incomes. These people feel less threatened and are less likely to engage in antisocial behavior.

The general availability of housing for whites and Negroes, and the type and condition of the housing in the specific neighborhood are also important factors, particularly when the Negro family is moving into an area near a Negro neighborhood.

But most important is how people act.

A homeowner or landlord should not consult with neighbors about whether he should sell or rent to a Negro. Although it is unlawful to discriminate, if the question of Negro entry is presented to the neighborhood, it is certain to draw negative reactions. In addition, asking the question implies that something is wrong with Negro entry and that the neighbors have a right to participate in the decision. Any such question is sure to bring a negative reaction which otherwise might not have occurred, including strong pressures not to consummate the transaction. The individual who asks such a question has nothing to gain; he can anticipate the response. But he has much to lose since those who most oppose integration may become unpleasant, possibly threatening. In short, the person who consults with the neighbors is either naive or seeks a rationalization to break the law.

Discussing the possibility of Negro entry with the neighbors has an additional disadvantage: those who oppose integration may have time to organize. Since the major impetus for a resistance movement is lost once a sale contract or rental agreement has been signed, the time should be minimized between knowledge of the impending sale and its completion. This not only shortens the period the seller or landlord may be under pressure, but decreases the chance that a resistance movement will develop to harass the black family. Incidentally, sellers seldom have been harassed when they have sold to blacks as required by law.[13]

The key to minimizing tension in a neighborhood experiencing initial Negro entry is for those who support equality to make their position known as soon as possible. This is the heart of a penetrating analysis made by fair housing worker James Tillman, who classifies people into three groups: the committed (those who strongly support open housing), the indifferent or uncommitted, and the hostile.[14] Initially most people are uncommitted. As the hostile — those who strongly oppose integration — organize resistance to entry of the Negro family, they are joined by some of the uncommitted, unless opposed by those who are committed. But positive action by the committed normally swings many of the uncommitted and neutralizes the hostile.

It is not easy to support an unpopular position in one's own neighborhood. But in other respects the committed inherently have a strong position. They stand for restraint as opposed to the rash action advocated by the hostile. They stand for what most of the community know is right. And they stand for the law. It is not surprising that in recent years the committed have almost always carried the day.

The effectiveness of a small minority in influencing the neighborhood is consistent with research studies which have shown that in other types of discrimination intervention by even a single white person often resulted in equal treatment.[15] These studies included carefully staged tests where a black attempted to obtain service in a tavern and a white member of the test team intervened in his behalf.

Indeed, more than anything else the rapid return to normal on Cindy Drive resulted from the stand taken by Priscilla and Warren Hammond. Their leadership paid off handsomely. One might not expect that the positive stand of only one or two families would swing a neighborhood, but experience has proven that it works.

One of the most important truths about equal opportunities in housing is that one man can make a difference.

The extent of tension in a neighborhood experiencing initial Negro entry is dependent on the preparation of the people in the neighborhood. About a year after a Negro family moved onto Cindy Drive one of the residents of that street who had been most strongly opposed spoke out in a discussion of a proposed open-housing covenant campaign. With great eloquence he urged that such a campaign be undertaken to prevent other neighborhoods from experiencing the tensions which had tormented the residents of his street because "we were not prepared."

If an effort is made, neighborhoods can be prepared for Negro entry before it occurs. In 1963 and 1964, HOME (Housing Opportunities Made Equal) in Buffalo faced a crisis almost every time a Negro moved into an all-white area. Fortunately, in addition to handling the crises, an educational program, as described in Chapters 5 and 6, was being carried out throughout the entire metropolitan area, so that eventually the moves no longer caused serious tensions. Two years later such moves attracted little attention.

If the white community is to be prepared to accept Negroes, it is important to understand that resistance to Negro entry results primarily from fear. This includes the fear that property values will decrease; the fear of Negro inundation; the fear that the neighborhood will physically deteriorate; the fear that the prevailing values will change; the fear that integration will lead to intermarriage.

These are the apprehensions expressed by otherwise reasonable people, the type who constitute a majority in most communities, the group Tillman labeled the uncommitted. There are other fears mouthed by the hostile which are too remote from reality to be worthy of comment. Finally, there is the fear which is hardly ever mentioned, but is one of the most important of all — the fear of loss of status.

The need for status serves as the social manifestation of the broader need of most people for ego support. When a person's ego is threatened by a loss of status, the result can be aggression, resentment, hate.

There are many symbols of status: a color TV set, a good repertory of jokes, skill or past glory in athletics, or the neighborhood in which one lives. The latter is particularly important for those who do not hold positions of status. For them, more than others, where they live is a symbol of their station in life. Their neighborhood not only meets certain psychological needs, but is of significance to friends, business connections and potential mates for their children.

The fear that a Negro family in the neighborhood will cause a loss of status is most clearly shown by a complete lack of objection on the part of white people to having Negroes live among them, provided these Negroes are not considered neighbors. Under these circumstances the status of living in an "exclusive" neighborhood is not threatened. Thus it is acceptable for a Negro to live next door — if that Negro is a live-in servant.

The fear that property values will decrease if a Negro family moves into an all-white neighborhood is probably the most controversial of the myths. Fortunately, the effect of Negro entry on property values has been studied in considerable detail. Unfortunately, the situation is very complex.

There is some substance to the fear. The so-called self-fulfilling prophecy occurs if, when a Negro family moves into a neighborhood, many of the homeowners, fearing that property values will drop, list their homes for sale. The result is panic, and the fears of the homeowners materialize since prices must be decreased to attract additional buyers to balance the unusually large number of sellers. Such panic often has been caused by speculators and unscrupulous real estate brokers, but can occur without external agitation if people act in haste and efforts to stabilize the neighborhood are ineffective.

But there is a great mass of evidence which clearly shows that Negro entry need not result in the price declines feared by many whites.

The most significant study on the effect of Negro entry on property values was that conducted by Luigi Laurenti, an economist who, under a grant from the Fund for the Republic, analyzed the sale prices between 1943 and 1955 of a test group of 5,417 homes in 20 formerly all-white areas in the cities of San Francisco, Oakland and Philadelphia and compared them with the selling prices of a control group of 4,495 houses in 19 comparable areas which remained all white.[16] However, Laurenti apparently did not include any areas in which real estate speculators operated. His results showed that in 41 percent of the comparisons the prices in the test group stayed within 5 percent of the control prices, indicating no significant difference in price behavior; in 44 percent, prices in the test group were higher than those in the control by margins of 5 to 26 percent; and in the remaining 15 percent, prices in the test group were lower than control prices by margins of 5 to 9 percent.

Other studies in Chicago, Kansas City, Detroit and Portland, Oregon, are in agreement with the Laurenti findings.[16] These studies consisted of smaller samples and used less rigorous methodology, but the results clearly reflect the same basic findings.[17]

Many other smaller studies are also in agreement with the Laurenti work. One of these was conducted in New Haven by two Yale professors.[18] Property values in eight of nine neighborhoods into which a Negro family had moved increased as much or more than the average increase in New Haven during a comparable period.

The Laurenti study, which also showed that price changes are not significantly related to either the price of the housing or the percentage of Negro entry, sometimes is cited by open housing enthusiasts as proof that Negro entry does not affect real estate prices. This is an oversimplification which is not correct; real estate prices often have been influenced. What the Laurenti report and the other studies indicate is that prices have increased more often than they have decreased, and that when decreases have occurred they usually have been relatively mild.

Even real estate brokers, long-time foes of integrated neighborhoods, have come to recognize that non-white entry does not mean declining prices. According to Eugene P. Conser, executive vice-president of the National Association of Real Estate Boards, "If there can be slow integration, we have no reason to believe this will affect prices. The problem arises when the whites panic."

The prices of real estate in a given area are governed by the law of supply and demand. If there are many sellers and few buyers, prices decrease. On the other hand, if the supply of buyers is increased so that it exceeds the availability of sellers, then prices rise.

After Negro entry, three factors affect the supply-demand ratio. One is the desire of the white people already living in the neighborhood to remain. Closely related is the desire of other whites to move into the neighborhood. If these two are high, prices will not decline, and, if the desire of Negroes to move into the area also is high, prices will increase substantially, Likewise, a strong Negro market will prevent a depression of selling prices even when there is a decrease in white demand.

The desire of white people to remain in the neighborhood is the product of the interaction of a number of complex factors, including whether forces in or out of the neighborhood create panic or leadership prevents panic. The degree of desegregation in the metropolitan area is also important: if blacks already have moved to many other white neighborhoods nearby, whites are less apt to run when Negroes move near them. The age and condition of the housing in the area are significant, because owners of old or dilapidated housing are more likely to leave. The availability of good alternative housing also favors flight by the whites. Finally, when the percentage of Negroes in the neighborhood reaches 30 to 40 percent, the exodus of the remaining whites usually is accelerated.[19]

The desire of whites to move into an integrated neighborhood is closely related but not identical to the desire to remain. Again the condition of the housing in the mixed area appears to be particularly important. For example, after Negroes started moving in large numbers to West Philadelphia, where the housing was good, whites continued to move there, but this pattern was not followed in the Strawberry Mansion area in North Philadelphia where the housing was poor.[20] When the housing in an interracial neighborhood is in good condition, but there is a large supply of attractive alternatives for whites in all-white neighborhoods, whites who are moving tend to go to the all-white areas, but those already in the interracial neighborhood remain rather than incur the expense and trouble of moving.

Proximity to areas with large Negro populations is one of the more important factors in increased Negro demand. Selling prices consistent with the purchasing power of large numbers of Negro families also are necessary to attract Negro buyers. If there is a shortage of other housing available to them, either because of discrimination in other neighborhoods or a housing shortage in existing Negro areas, then the demand by Negroes will be high in those neighborhoods where they can get something. Finally, conditions which make housing desirable to whites, such as well-kept homes and good community facilities, increase Negro demand and their willingness to pay higher prices.

There is an enormous difference between what is likely to happen in an upper middle-class suburban neighborhood and in a center city neighborhood with less expensive housing in close proximity to Negro areas. Not many Negroes can afford high-priced homes, and, as discussed in Chapter 9, most of these Negroes are not in the market for suburban housing. Since there is not much Negro demand, real estate prices in the suburban neighborhood depend almost entirely on the response of the whites. In fact, one can only speculate why in some studies there appeared to be a relative increase in the price of suburban housing because of Negro entry. Perhaps the apparent increase in price really was not significant; perhaps there are enough families who prefer to live in a neighborhood which has at least one Negro family to increase demand significantly; perhaps when a house in these desegregated areas was for sale some of the neighbors, fearing further Negro entry, helped in the selling process to a degree not experienced in neighborhoods without a Negro family.

However, when the neighborhood is close to the ghetto and the price of the housing is in a range that many Negroes can afford, Negroes will compete for the housing. What happens is determined by the interaction of the complex factors previously described. But whatever the situation, the people in the neighborhood will be better off financially if they prevent panic.

There are questions the available data do not resolve. Is there a difference between the house next door to a Negro family and others in the neighborhood? Does it take longer to sell a house in an integrated neighborhood? Perhaps studies should be made to determine the facts. But would it be worth it? The available information conclusively shows that catastrophic long-range price declines do not occur, but the entry of Negroes into a previously all-white neighborhood has, at times, caused decreases in property values. However, such decreases need not occur.

The fear of Negro inundation also has some substance. As we have seen, in neighborhoods which are close to areas with large Negro populations the entry of a Negro family often is followed by others, and frequently such a neighborhood eventually becomes predominantly Negro.

However, in neighborhoods well away from the ghetto, inundation is rare. Statistics from the Buffalo area demonstrate this well. Between 1964 and 1968 Negroes bought homes in about 250 neighborhoods which previously were all white. In all but three of these neighborhoods only one Negro family moved in, and in two of the others only two families. However panic developed in the third, a block on Voorhees Street. After a second house on the block was purchased by a Negro family, two others were listed for sale and also bought by Negroes. Then more houses went up for sale. The situation was aggravated by the fact that real estate brokers rarely showed white families any of the listings; in effect, white homeseekers were not given the option of buying on a street containing four Negro families. As a result, at the end of three years over half the residents on the block were black and the transition was continuing. But the houses which were sold brought excellent prices. Although the whites panicked, they did not sell hastily and, since the homes were relatively new, the $18,000-$20,000 price range was one which many Negroes could afford, and the neighborhood was not far away from the ghetto, the result was heavy Negro demand and good sale prices.

Buffalo's experience has been repeated in many other places. For example, in suburban Philadelphia a careful study was made of seventeen neighborhoods into which Negro families moved between October 1957 and November 1960.[21] Prices of homes in these areas ranged from averages of $10,000 to $18,000. In fifteen of these neighhoods no other Negro family followed the move of the first. In one area, two other Negro families rented temporarily, then moved away. In the other area, one additional Negro family bought a home. However, during the period of the study a total of 346 white families purchased houses in these neighborhoods after the Negroes moved in. In over half of the neighborhoods white families bought homes either next door to a Negro family or across the street.

This example also demonstrates the willingness of whites to move into an area after Negro entry. Similar results have been reported in the Chicago area. Since 1959 over a hundred Negro families and several thousand white families have moved into suburban Park Forest.[22] With the one exception previously noted, strong white demand continued in the 250 neighborhoods to which Negro families moved in the Buffalo area. When the housing is in good condition, white demand often continues even in fringe areas with moderate Negro populations (under 30 percent) as evidenced by studies in Philadelphia[23] and Buffalo.[24]

The residents of a neighborhood affect each other. Schools and cultural activities reflect the values and tastes of the community; children mirror the mores of the other kids in the neighborhood. For these reasons, as well as snobbishness, most people wish to avoid living in close proximity with "low-class" people — those with educational levels, occupations and cultural interests below their own. Unfortunately a disappointingly large number of these people equate all Negroes with this "low-class" and assume that a Negro's values will differ from their own.

While it is true that the percentage of "low-class" people is higher among Negroes than it is among whites, this is as irrelevant to the issue as the almost universal opinion among social scientists that this is not a characteristic of race but the unfortunate product of exploitation and discrimination. What is pertinent is that, with rare exceptions, "low-class" Negroes do not seek housing in all-white areas. In fact, it has been well established that the Negro families who buy or rent in all-white areas average better educations and jobs than their white neighbors. For example, in the New Haven study previously cited this was true in all nine neighborhoods where blacks moved.[18] The fifteen Negro families in the study averaged 1.7 on the Hollingshead Occupational Scale — where one represented the highest rating and seven the lowest — while the whites in the same neighborhoods averaged 3.4. Similar results were obtained in an earlier study in Kansas City where a marked superiority in educational background, occupational level and income was noted for the Negro families.[25]

There are several reasons why this occurs. Many Negroes have lower incomes than whites with similar educations and occupations. In addition, some Negroes planning to move to an all-white area sense there will be advantages to a neighborhood where they are at least equal in status to most of their neighbors.

Thus what has happened has been the opposite of what some whites fear. However, as discriminatory practices decrease, the status of Negro families moving into white areas probably will tend to match the status of those already in the neighborhood.

The myth that Negro entry into an all-white neighborhood will physically deteriorate the area is derived from the conditions which exist in overcrowded Negro slums. Overlooked, however, are the reasons why the slums become that way. Conditions in the slums have no bearing on the behavior of Negroes who move into white areas.

Almost all of the Negroes who live in slums are renters. It is not they but their landlords, most of whom are white, who fail to maintain properties. Slumlords generally are only interested in profits.

At the same time it must be acknowledged that much of the deterioration in Negro slums is caused by the people who live in them. Many from depressed rural areas have never been exposed to conventional standards of cleanliness and maintenance.* However, as previously pointed out, these people are not likely to move into a white area. A Negro family seeking housing outside the ghetto usually is as different from the Negro slum dweller as middle-class suburbanites differ from those low-income whites who continue to live in squalor.

Thus it is not surprising to find ample evidence that Negroes who live in integrated neighborhoods maintain their properties at least as well as their white neighbors. In fact, there is evidence that in some neighborhoods they have done a better job. There has never been any evidence to the contrary.

A 1954 study of 202 families in a Kansas City neighborhood which was half white and half Negro showed that a higher percentage of Negro homeowners had made or were making repairs and improvements than were white homeowners of comparable properties.[25] Laurenti also reports finding much evidence of Negroes keeping up properties.[27] This evidence consisted of visual inspection of both the exterior and interior of over a hundred homes in test areas; a correlation of major exterior improvements projects (such as painting, reroofing or extensive landscaping) with the race of the owner in all of the test areas in San Francisco; and comments by scores of real estate brokers familiar with the test areas. All indicated that Negroes keep up their property. Today additional evidence can be seen in interracial housing developments, in the thousands of well-kept homes where Negro families live in white areas and in the excellent

*The basic nature of this problem is demonstrated by the report of a Chicago building inspector which reads, "The tenants seem to wholly disregard personal cleanliness, and the very principles of decency, their general appearance and actions corresponding with their wretched abodes. This indifference . . . is doubtless acquired from a long familiarity with the loathsome surroundings . . ." The report was published in 1864 about an Irish neighborhood.[26]

maintenance of houses in many middle-class Negro areas.

An important reason why Negroes in interracial areas often take better care of their property than do the whites is that the Negro families usually are of higher status and have more money than the average white family in the area. Negro pioneers are also aware that their neighbors will be judging them and their race by the appearance of their home. Finally, the Negroes who move into white areas are not a random sampling of Negroes with similar socioeconomic status, but by self-selection are those who particularly value a good home.

The resistance to integration, based on the fear that it will lead to interracial marriages, stems more from the emotional hostility of large elements of the white population to intermarriage than from any statistical frequency. In the United States, only about one marriage in a thousand involves people of different races.[28]

The low rate of intermarriage is caused by the tendency of most people to marry within their own race. In part this is a matter of personal preference, but it also is a consequence of the intense disapproval of such liaisons by the great majority of Americans, including those in minority groups. In his An American Dilemma, Gunnar Myrdal found that intermarriage and sexual intercourse with white women were the areas in which whites most opposed Negro equality. Twenty years later Louis Harris obtained the same result: 94 percent of white Americans said they would oppose their teenage daughter dating a Negro.[29] However, there is no evidence that intermarriage increases in integrated housing situations and, if residential propinquity has not been a significant factor in interracial marriages in the past, it is even less likely to be one in the future since marriages are occurring less on a neighborhood basis.[30]

43

But eventually integration in housing probably will lead to more interracial marriages as the result of changes in attitudes resulting from integration. What will happen if interracial marriages become common? Neither science nor theology give any reason for concern, and miscegenation is not new to our country: about 80 percent of America's Negroes already are racially mixed.[30] In the long run widespread intermarriage could eliminate the racial polarization which is occurring in the United States.

There are other concerns that whites express about Negro entry into their neighborhoods.

"Who is in back of this?" is a question which frequently has been raised when a black family has bought a house in a white neighborhood. Often the NAACP has been singled out as the culprit by those who believed that the Negro family was being subsidized by a civil rights organization as part of a plot to integrate the community or even to take it over. But the only times Negro entry has been part of a plan to change significantly the racial complexion of a neighborhood have been when unsuspecting Negro families were used to "break a block" in areas where there would be a high demand by Negroes and where whites might easily be panicked into selling their homes cheaply.[31]

"Neighborhoods should be homogeneous; people who live together should be alike" is another comment sometimes made. This thesis, when used to justify the exclusion of Negroes from white areas, suffers from the obvious weakness that white neighborhoods are heterogeneous in many respects other than race. In addition to the impossibility of creating truly homogeneous neighborhoods in a free society, residential segregation deprives the residents, particularly the children, of enriching contacts with others of different backgrounds. It is noteworthy that universities and even "exclusive" private schools, by admission policies and scholarships, attempt to attract people of all backgrounds.

"Negroes are dirty." Yet, among those who can afford it, many hire Negroes to clean their homes, cook their food, and nurse their children . . . "Negroes will hurt the schools." Yet the most prestigious universities in the United States now have a greater percentage of Negro students than do most suburban schools . . .

Many whites are not aware of the extent to which open housing is supported by other whites. Whereas in 1942 only about one-third of the whites in a national sample said it would make no difference to them if a Negro family of the same education and income moved onto their block, by 1965 about two-thirds of a similar sample voiced no objection.[32]

In 1963 Louis Harris found that 45 percent of whites in the United States would not object to having a Negro living next door.[29] Gallup in 1963 found that only 45 percent would even consider moving if a Negro family moved next door; moreover, by 1965 that percentage decreased to 35 and only 13 percent said they would definitely move.[33] A similar result was reported in a *Look* survey about the same time: Only 15 percent of a national sample said they would move, while 19 percent said they would welcome the Negro family and treat them the same as they would treat white neighbors.[34] Early in 1968, 62 percent of the white inhabitants of fifteen large cities stated they believed Negroes had a right to live anywhere, and only 30 percent felt whites had a right to keep blacks out.[35] In this survey 49 percent said they would not mind at all if a Negro family moved next door.

In Buffalo, surveys taken in 1964 by HOME (Housing Opportunities Made Equal) in suburban Amherst indicated that 41 percent opposed a Negro family moving onto their block.

As a result of the strong efforts directed at open housing, by 1968 the opposition had decreased to 15 percent. These surveys also indicated that between 1964 and 1968 those who would participate in action to keep a Negro family out of their neighborhood declined from 21 percent to less than 5 percent. By 1968 only 5 percent said they would even consider selling their home if a Negro family moved onto their street.

One of the most interesting results of the Buffalo surveys was their demonstration of how much is required for people to become aware of facts. For example, 47 percent of the residents of the suburb of Amherst did not know there was a law against discrimination over two years after the Metcalf-Baker antidiscrimination law became effective in New York State. At that time there were seventeen Negro homeowners well-scattered throughout the town, yet 42 percent of those polled did not know whether there were any Negro families in Amherst and only 22 percent were aware that there were more than five such families. Those who were better informed were found to be more favorable to Negro entry than those who were not well informed. However, the survey information does not differentiate whether this support for open housing resulted from the knowledge itself or because those people who are better informed about the community also are less prejudiced toward Negroes.

The results of attitude surveys can, of course, be misleading. A great deal depends on the way the question is asked. Arnold M. Rose of the University of Minnesota has demonstrated that expressed attitudes on the race issue are frequently contradicted by other expressed attitudes or by reports of behavior.[36] He found that in an interracial neighborhood in Minneapolis only 8 percent mentioned their neighbors when asked in what respects they were dissatisfied with the neighborhood. Also, when asked an open-ended question regarding the characteristics they would seek in a future neighborhood, only 11 percent said they would want an all-white neighborhood. However, when asked specifically how they felt about neighborhoods with regard to racial composition, 74 percent expressed a preference for an all-white neighborhood. Yet only 19 percent said they objected to living in a neighborhood where there were one or two Negro families who kept up their homes and tried to be good neighbors.

The specifics of the questions asked are important. Thus while Gallup found that only 13 percent said that they would definitely leave if Negroes moved next door, in the same survey 40 percent said they would move if Negroes came to live in large numbers in the neighborhood.[32] A survey taken in Philadelphia in the 1950's indicated that while only 4 percent of whites would strongly disapprove of Negroes living in the same "neighborhood," 14 percent disapproved of Negroes on the same block and 31 percent disapproved of Negroes next door.[37]

The statistics from these surveys can become confusing. But three conclusions stand out clearly: there is more support for open housing than is generally realized; those who strongly oppose open housing are a relatively small minority; and white people are becoming more tolerant.

Because attitudes change slowly, it is widely believed that ending discrimination in housing will take a long time. But while attitudes about minority groups may change relatively slowly, *discriminatory practices can be ended with great rapidity.*

The great majority of people act in accord with what they believe is expected of them. If discrimination is the established pattern, even many of those who believe that such a practice is wrong will discriminate. Conversely, if equal opportunity is the accepted practice, even those who would

47

prefer to discriminate will act in accordance with what is required. Long before any of the barriers of segregation were lifted in the South, Southerners who visited New York City would dine in restaurants which served Negroes and would sit next to blacks in theaters. They may have felt uncomfortable, but they recognized that this was the way they were expected to behave in New York.

Social scientists have shown, beyond doubt, that practices of discrimination often are unrelated to intensity of prejudice. There are many cases where influential persons, who had the authority to determine policies, quickly and successfully ended discriminatory practices even though such practices were strongly supported by most of the community. For instance, fifteen years ago, although Phoenix, Arizona, still had segregated schools, the YWCA and USO had integrated canteens with interracial dancing.[38]

The denial of equal opportunity in housing is as much the result of conformity as of prejudice. That such practices continue is, above all else, a failure of leadership.

3 / The Villains and the Mavericks

How, in a country dedicated to the concept of equality, did housing discrimination become so severe?

The combined activities of government, real estate brokers, builders, landlords and bankers were responsible. But housing discrimination also was the result of how men often behave: fearful of those different from themselves, narrow in interest and perspective, more influenced by greed than love.

In the decade following the Civil War, the United States attempted to insure that those who had been slaves would enjoy full citizenship. The Thirteenth Amendment abolished slavery. The Fourteenth Amendment withdrew from the states the power to abridge the "privileges and immunities" of United States citizens or to deny any person "the equal protection of the laws" or "due process of law." The Fifteenth Amendment protected the right to vote. To implement these amendments, Congress enacted a series of civil rights laws providing for equal treatment of citizens of every race in property rights, voting, jury service, public accommodations and transportation.

Unfortunately, protection of Negro rights quickly became a farce because of decisions made by the Supreme Court and the failure of the entire policy of Reconstruction. The majority of those in the federal government supported the concept of Negro equality, but their attention was focused on other matters, particularly economic expansion. However, in the South, continued subjugation of the Negro was the absorbing issue.

The first of the Supreme Court decisions which made discrimination possible came in 1873 when the Court distinguished between two kinds of citizenship, federal and state, and held that the Fourteenth Amendment placed under federal protection only the "privileges and immunities" of federal, but not states' citizenship. Ten years later the Court held that the Fourteenth Amendment applied only to "state action," not to the acts of private persons, and that the federal government had no power to restrain individuals from violating the civil rights of others. Then, having determined that limits on discriminatory acts only applied to government action, the Court was called upon to specify how far government could go in discriminating against a racial group. In 1896, in *Plessy* v. *Ferguson*, the answer came in the doctrine of "separate but equal."

"Separate but equal" provided a judicial base for racial segregation. Beginning in 1898 and continuing into the 1940's, Southern legislatures adopted hundreds of "Jim Crow" laws which extended compulsory segregation into every area of life. Additional laws were passed which in effect deprived the Negro of the right to vote. Often legislated discrimination was supplemented by murder and terror. One measure of the results is that between 1896 and 1904 the number of Negroes registered to vote in the state of Louisiana fell from 130,000 to 1,300.[1] In practice the doctrine of separate but equal was a courtroom legalism used by whites to subjugate and exploit the Negro.

But American racism was not confined to the South. When Negroes migrated in significant numbers to Northern cities during World War I and the years that followed, they encountered the same bigotry which in the West was being directed at Orientals and Mexicans and which culminated in severe national restrictions on immigration. This racism was also translated into actions and policies by the nation's real estate brokers and their professional organizations. The restrictive policies already instituted by many local boards became national policy in 1924 when the National Association of Real Estate Boards (NAREB) adopted as part of its code of ethics the declaration that, "A Realtor* should never be instrumental in introducing into a neighborhood . . . members of any race or nationality, or any individuals whose presence will clearly be detrimental to property values in that neighborhood."

Through this code America's Realtors became committed to segregated neighborhoods. Even when a homeowner was willing to sell to a Negro, the Realtor was prohibited from being a party to such a transaction.[2] Moreover, the influence of the real estate industry extended beyond what the Realtors did directly. Realtors conceived of restrictive covenants and spread their use. These were agreements which, once made, legally prevented subsequent owners of the property from selling to members of specified minority groups.[3] Real-

---

*A Realtor is a real estate broker who, upon meeting certain professional requirements, is elected as a member of a Board of Realtors. Most real estate brokers are not Realtors, but most heads of large real estate firms are Realtors. The National Association of Real Estate Boards is the national organization of Realtors. There is also the National Association of Real Estate Brokers which is a professional organization of Negro brokers whose members are known as Realtists.

tors also influenced the adoption of government policies of discrimination which further heightened the walls of the ghettos.

In a way real estate brokers did for discrimination what the mosquito did for malaria. While brokers were not the basic cause, they were the vector. And, like the mosquito, they eventually received a disproportionate share of the blame.

Government action often caused segregation. Beginning with Baltimore in 1910, many Southern and border cities passed laws which specified the districts in which Negroes would be allowed to live. While these ordinances were declared unconstitutional by the Supreme Court in 1917, municipal governments continued as effective instruments in the creation of segregated communities by condemning property, withholding city services, not building roads and sewers, leveling high assessments, filing building violations and changing zoning regulations.[3] Local governments also were responsible for segregating most public housing.

Another form of government action which helped create the ghettos was the enforcement by courts of restrictive covenants. It was not until 1948 that the Supreme Court, in *Shelley* v. *Kraemer*, ruled unconstitutional the enforcement of such covenants.

But the greatest damage, because of the number of housing units involved, was caused by the Federal Housing Administration (FHA), an agency whose purpose was to provide for the housing needs of a rapidly growing nation by insuring mortgages on private dwellings. When the FHA was created in 1934, its founders recognized that the agency's ultimate success required that its operations be based on sound economic principles. Unfortunately, the assumption then was made that the economic stability of property dictated that neighborhoods be homogeneous. The FHA underwriting manuals stated, "If a neighborhood is to retain stability, it is necessary that properties shall continue to be occupied by the same social and racial group." The manuals recommended racial restrictions and even provided a model restrictive covenant. Urbanologist Charles Abrams points out that "Pigpens and unwelcome races were classed as equally objectionable."[3]

Thus for fifteen years the United States government officially sanctioned segregation in housing. Since FHA insurance was more likely to be given to houses covered by racial covenants, builders were pressured into adopting policies of racial exclusiveness. From 1934 to 1949 approximately fifteen million new housing units were constructed, almost 100 percent of which became all-white preserves. For example, until 1949 only one Negro in the entire Miami area was able to get an FHA commitment to build a home, and there is evidence that he was not recognized as black.[4]

An illuminating example of how FHA operated during this period is the experience of a group from one of the major unions in the motion picture industry which in 1946 formed a cooperative to build housing.[5] For over three years FHA toyed with them as they attempted to get an insured loan. Finally the project was abandoned. Officially FHA talked technicalities and requested changes in plans, but unofficially FHA expressed concern over the interracial nature of the proposed development since membership in the union was 6 percent non-white and FHA agreed to "go along" if restrictive covenants were placed on all but twenty lots. In one meeting an FHA official said he was a friend of the Negro people and would do everything to help, but his agency could not help democratize America.

More and more Negroes were migrating in the 1940's to Northern cities to take advantage of better job opportunities.

The separate-for-white-essentially-nothing-for-black housing policy of the federal government, which could not help but have enormous implications on the actions of individual citizens, gave black Americans no choice but to overcrowd whatever housing was available.

In the wake of the 1948 Supreme Court decision that racial covenants could not be enforced, and in response to increased national support of nondiscrimination, FHA gradually changed its policies until a reversal had occurred by the early 1960's, and the official policy called for active encouragement of equal opportunities. Nevertheless the federal government continued to be instrumental in the building of segregated communities.

Consider Houston. During the five-year period after November 20, 1962 — when President Kennedy issued Executive Order 11063 which explicitly prohibited discrimination in new houses receiving federal aid and in all housing owned by the federal government — there were 212 new subdivisions insured by the Houston FHA office. Thirteen of these developments, containing 466 houses, became exclusively Negro; in the other 199 subdivisions, with 11,734 houses, there was a total of five Negro families.

The events in Houston were not atypical. The American Friends Service Committee (AFSC), in a scathing report, has carefully documented FHA's failure to properly implement the executive order.[6] Among AFSC's findings: FHA failed to counsel the building industry on required action; the performance of builders receiving loans was not reviewed; Negroes were not informed of their rights; the properties covered by the executive order were not identified as such to homeseekers, and often this information was difficult to obtain. Even when specific discriminatory practices were brought to the attention of FHA, little was done, and, on the very rare occasions when sanctions were imposed, they were trivial. In fact, for a Negro family to obtain its rights under the executive order it often needed powerful outside support. In a case in the Washington, D.C. area, AFSC's staff made sixty-nine telephone calls, attended thirteen meetings, wrote ten letters and hired an attorney before the house was made available to the Negro family.

The AFSC also documented that FHA and the Veterans Administration allowed government-owned properties, obtained as a result of foreclosures, to be sold in a discriminatory manner. In 1966 an example of this was brought to light in Kansas City by a white couple, Mr. and Mrs. Dwight Davis. When they inquired about an FHA-foreclosed house, the "managing broker," whom FHA had hired to get the house ready for sale, sold them the house before it officially was placed on the market. According to both Mr. and Mrs. Davis, the broker candidly stated that one of the reasons he was doing this in violation of FHA rules was "we have to work to keep the Negroes out of these areas." (An unstated reason was that it was financially profitable to do this because of the commission.) Because Mrs. Davis was a committee chairman of the Greater Kansas City Council of Religion and Race and because that organization waged an intensive campaign for reform, ripples were created which reached Washington and resulted in procedural changes. However, the broker received no punishment other than being warned he would lose his contract with FHA if he were again found pre-showing or pre-selling.

FHA remains today more of an instrument of segregation than integration because of the background of the people in that giant government bureaucracy. Almost without exception they are men who are oriented toward economic rather than social concerns and, despite the barrage of policy pronouncements about equal opportunity, the talk has not been supported by programs geared to prepare the agency's staff for their new responsibilities. The result is that almost all FHA offices continue to function more as ghetto builders than ghetto dissolvers.

The control by individual builders and apartment owners of up to thousands of new units was an important factor in the growth of the ghettos. Entire neighborhoods and entire communities came into being without any black inhabitants. The decision of a single builder created Levittown, Pennsylvania, as an all-white community of 60,000 people. Between 1942 and 1962 the Metropolitan Life Insurance Company, which owned the Parkchester Development in New York City, excluded Negroes from this city of 40,000 within a city. Metropolitan Life created another all-white neighborhood of 25,000 people when it built Stuyvesant Town in New York City in 1947.

The discriminatory policies which for many years were practiced by lending institutions also reinforced patterns of segregation. Most banks* made loans to Negroes only if the purchased property was in an established Negro neighborhood or an already mixed area.[7] Some banks discriminated to protect property investments against the supposed destructive effect of non-white entry; other banks were aware that a Negro purchaser would not hurt property values, but discriminated to maintain good relations with white homeowners and white real estate brokers.

While builders, apartment owners and bankers all have engaged in widespread discriminatory practices, real estate brokers are still viewed as the prime villains, largely because of the practice of blockbusting and the almost psychotic battle waged by the real estate industry against fair housing legislation.

*Exceptions included the Bank of America and the Bowery Savings Bank of New York.

If real estate organizations had not opposed fair housing legislation, they would have violated some basic laws of behavior. Any proposal to regulate an industry invariably meets resistance among the members of that industry. The fact that hundreds of thousands of dollars (perhaps more) were spent fighting such legislation is not surprising either. There are over fifteen hundred local Boards of Realtors in the United States, and their total membership exceeds ninety thousand. But what appears indefensible is the hysteria with which fair housing was fought and the inconsistencies in the Realtors' position.

Realtor campaigns against fair housing legislation have all had pretty much the same flavor, whether opposed to local, state or national legislation. In 1966, when Congress gave serious consideration to a national fair housing law, a prominent Realtor told a Senate subcommittee that "forced housing provisions of the proposed civil rights bill flout the United States Constitution." Earlier NAREB's president, Jack Justice, had warned Realtors of their obligation "to alert the public against an attack on human rights . . ." NAREB's official publication, *Realtor's Headlines*, carried in large type on page one, "You, personally, and your sales people, are threatened by a bill to impose restrictions against which you cannot protect yourself; few people are aware how easily harassment of you in your work, and time consumed in defense against federal charges, could result in alienation of your clients, blasting of your reputation and destruction of your business."[8]

In this same issue of *Realtor's Headlines* Mr. Justice elaborated in detail the dire consequences if the fair housing bill were passed. He claimed, "You could not call attention to the desirability of a nearby parochial school . . . without being in violation of the law." Justice warned, "Your business now is your own, to serve according to the standards *you* set.

But not in the future! If an applicant for your services is unhappy with them, he could take you into federal court. . . ." And he stated that a fair housing law would result in "economic, social and political turmoil."

Local boards, through newspaper ads and other means, relayed the message to the public, often concocting a few additional misrepresentations of their own. The result was a tremendous barrage of mail in opposition to the proposed fair housing law, a campaign which may have been the reason Congress did not pass the bill.

It was a Pyrrhic victory for NAREB. Its misrepresentations in 1966 soiled the Realtors' image among many moderates, while the ferocity of the campaign made the hypocrisy of the Realtors' position all the more revolting to fair housing activists. The fundamental thesis the Realtors advanced was that homeowners had a right to dispose of their property as they wished; yet the position of real estate boards frequently has been to forbid sales to minorities even when the seller was willing, and one board expelled two of its members for participating in such sales.[9] In addition, even in the absence of restrictive policies most brokers have ignored requests by homeowners to sell on an unrestricted basis.[10] Additional evidence of this hypocrisy has been the virtual exclusion of Negro brokers from real estate boards, thereby making it difficult for white homeowners to do business with black buyers.

The opposition by the real estate industry to fair housing legislation on the basis that such laws violate the "right" of homeowners to do business with people of their own choosing also is completely inconsistent with the strong Realtor support of restrictive covenants, which by preventing sales to members of minority groups legally forbade homeowners from exercising this same "right" to dispose of property to whomever they wished. Indeed, there is no record of any real estate organization ever criticizing the use of restrictive covenants and, when the Supreme Court finally ruled restrictive covenants unenforceable, there was talk within the real estate industry of sponsoring a constitutional amendment to validate such covenants.[3]

If Realtors did not fight fair housing legislation to preserve the rights of property owners, the question arises as to their real motivation. While there certainly was anti-Negro sentiment among many real estate brokers, there is no evidence that brokers as individuals have been more guilty of racism than other Americans of similar socioeconomic status. In fact, in 1944, long before most white Americans were thinking of the plight of their black countrymen, NAREB recommended to local real estate boards that they undertake programs to provide better housing for Negro families and listed as problems to be solved, "adequate financing," "construction of Negro housing" and "management of Negro rental properties . . . on a parity with that given to other types of property."[2] Shortly thereafter NAREB publicized the results of a study which said that experience indicated "As a class, the Negro home buyer meets his payments faithfully — often more faithfully than other race groups in the same economic level — and that if his property is in good repair when he obtains it, he takes care of it after he buys it. As a tenant, he takes as good care of such premises as other tenants of his economic class."[2]

In a half century of otherwise inconsistent positions, there has been only one constant in everything that Realtors have done — they have always supported mechanisms which encourage ethnically homogeneous neighborhoods.

And why not! Finding the "right neighborhood" for a client always has been one of the foundations on which real estate businesses were built. But since it never was possible to create homogeneity in neighborhoods other than along economic and ethnic lines, that which threatened to destroy ethnic homogeneity was a threat to the Realtor — a threat to the need for his services and the satisfaction he would derive from his work. Given the choice of self-interest versus public need, the real estate brokers made the same choice that virtually every other group has made when similarly confronted, and they clothed their position in rationalizations which made that choice appear to be for the good of the republic.

Most real estate brokers no more desired the evils of housing discrimination than doctors, teachers, railroad workers, electricians and many, many others have favored the unfortunate public consequences of their organized activity in behalf of their own special interests.

A few real estate brokers have made enormous profits by skillful use of the fears of whites concerning Negro entry into their neighborhoods.

"Blockbusting" is the tactic of causing white people to move from otherwise satisfactory housing because of fears of racial transition. The opportunity for profit has been substantial. Some blockbusters settle for the commissions they receive for selling houses, others make a much bigger killing by buying the houses themselves at low prices and then selling them to Negroes at inflated prices. Such speculators often increase their profit further by financing purchases at high interest rates. According to one experienced practitioner, "If anybody in this business doesn't earn a hundred thousand dollars a year, he is loafing."[11]

The blockbuster usually strikes in an all-white block near a Negro neighborhood. His standard procedure is to scare everyone on the block into wanting to move, and his techniques for doing this and for attracting buyers from the black community have become highly developed. Sometimes a black family buys a home on a white block through normal channels and then the blockbusters move in to create panic. But, if the blockbuster is looking for business, he may initiate the panic himself on a block felt to be suitable.

The usual practice is to buy a house and get blacks into it, preferably those of a lower socioeconomic level than the whites in the neighborhood. One technique is to buy a single-family home and rent it to two low-income families. Another is to sell it to a low-income family (probably after having misrepresented costs). This family then either meets payments by taking in roomers or another family, or defaults and gives up the house; by the time the latter happens, panic has been created. Another technique is to rent a house temporarily to a low-income family at a reduced rate. In Baltimore, a well-known blockbuster initiated panic by buying a house and putting up a large luminescent "sold" sign even though the house had not been sold.

Blockbusters have learned how to place the white people in a target neighborhood under tremendous pressure. They knock on every door, offering quick cash deals and warning that prices will fall $1,000 a week because Negroes are moving in. Once panic is under way as many as thirty speculators have attempted to get a piece of the action on a single block, knocking on doors, telephoning, sending mailings.[11] No technique is too deceitful. Blockbusters have hired Negroes with old, noisy cars to drive around a neighborhood, and they have paid black women on welfare to walk their children along the street. In Houston, one panic formula was to telephone late at night — "I wanted to get hold of you immediately because . . ." In suburban New York a blockbuster told a White Plains housewife her husband wanted to sell after he had told the husband (who did not wish to sell) that his wife wanted to sell.

Black buyers have been badly misled. Often a family used to create panic was deceived by a blockbuster into believing that there already were other black families on the block. In Baltimore, in 1958, blockbusters advertised in the real estate sections of the newspapers, "Ashburton — colored" although the area was 95 percent white.[12] Worst of all, Negro families were given gross misrepresentations of their monthly costs and the possibilities for income. For example, they might be assured that for a few hundred dollars a basement could be converted to an apartment which would yield $80 per month rent, but discovered later that such an apartment was against fire regulations, or would cost $3,000 to build. As a result, in order to meet their payments such families often took in roomers, thereby overcrowding the premises and causing deterioration.

The exploitation in blockbusting has been almost unbelievable. For example, between April 1965 and July 1966 one real estate operator in Baltimore purchased twenty-three houses in the 2700 through 3000 blocks of the Alameda for between $5,200 and $7,500. By 1968, ten of these houses had been sold at prices between $11,950 and $13,-550. The others were all rented. The profits from these rentals also were high; when a two-apartment house was purchased by a speculator for $7,300 the $75 per month rent for an upstairs apartment immediately was increased 50 percent.[13]

In Chicago the Commission on Human Relations made a detailed analysis of what happened on one block.[14] The average increase between the price paid by the speculator to the white family and the price charged the Negro family was 73 percent. The markup never was less than 35 percent and, in one case, was 115 percent. A relatively typical transaction took place at 6933 South Princeton. The speculator purchased this house for $9,500; two months later he sold it to two Negro families for $18,300. The speculator needed only a $500 down payment, the remainder coming from a low-interest loan; the Negro families paid $1,500 as a down payment and then paid a higher rate of interest to the speculator than he was paying the bank. In addition, most Negro families bought on contract, which meant that they did not receive title to the house until they had made full payment and, if they defaulted, they lost their entire investment.[15]

Blockbusting of this type, with minor variations, has taken place in many cities. While only a small fraction of real estate brokers profited directly from such operations, it was largely the actions of the entire real estate industry which made this exploitation possible.* Brokers made Negro homeseekers desperate by shutting them off from most available housing, and made rapid racial transition of neighborhoods a self-fulfilling prophecy by not showing housing to whites in neighborhoods to which Negroes had moved. In addition, the real estate industry failed to demand government action to end blockbusting practices.[16] Not until 1963 did NAREB draft model antiblockbusting laws, and even then very little effort was made to secure their passage. Moreover, as individuals, Realtors have opposed such legislation more often than they have supported it. Some of the opposition was to protect profits which accrued not only to blockbusters but to all real estate brokers, since whites scared into moving by blockbusters bought houses in other areas. The phobia that an antiblockbusting measure would be a foot in the door for fair housing measures also caused opposition.

While Negroes seeking housing in white areas faced massive institutional discrimination supported by the actions of well over 95 percent of white Americans, some whites went against the tide.

---

*Other major culprits were the FHA, which usually did not insure houses in Negro neighborhoods or those undergoing racial transition, and those lending institutions which provided speculators with financing.

In the decade which followed World War II about fifty privately-developed interracial housing developments were built in the United States: approximately eight thousand units of the ten million constructed during this period.[5] These units, and some much larger interracial developments which followed, which were purposely marketed to both whites and blacks, clearly showed how dependent is the racial makeup in housing developments on marketing techniques.

White or Negro, homebuyer or renter, people respond to affirmative marketing policies. Thus, developers who skillfully control marketing usually have been able to exercise control of the racial mixture. In Rochdale Village, a six-thousand unit cooperative development built in the middle of a Negro slum in New York City, there was concern that there would be a disproportionate number of black applicants. Consequently initial promotional efforts were beamed at the white community by advertising in the *New York Times* and the *Post*. As a result, very few applications were received from Negroes until ads were placed in the Negro press. Another technique was to hold meetings for prospective tenants to discuss the nature of a cooperative, which also tended to assure both whites and blacks that the racial distribution would be in an acceptable range. The final result: Rochdale Village had 15 to 20 percent black occupancy.[17]

Integration, per se, does not have much appeal in the marketplace. In an extensive study of integrated housing developments, Schermer found that while some lived in such developments because they wished to be in a racially integrated area, most chose them simply because of factors such as location, convenience, design and price.[18] Also, attempts to market interracial housing through civil rights groups have been disappointing.

Although integration may not have proved to be much of a selling point, neither has it been a strong deterrent to sales or rental of housing. For example, in California in the 1950's a rental development, originally built for Negro occupancy only, had almost two hundred vacancies out of three hundred units because of a miscalculation by the original developer on the size of the black market. When a new owner strongly marketed the housing to whites, all of the vacancies were filled and white demand continued strong for a development where about 30 percent of the residents were Negroes.

In addition to the builders and landlords who actively planned interracial developments, there were a few others who did not discriminate. While their competitors were claiming that an open housing policy meant economic ruin, these men were demonstrating the opposite.

One of these builders, Edward Eichler, the former president of Eichler Homes, does not believe that sales to Negroes hurt his business (seven hundred houses a year in California of which thirty or forty were purchased by blacks).[19] Among the techniques which appear to have helped Eichler were the unemotional manner in which he approached the problem, his willingness to buy back at original prices the house of anyone who wished to move because a Negro had bought in his neighborhood (an offer hardly ever taken), and his policy of minimizing the time between when people first learned they were going to have a Negro neighbor and when the black family actually moved in.

However, Eichler also was helped by the kind of house he built, an ultra-modern middle-income dwelling which was popular with unconventional professional people who were not likely to object to a Negro neighbor. Most builders who practiced open occupancy report they did pay some penalty; in particular, a house next door to a Negro family required extra selling effort. There also appear to have been instances where a builder failed to obtain needed cooperation (e.g., a zoning change) from local government officials because the developer had practiced open occupancy. During the years that discrimination was not against the law, practicing open occupancy was not as easy for a builder as many civil rights activists represented. On the other hand, the fact that those who did not discriminate before open housing was required by law did not encounter serious problems makes indefensible the violations of law which occur today.

The impact of open-occupancy practice by real estate brokers on their own businesses was more complex. In those few places, such as Boston, Denver and the San Fernando Valley, where sentiment for open housing was relatively strong among Realtors, individual brokers could give nondiscriminatory service without encountering serious difficulties. On the other hand, in most areas a broker known to assist Negroes lost business because of decreased cooperation by other brokers. Such cooperation was important to business success because so many sales involve two brokers — one representing the property owner and the other the buyer. In addition, at least one local board expelled members for nondiscriminatory practices.[9]

Another factor was the way the broker practiced open occupancy. In Chicago, John Baird, the president of Baird and Warner, publicly supported fair housing legislation and sold houses to blacks. However, since the law permitted discriminatory practices, Baird's firm also accepted restricted listings.[20] Whether it was the limited nature of his open housing policy, or the tact with which Baird handled his relations with other Realtors, or luck, Baird and Warner did not suffer. Sales volume grew every year and in 1968 the firm was selling 80 percent more houses than in 1962.

In Baltimore, Mal Sherman, the head of what was then one of the five largest real estate firms in the city, had an entirely different experience. When in 1964 he publicly declared he would do business with any qualified buyer, other Realtors told potential clients, "Don't list with him; he'll sell to a nigger." Within six months the volume of Sherman's business had dropped by two-thirds. Yet, although he lost a great deal of money, if he could relive that decision Sherman would do it again. The entire nature of his business changed: in one year he sold one hundred houses in many previously all-white areas to blacks.[21]

Of those in the housing industry who fought discrimination, one stands out above all others. Morris Milgram cannot properly be classified as a businessman with a strong social conscience; he is a social reformer who entered the housing business in order to do something about discrimination.

Bright, energetic, intense, Milgram spent nearly ten years as a professional defender of labor and minority rights before 1947 when he joined his father-in-law, a builder in Philadelphia, on the stipulation that he would be allowed to build houses open to anyone. Four years later, having apprenticed the housing business, he raised $150,000 to finance his first integrated developments.

The result was Concord Park, 139 single-family houses just outside Philadelphia, and Greenbelt Knoll, 19 houses in northeast Philadelphia. Both were financial successes; investors got their money back plus 6 percent annual profit. And both became genuine interracial communities with whites slightly outnumbering blacks. While Milgram had to impose quotas to prevent these developments from becoming predominantly Negro, he learned rapidly how to market integrated housing by selective techniques. In his next two projects, both of which were in Princeton, New Jersey, ten of the forty purchasers were Negro without resorting to quotas. In fact, in all of his subsequent work Milgram was able to keep the housing racially integrated by marketing techniques alone.

After Princeton came some painful lessons. In 1959 in Deerfield, Illinois, an all-white Chicago suburb, the two sites Milgram had bought were condemned for public parks when his plans became known. It was a costly defeat, made all the more expensive by the loss of a long series of court battles.[22] Another costly debacle followed in Waterbury, Connecticut. As a result, Milgram shifted his emphasis to M-REIT (Mutual Real Estate Investment Trust), a real estate trust he organized which purchases apartment houses far from black ghettos and then slowly builds up Negro occupancy to a respectable minority. By 1970 almost ten thousand investors had subscribed over ten million dollars; M-REIT owned seventeen properties in five states, a total of three thousand units, and was in the process of purchasing more.

M-REIT is having successes: the Ford Foundation invested a million dollars and, according to the 1968 annual report, vacancies in every building have declined under M-REIT ownership. But M-REIT also faces severe problems, the most important of which is that although it has yet to reach maturity, in some ways it is outdated. The need to demonstrate that integrated housing developments can be successful is past. Now the need is for integrated housing projects on a scale a hundred times greater. The M-REIT approach ties up too much capital for the integration accomplished to merit a high priority for money being risked on behalf of integration; on the other hand, M-REIT has not yet established itself as an attractive enough investment to command substantial support from investors whose major concern is their return on money invested.

Another of Milgram's accomplishments is that he has successfully motivated many others to work on behalf of equal opportunities. For Mal Sherman it was Milgram who tipped the scales and caused him to start doing what he believed. It was Milgram — sitting across the aisle from a young United

Church of Christ clergyman as both rode a bus from New England to march for civil rights in Washington — who motivated a change in direction for the Reverend Howard Smith, now the director of the housing program for Chicago's Conference of Religion and Race, a man many in Chicago believe has accomplished more than anyone else in behalf of equal housing opportunities in the nation's second largest city.

Indeed, in the long run Milgram's greatest contribution may be what he causes others to do in bringing about what he has termed "The Achievable Dream."

The federal government, real estate brokers, builders, landlords and bankers may have been important agents in forming and maintaining the ghettos, but they were not the only causes. One man's misery frequently is another's profit. The slumlords and slum merchants had a vested interest in the ghetto. So did many black leaders at the community level. Although they often decried the evils of the ghetto, few black clergymen and black politicians have tried to break down the walls which contained their base of power and influence.

Finally there were the millions of white Americans who acknowledged that it was wrong to deny a family housing because of its race, but who never did anything about discrimination. While these people were preoccupied with their own personal and family concerns, they demonstrated Edmund Burke's observation, "All that is required for the triumph of evil is for good men to remain silent." Racial segregation in housing has complex causes — including prejudice, fear, myths, and greed, but, perhaps more than anything else, the terrible injustices are the product of apathy.

4 / The Law and Its Enforcement

IT IS AGAINST THE LAW to discriminate on the basis of race in the sale or rental of any housing in the United States.

On June 17, 1968, the Supreme Court declared that Congress meant exactly what it said in Section 1982 of the 1866 Civil Rights Act: that all citizens, regardless of race or color, have "the same right" to purchase and lease property "as enjoyed by white citizens." This interpretation of the 1866 act in the *Jones* v. *Mayer* decision permits a Negro who has encountered discrimination to enforce the law by bringing a private suit in federal court.*

Other laws make it illegal to discriminate in housing transactions because of religion, national origin or race and include provisions for government enforcement. Most housing is covered by federal legislation: Title VIII of the 1968 Civil Rights Act. There also are fair housing laws in twenty-four states and about two hundred local communities, including most large cities.

But laws and decisions alone do not end discrimination. In

*See Chapter 7, particularly pages 171 and 172.

most communities there is very poor compliance with fair housing laws. In Chicago over 70 of 104 landlords contacted by the Leadership Council for Metropolitan Open Communities admitted they would not rent to Negroes despite the Chicago fair housing ordinance.[1] A committee appointed by Governor Nelson Rockefeller to review New York State's laws and procedures concerning human rights reported early in 1968:[2]

> The laws are unknown or ignored by many persons in the state. Active, blatant acts of discrimination occur and recur, often without relief for those discriminated against. . . . The State Commission, charged with enforcing the law, has been timorous and relatively ineffective. [It] has become a target of ridicule in the communities it was designed to serve.

In Hartford, Connecticut, a black man told a reporter, in reference to housing in the all-white south end of the city, "Yeah, the governor says I can get a house down there; he ought to go with me when I try."[3]

However, laws can be effective in ending discrimination. What happened in most communities has not happened everywhere. In Buffalo adequate legislation, backed up by reasonable enforcement, ended much of the housing discrimination with surprising rapidity.

The effectiveness of a law depends on the degree with which people voluntarily comply with it. Even such serious crimes as murder, kidnapping, rape and armed robbery have not been eradicated. Regulations pertaining to gambling, narcotics, driving speeds and the sale of alcoholic beverages are violated frequently. Some laws are almost completely ignored even by the authorities, such as the laws in forty-eight states which prohibit fornication.[4]

71

The extent to which any law is voluntarily obeyed appears to involve four separate but interrelated factors: the extent to which people in the community believe in the law; the vigor with which the law is enforced; the penalty imposed on those who break the law; and the gain realized by those who break the law.

The most important reason why fair housing laws usually have failed to halt discriminatory practices is that there has been insufficient public support. This lack causes legislatures to restrict the coverage and enforcement provisions of fair housing laws and to provide inadequate funds for their enforcement. Insufficient public support also encourages government officials charged with the responsibility of enforcement to go easy lest they stir up trouble; it reduces the independent citizen action always needed to assist government officials in enforcement; and, because most people act in accord with what they believe others to expect of them, apathy encourages violation of the law.

But it is not necessary that a law be supported by a majority. With effective leadership desegregation of public schools has been successfully accomplished in some school districts in border states where less than one-third of the white population supported such action.[5]

One of the reasons for the lack of enforcement is that most of those who favor the law do not support it actively. Roy Wilkins, executive director of the National Association for the Advancement of Colored People, has observed, "One of the great handicaps in the civil rights movement . . . is . . . we can't arouse people to work assiduously on implementation as much as [they do] in the fanfare of a campaign to get a law enacted."

One active supporter is equivalent to many inactive ones. Visible supporters are needed because there are many who oppose fair housing legislation. Referenda opposing fair housing laws have been approved in the state of California and in several cities, including Seattle and Akron. Public opposition also has been demonstrated by the frequent defeat of fair housing legislation in state and municipal legislatures, and the weaknesses of most of the legislation which has emerged.

Some oppose fair housing laws because they recognize the potential effectiveness of such laws. They do not wish to see discriminatory practices end. The opposition of many others stems from the mistaken belief that such laws are not the way to end discrimination because they abridge the "rights" of the owners of private property.

But the unfettered use of private property has continually been rejected by the courts in favor of the proposition that one cannot use what one owns in a fashion harmful to others. Over twenty years before the first fair housing law was passed, the United States Supreme Court declared, "Government cannot exist if the citizen may at will use his property to the detriment of his fellows." Thus it is not surprising that the constitutionality of fair housing laws was upheld in court cases in seven states prior to the 1968 decision of the Supreme Court.

One author recently listed twenty different aspects of law in which the absoluteness of property rights has been rejected.[6] A property owner may not violate building codes or zoning regulations; he must grant certain types of easements; he must share the benefits of water on his land; he must conform to standards of conservation; he may not violate sanitation regulations; and he must maintain certain standards of morality. Even an owner's power to dispose of his property is limited. For example, he may not make an inheritance depend on the marriage or the occupation of his heirs.

Antidiscrimination laws are just another restriction on

73

property owners, an acknowledgment by society that unfettered property rights do not take precedence over human rights.

City, state and federal action to end housing discrimination has been deficient in three respects: in coverage, enforcement and in deterrents.

Under the *Jones* v. *Mayer* decision of the Supreme Court, the 1866 Civil Rights Act makes it unlawful to discriminate because of race in the sale or rental of any housing in the United States. However, since there is no provision for enforcement of this by government action, additional federal and state legislation is required. Perhaps it is reasonable to exempt the rental of one or two rooms in a private home on the basis of the very close relationship which does exist between landlord and tenant in such circumstances. But in all other types of housing the relationships are more distant, and discriminatory practices based on personal preferences cannot be justified. Yet Title VIII of the 1968 Civil Rights Act does not give this coverage, and of the twenty-four states which have fair housing laws only three states — Alaska, Colorado, Michigan — have gone this far.*

A more serious problem with fair housing legislation to date is that it often fails to include adequate provisions for enforcing the law. Five years ago such deficient legislation could be excused on the basis that requirements were not really known. The first fair housing law in the United States only went into effect in New York City in 1958, and until 1961 only four states and two cities had fair housing laws.

---

*The other states which have fair housing laws as of this writing are California, Connecticut, Delaware, Hawaii, Indiana, Kentucky, Maine, Maryland, Massachusetts, Minnesota, New Hampshire, New Jersey, New York, Ohio, Oregon, Pennsylvania, Rhode Island, Vermont, Washington, and Wisconsin.

But today there is sufficient experience so that this excuse is no longer valid.

The required legislation and associated administrative policies should be responsive to the needs of black families who are not freedom fighters but people in need of a place to live. Experience shows that very few Negroes are willing to become involved in legal action to secure housing rights. This hesitancy occurs not because blacks do not want these rights, but because they must balance the gain of a better place to live against time lost from work, the emotional tensions of a legal battle, and the repercussions, both real and imagined, that might ensue.

A critical component of effective enforcement procedure is speed. Frequently the family seeking a home must move by a certain date and must settle for an alternative if its first choice cannot be made available. Even when the Negro family has the option of waiting, tardy action will result in the housing being sold or rented to someone else.

If a fair housing law is to be effective an agency which has the necessary legal powers and funds must be responsible for enforcement. This has very seldom been the case. For example, in September 1967, less than half of such state agencies had the power to obtain injunctions to prevent disposition of housing sought by a complainant.[7] Many agencies with injunctive powers are saddled with restrictions which prevent them obtaining injunctions quickly.

The inadequate budgets of almost all government bodies with responsibility for enforcing fair housing laws have been well summarized by Feingold and Harris, two University of Michigan professors who have made a detailed study of the administration of fair housing laws.[8] These investigators found the median budget for the twenty-two states with such agencies to be only a little over $100,000 and, in general, these organizations had to deal with a wide scope of problems of which fair housing was only one. Most city agencies had much smaller budgets.

Inadequate funding has not been the only cause of poor performance. Agencies can only function properly if their staff members are competent and committed. Low pay is often a problem; the use of jobs as a reward for political service is another. Even in the civil service initial appointments are often made on a political basis. As a result, complaints have been handled by people who lacked the basic verbal skills to effectively transmit to paper the essential facts, and investigations have been made by employees who lack the analytical ability to determine whether discrimination occurred. Another bad effect of patronage appointments is that since it was political service which landed the job, political service continues to take priority.

In some agencies, despite all these factors, the employees are competent and dedicated to equal opportunity, but the effectiveness of the enforcement of the law is decreased by bureaucratic behavior. Government employees, like others, try to please their bosses — political officeholders who are trying to please everybody. Since strong enforcement of fair housing laws will displease politically powerful elements in the community, the officials of the enforcement agency view their self-interest as best served by not rocking the boat.

A surprise for many who have been active in the fair housing movement has been the discovery that the personnel of an enforcement agency are not necessarily on their side. The same discovery has often been a bitter one for Negro homeseekers, such as the family that was asked by a staff member of New York State's Commission for Human Rights, "Why do you want to go where you aren't wanted?"

The overall result is that fair housing laws have been enforced very poorly. Complaints are processed too slowly and investigations are not thorough. In addition, when respondents have been ordered to take corrective actions, compliance has not been properly monitored. Feingold and Harris observed that often the situation was so bad that staff members held their own agency in low esteem.[8]

However, even if an enforcement agency pursues complaints vigorously and effectively, it can only do its job properly if it also supplements case-by-case enforcement with broad, long-term programs to end discriminatory practices. Voluntary compliance with the law will be achieved only when there are well publicized deterrents to breaking the law. Until then, many whites will regard fair housing laws as a gesture to placate blacks and most blacks will continue to regard enforcement agencies as another symbol of white hypocrisy.

The national fair housing law passed by Congress in 1968 suffers from the same weaknesses as most state and local legislation. Coverage is limited: single-family houses being sold or rented by the owner without the services of a real estate broker are not included,* nor are apartments or rooms in owner-occupied dwellings occupied by two to four families. But the greatest weaknesses lie in the lack of provision for enforcement powers and deterrents.

Federal jurisdiction will not normally be exercised where state or local fair housing laws are applicable. In other areas a person can either bring a private lawsuit or file a complaint with the Department of Housing and Urban Development (HUD). However, HUD's powers are limited to conference, conciliation and persuasion. If these fail, it is possible for HUD to refer the matter to the Attorney General, who

*More technically, single-family houses owned by a private individual owner of three or less are excluded where (1) a broker is not used to sell or rent; (2) discriminatory advertising is not used; (3) no more than one house in which the owner was not the most recent resident is sold during any two-year period.

can bring a civil suit in the federal district court, but such actions will be very limited because of limited staff. Thus the federal law represents a compromise between what civil rights activists wanted and what they could get, a law better than some state and local fair housing legislation, poorer than the rest. Amended it could be an important step toward an open society; as is, it will be another unkept promise to America's blacks.

When New York State's fair housing law was expanded on September 1, 1963, to include most housing it, too, was a compromise with many imperfections. In spite of these, there was great change in Buffalo and its suburbs during the next few years.

The New York State law and its administration is similar to that in most communities. After an aggrieved person files a complaint there is a preliminary investigation which usually includes a conference to which both the complainants and respondent are summoned. If "probable cause" is found to substantiate the complaint, conciliation is attempted. If this is unsuccessful, a public hearing is called to review all the evidence. If discrimination is found, the respondent is ordered to cease the discriminatory practice. This order can be enforced, if necessary, by a court action where the respondent has the right to appeal.

Prior to September 1, 1963, it was the policy of the Greater Buffalo Board of Realtors, to which most of the large real estate brokers in the Buffalo area belonged, that members would not show houses in all-white areas to Negro families. There were no exceptions, even if a seller wanted his home to be available to Negro buyers. On September 1, 1963, this official policy had to change.

But not much else changed at that time. A few real estate firms, including one of the largest in Western New York, did adopt nondiscriminatory policies. Most evaded the law. They stalled a Negro client in a variety of ways, showed only the advertised listings which had brought him to the office, emphasized and fabricated undesirable features of houses in which he expressed an interest, misrepresented the required down payment and, of course, never gave any indication that the asking price was negotiable. If this barrage of discriminatory actions still did not deter the Negro family from making a purchase offer for the asking price, there was another arsenal of tactics on which the brokers relied: someone else had made an offer, the owner had decided he was not going to sell the house, the owner was out of town and had not yet answered the letter the real estate broker had sent him, the real estate agent was out of town. . . . If the Negro family did not offer the asking price, the offer would, of course, be turned down.

A few real estate firms were not even subtle. If a Negro came in, there was nothing available; if there was a specific inquiry about a house just advertised, it was represented as sold.

It was about this time that the fair housing group HOME was founded in the Buffalo area. In order to bring such practices to a halt, or at least make them less frequent, the initial strategy of the new organization was to work closely with the Greater Buffalo Board of Realtors and the State Commission for Human Rights (the enforcement agency for antidiscrimination laws in the state of New York, now called the Division of Human Rights).

A few days after the first newspaper article about HOME, the Board of Realtors invited the leaders of the newly formed fair housing group to lunch. HOME's leadership enthusiastically accepted the invitation. They were exhilarated. This was the answer: getting reasonable people together to work out the problems.

The luncheon seemed a success. There was a good dia-

logue. The Realtors emphasized that they were not prejudiced, but that prior to the new law they had followed discriminatory policies because of community pressures. They
went on to point out that there still were many fears about
integration and that HOME could provide a valuable service by educating the community. At the same time, the
Realtors promised to do what they could for the common
goal.

But that was as far as the working relationship went. The
exhilaration changed to disenchantment as the HOME leaders saw mounting evidence that the Realtors did not share
their goals. A request for a public endorsement of open housing met with no action. A request for a statement about what
had happened to property values in the neighborhoods into
which Negro families had moved met with no action. Requests for action within the Board of Realtors to eliminate
discriminatory acts were brushed aside with the claim that
there was no discrimination. Strong evidence of discriminatory practices based on sworn statements of reputable citizens was categorized as the fabrication of troublemakers.

If there was any doubt that the Board of Realtors was not
going to make much of a contribution toward equal opportunities, it was resolved by Cleon Service, an urbane Negro
Realtor who owned and operated the Newton Realty Company.

Although his firm was one of four Negro-owned real estate
companies associated with the Board of Realtors' "multiple
listing" service, thereby having access to many properties in
white areas, Service was the only Realtor, black or white,
who made any effort to develop that segment of the Negro
market which sought to buy outside of the ghetto. His interest was partly motivated by profit — a good judgment since
his commissions from this segment of his business have averaged almost $10,000 per year during the last four years. But

equally important was his strong desire to be an active participant in the battle for equality and his personal conviction that equality required integration in housing.

On October 8, 1964, Service telephoned the office of Harrington, Smith and Cornwall* and requested an appointment to show one of their listings to a client. The woman who answered the telephone promptly made the appointment. A short while later, however, Mr. Cornwall called and requested a qualification sheet on the buyer be brought to their suburban office for approval. Service gave the information on the telephone, but this did not satisfy the real estate firm. They insisted that he personally bring the information to them for approval — a request Service interpreted as aimed at discouraging him from using their listings.

This was, for Service, the straw that broke the camel's back. It was thirteen months since the passage of the law which had given him the right to show homes in white areas to Negro clients. But, with the exception of a very few firms, it was a struggle just to get an appointment, let alone to get an offer accepted. After several days of thought, he wrote a letter to the Practice and Ethics Committee of the Board of Realtors asking that Harrington, Smith and Cornwall be directed to make appointments for his office in the same manner as for other Realtors. At the time he touched on other grievances without naming specific firms or incidents.

Nothing happened. Months went by and still nothing happened. He wrote another letter and made numerous telephone calls, but still nothing happened. He pointed out that the bylaws of the Board of Realtors required that a hearing be held on a complaint of the type that he had lodged, but still there was no response. More drastic action appeared to

*Fictitious names have been substituted for the real names of brokers accused of discrimination.

be necessary; but more drastic action involved a risk to his means of livelihood.

After eight months without a response, Service filed a complaint with the New York State Commission for Human Rights directed against Harrington, Smith and Cornwall. At the same time he also filed a complaint against Petty, Joseph and Richards, one of the largest realty firms in the area, in which he cited ten different discriminatory acts by the firm involving six different properties. Among the complaints: twice he was told the key to a vacant home was not available but once, when a white couple asked fifteen minutes later to see the house, the key was immediately at hand; on another occasion a key was given for a house, but it was the wrong key; once when Service telephoned he was put on "hold" for twenty minutes and then was told that the owner would have to be contacted, but the call was never returned; a Negro client who was able to see a house and subsequently made an offer at the asking price received no response over a ten-day period, at which time the discouraged family withdrew the offer.

Suddenly the Board of Realtors came to life. Jack Donovan, the executive vice-president, told Service that unless he withdrew the complaint to the State Commission he faced expulsion from the Board of Realtors. But Service, aided by one of HOME's lawyers, called the bluff and replied that, if expelled, he would seek reinstatement and damages in court.

There was no further move toward expulsion. The Board of Realtors' Practice and Ethics Committee reviewed Service's complaints, found in his favor, and warned the offending Realtors to cease discriminatory practices. Having achieved what he wanted, Service dropped the charges he had filed with the State Commission. He never had to file a complaint again. Other events were occurring which made it undesirable for Realtors to have complaints lodged against them, and Cleon Service had clearly declared his intent not to let acts of discrimination be ignored.

HOME's original strategy of working closely with the New York State Commission for Human Rights to obtain broker compliance also was a failure. When complaints were filed with the Commission it took weeks, sometimes several months, before even an initial conference was held. Then more time, sometimes many months, would elapse before a decision. Since HOME only submitted cases to the Commission where good evidence was available, the determination almost always was that discrimination had occurred. But no action sufficient to stop discrimination resulted. At the most, the real estate broker would post a sign in his office saying that discrimination was against the law, write a letter of apology for the "misunderstanding" and offer to serve the complainant on some future occasion.

It was an agonizing period for the whites who were active in HOME. They were less accustomed to such frustrations than were Negroes. Their efforts were like trying to move a giant sponge which was glued to the floor. There was a yielding when pressure was applied, but no overall progress.

A new strategy was needed, one that would compel brokers to cease discrimination. Disciplinary action by the licensing agency — the New York Department of State — was a possibility. HOME's lawyers studied the powers vested in the State Department and concluded that new legislation was not necessary since "untrustworthiness" was a ground for suspension or revocation of license, and the actions of discriminatory brokers fitted a definition of untrustworthiness.

The legal power was there but not the willingness to use it. Letters to Governor Rockefeller, Secretary of State John

P. Lomenzo and George H. Fowler, Chairman of the State Commission for Human Rights, brought polite, noncommittal replies. Telephone calls were parried. A large public meeting sponsored by HOME in November 1964, which dramatically revealed the widespread violation of state law by local real estate brokers, got good press and TV coverage, but still no action.

Fortunately, other fair housing groups throughout the state were also pushing for disciplinary action against licensees who discriminated. Particularly active were the Yonkers Fair Housing Committee and a group in Brooklyn called FOCUS. As a result of these pressures, Lomenzo and Fowler met in December 1964, and agreed that brokers who repeatedly violated the law would be referred to the Department of State for disciplinary action. However, this step was regarded as a token by the fair housing interests who recognized that it would promote change very slowly.

In the end, the actions of government are the actions of men. Chairman Fowler, an able Negro lawyer, believed that discriminatory practices were better ended by conciliation and persuasion than aggressive enforcement of the law. He also held political ambitions beyond the high office he had already achieved — ambitions he might realize by winning acclaim in the white community for his responsible administration of the State Commission and by the favors he was able to do for party leaders by virtue of the patronage he controlled. Ambition and pride made him unreceptive to delegating a part of the responsibility for the fight against discrimination to another state agency; caution prevented him from making the Commission the instrument of change that it might have been.

Secretary of State Lomenzo was a different type of man. A former judge in Rochester, he was more liberal than most upstate Republican politicians — a Rockefeller Republican with a tremendous admiration for the Governor. In Lomenzo's view, the political interests of Nelson Rockefeller, in New York State and the nation, would best be served by enforcement of the law, although hopefully with a minimum of disturbance in the real estate community. As a result, when civil rights advocates continued to protest violations of the law, Lomenzo decided to act unilaterally. On June 3, 1965, he established a special six-man civil rights unit to investigate complaints of discrimination against real estate brokers and salesmen and to discipline offenders. In the next three years this unit investigated over four hundred complaints which resulted in hearings for ninety-nine brokers and salesmen. Seventeen of these had their licenses revoked and fifty-three others received suspensions.

In Buffalo, once HOME had adopted the strategy of seeking suspensions, it was felt desirable to develop a well-documented case against one broker rather than to bring relatively weak cases aginst many firms. The task of selecting the target firm was not taken lightly. It was recognized that it would not only be unfair, but might be harmful to the overall objective if the selected target were not one of the more serious offenders. A real estate broker named Richard Howland made this choice an easy one.

In July 1964, George Clarke, a Negro who held a managerial position with a local company, telephoned the office of Howland Real Estate to inquire about a home which had been advertised that day in the Buffalo *Evening News*. The salesman suggested he come to the office immediately so that he could be taken to see the house. Clarke said he would be there in fifteen minutes. Fourteen minutes later, when Clarke and his wife arrived, two men were standing in front of the office. Since there was no parking space available in front of the office, the Clarkes went around the cor-

ner, parked and walked back to the agency.   ow the men
were gone and the office was deserted. Not until almost
thirty minutes later did someone appear. When Clarke asked
for the salesman with whom he had spoken, he was told
that the salesman had not been in the office for several
hours; when Clarke said he had talked to the man less than
an hour earlier, he was told that the salesman must be out
showing houses to other people. Clarke left his name and
telephone number, but he never received a call.

At that time, almost one year after discrimination of this
type became unlawful in New York State, such violations of
the law were still common in the Buffalo area. In order to
concentrate the feeble efforts of the State Commission on
the most important cases, HOME had temporarily adopted a
policy of filing complaints only when the Negro family specifically wanted to overcome the discriminatory act they had
encountered. In this particular case the Clarkes did not wish
to do so and consequently no complaint was lodged.

The next encounter with Howland Realty was more unusual. On September 26, 1964, Mrs. Alan Sterns listed her
home with Howland. Shortly thereafter a Negro real estate
broker named Mary Fisher called Mrs. Sterns to see if she
could show the house to a prospective buyer. Mrs. Sterns informed her that the house now was listed with Howland and,
at Mrs. Sterns's suggestion, Mrs. Fisher telephoned Howland,
received permission to show the house, and arranged an
appointment with Mrs. Sterns. Although Mrs. Fisher and
Howland had never met, arrangements such as this between
brokers were common. If a sale resulted, the commission was
shared.

A few minutes after Mrs. Fisher and her Negro client arrived at Mrs. Sterns's home the telephone rang. "They're
white, aren't they?" a representative from Howland asked.

Mrs. Sterns told him that they were Negroes. The caller sounded surprised and upset and, while Mrs. Fisher and her client were still inspecting the house, he called again. He told Mrs. Sterns that she did not have to sell to Negroes. She said she did not care if a Negro bought the house. He persisted and emphasized that there were ways of getting around selling to Negroes; she reiterated that she wished to sell on an open basis.

Later that evening Howland and one of his salesmen called on Mrs. Sterns. He told her that if an offer were tendered by a Negro that he would represent the house as sold. Mrs. Sterns stood her ground and cited the antidiscrimination law. Unable to pressure her, Howland and his salesman removed the "FOR SALE" sign from in front of the house; a few days later Mrs. Sterns received notice that her contract with the real estate firm had been terminated.

Within a month there was yet another complaint against Howland. If someone were to be singled out by HOME, Howland seemed the logical candidate, particularly after an investigation indicated that his overall reputation was not one that would discourage such action.

In order to present as strong a case as possible, two Negroes acting as testers attempted to see houses listed by Howland. Mrs. George W. Clay, Jr., wife of an electrical engineer, made an appointment to see a five-bedroom house which was advertised in the paper. While making the appointment by phone she was asked where she lived; later that day the appointment was canceled because "the house was sold." However, the same house was available to a white checker the following day. Meanwhile Mrs. Clay attempted, by telephone and a personal visit to the Howland office, to see another five-bedroom house, but was told none were available. The white checker, however, was shown

another five-bedroom house. Mrs. Clay described the salesman with whom she talked as "friendly, but he made it clear
he did not want to do business with me."

Another Negro, William H. Scurry, called the Howland
office at 8:00 P.M. a few days later. He noticed there were
three people in the office when he drove up. They hastily put
up a "closed" sign on the front door, turned off all the lights
in the office, and hurried into a back room. By the time he
reached the front door all was quiet inside. After waiting
several minutes, he left.

The HOME leadership was satisfied with the evidence.
Complaints were filed with the State Commission and cop-
ies, with other evidence, were sent to the Department of
State on November 19, 1964.

Days, weeks, months went by. The State Commission
held preliminary hearings, found probable cause on all complaints, held public hearings, and, in June 1965, obtained
a court order restraining Howland from engaging in future
unlawful discriminatory practices. But the Department of
State took no action until June 30 when a letter was written
to HOME stating that since the State Commission had gotten
a court order "further action by this Department. . . . would
not be appropriate."

The letter was not well received. Unaware of the inter-
departmental and interpersonal problems involved, the
HOME people looked with suspicion on the explanation offered privately that there was uncertainty of jurisdiction. But
they did listen attentively when Patrick J. Cea, the head of
the newly-formed civil rights group in the Department of
State, suggested that another complaint against Howland
probably would result in a disciplinary hearing.

On August 3, 1965, Floyd F. Cumberbatch, a Negro
chemist who held a responsible position with the Food and
Drug Administration, inquired of Howland Realty about a

house just advertised. He was referred to an agent named Joseph R. Moynihan who worked part-time selling real estate. Moynihan showed him the house and gave the price as $28,500. Cumberbatch said he thought the price was too high and pointed out that the newspaper ad listed the house in the "low twenties." Moynihan's response was, "Well, it's under thirty thousand dollars."

On the afternoon of August 9 — with a well-known Buffalo musician listening on an extension — Cumberbatch called Moynihan and told him he was interested in the house. At Cumberbatch's request Moynihan verified that the asking price was $28,500. When Cumberbatch asked if the price was negotiable, Moynihan said it was not since the owners were not being forced to move. Meanwhile, Bill Harrell, a professor at the State University of New York at Buffalo and white, was told that the asking price for the same house was $22,900 and the price was negotiable.

A complaint was filed with the State Commission and the evidence was presented to the Department of State. But, having been frustrated for so long, HOME's board of directors decided that this time they would apply additional pressure. Consequently a letter was sent to Governor Rockefeller which also was released to the news media. This letter, which received wide publicity, said what HOME had never before said publicly, but every active fair housing group in the state of New York felt at that time:

> . . . Your administration has failed or refused to enforce the New York State laws against discrimination in housing. . . . Each of these complaints results from a violation, as brutal as any physical assault, against a responsible citizen of our community. . . . This situation exists because of the failure of your administration to punish those who break the law. . . . We are weary

89

of . . . misleading statements by state officials . . . when in fact compliance with the law has not been achieved. . . . We hope that you will match your words with deeds.

Within a few days word was received that there would be a hearing by the Department of State on the Howland case.

The hearing was a great victory for HOME even though Howland, guilty as he seemed to some, received no punishment. The hearing officer ruled that while Moynihan was guilty of untrustworthiness, there was no evidence that Howland was aware of his employee's actions. HOME's objective, however, had not been to punish a specific broker but to end discriminatory practices by all brokers. As an indication to the real estate industry that those who broke the law would be punished, the disciplining of Moynihan was a giant step.

It was only the beginning. The policy of HOME, explicitly stated by letter to all real estate brokers in the area, was to bring any discriminatory act to the attention of the Department of State and to press key staff members, and Secretary Lomenzo himself, to take action. During the next year five more brokers were disciplined in the Buffalo area, and two other cases were in process.

The result of these disciplinary actions was that the practices of real estate brokers changed to an extent that even the most optimistic leaders of HOME had not expected. During the three and one half year period up to March 1970, only three brokers were caught discriminating, and since two of them lost their licenses* the violations will probably be even fewer in the future. Moreover, most real estate bro-

*License revocations in New York State often amount to a suspension of one year since a person whose license has been revoked can apply for a new license after one year.

kers have gone well beyond the minimum required by law. Although none of the white brokers has solicited Negro business for nonghetto housing, Negro clients have been treated much the same as whites. One large real estate firm, in which two of the partners have long-standing reputations as bigots, has joined a growing list of brokers who will not take a listing unless the seller explicitly agrees beforehand not to discriminate if an offer is received from a Negro.

A disciplinary action of particular interest taken by the New York Department of State was against a grandmotherly lady with over twenty years of experience in the real estate business. Mrs. Sara Cameron, while attempting to obtain a listing, had urged a homeowner not to sell to Negroes. "I respect the rights of the people in this neighborhood," Mrs. Cameron was quoted as saying. Because she strongly opposed discrimination, Mrs. Robert Bradford, the seller, got in touch with HOME and was advised to write a description of the incident to the Secretary of State.

Frances Bradford received a polite reply, but nothing further happened. However, HOME officials recognized the potential in this different kind of case, one which involved advice to discriminate rather than a discriminatory act, and when HOME threatened to make a public issue of it, the State Department agreed to conduct an investigation. By this time Mrs. Bradford had sold her home and moved to Columbus, Ohio. This gave the State Department a new excuse not to do anything, but when Mrs. Bradford was contacted by HOME and declared her willingness to return to Buffalo for a hearing the maneuvering was over.

There was an interesting sequel to the Cameron case. On the day after it was announced that Mrs. Cameron had been found guilty of untrustworthiness and had received a thirty-day suspension of her license, the minister of a large suburban church placed a call to a HOME officer to whom he felt he could talk freely. The clergyman was very disturbed; Mrs. Cameron was a member of his church whom he had known as a fine churchwoman for many years. He noted that Mrs. Cameron had denied what Mrs. Bradford claimed and that there was no evidence that Mrs. Bradford was telling the truth and Mrs. Cameron was not. He pointed out that he was a member of HOME, but that he could not support an organization, no matter how worthy its objectives, if it victimized an innocent person.

Little could be said at the time except that Frances Bradford had seemed to be a fine person who had no reason to do what she did unless her claims were true. Fortunately, in the next couple of days there were several other reactions. "I'm glad you got that old witch," said one woman well known in the community. "Eight years ago when my husband and I were looking for a home, Mrs. Cameron tried to sell us one on the basis that it was in an area where she and the other real estate brokers had been able to keep out Jews."

The information was relayed to the clergyman, who maintained his membership in HOME.

It is useful to review what actually was required in the Buffalo area to change the practices of real estate brokers from a position where at least 75 percent were violating the law to compliance so nearly complete that in over three years there were only three complaints about discrimination by brokers. Not only was the transition time short, but most of the penalties imposed were very light, almost token. Several lawbreakers, such as Moynihan, lost their licenses, but in all cases they were either part-time salesmen who, for other reasons, decided they had enough of the real estate business, or they were in a phase of the business where they did not need a license. Of those whose license was essential to their livelihood, the most severe punishment was a sixty-day suspension, and even then there was an option to avoid the suspension by payment of a $258 fine. In one case the dates of the suspension were adjusted so that it coincided with the broker's vacation.

There were some in the civil rights movement who thought the penalties during this period should have been harsher. However, the leniency initially shown by Secretary of State Lomenzo appears to have been justified. Light penalties, coupled with the threat of more severe sanctions in the future, were sufficient to effect most of the required changes. And, reprehensible as were their actions, to a certain extent the brokers who discriminated were responding to pressures and prejudices in the community.

The voluntary compliance so rapidly achieved was partly the result of community education toward acceptance of the law,* partly the imposition of sanctions against those who broke the law, and largely the realization by real estate brokers that they had nothing to gain by breaking the law. Once it was obvious they had something to lose and nothing to gain, brokers complied with the law.

On the other hand, what happened in Buffalo should not be understood as being easy to accomplish. By 1966 HOME had grown to over one thousand members, and thousands of others could be counted on to cooperate. There were too many people such as Frances Bradford, who believed that the law should be enforced and knew where to go to have injustices corrected, for real estate people to take a risk.

Another element which contributed to success in Buffalo was the relatively good relationships which HOME's leadership maintained with the state officials whose cooperation was needed to get the law enforced. These relationships were not achieved by compromising principles or retreating from what needed to be done; in fact, the relationships were

*See pages 121-124 and Chapter 6.

often purposely strained. But at all times there was a strong effort at good communication, a serious attempt to appreciate and allow for the problems of state officials, a willingness not to press matters of small importance, and a positive response to requests for information or assistance by state employees. Perhaps most important, when public criticism was leveled, personalities were avoided; whenever there was any reason for praise, it was loud and clear.

The enforcement of antidiscrimination laws concerning the sale of new houses by builders was a different type of problem that confronted HOME. Builders are not licensed by the state and builders constructing new developments were even more fearful about doing business with Negroes than real estate brokers.

Some of the difficulties experienced by Harold Amos — the first Negro in Buffalo to obtain newly built housing under the law — have already been mentioned on page 6. The mechanism of the law worked so slowly that the builder was able to sell almost all the other houses in the subdivision while he kept the Amos family waiting. Even then, if left to himself, the builder would have continued to resist selling to the Amoses, but his lawyer persuaded him not to fight the law.

Confrontation also was avoided by the developer from whom Dr. Wayman McCoy, a Negro physician, bought his home. This developer had high moral principles and genuine sympathy for the Negro position. As a result, when Dr. McCoy said he wanted to buy a house, there was none of the lying and misrepresentation which customarily occurred. Instead he was ushered into the builder's office and the conversation was opened by the builder with "We are all Christians . . ."

Nevertheless, the builder told Dr. McCoy he would not

sell him a house because he feared an adverse effect on the sale of other houses in the development. It was a somewhat tortured "no." Dr. McCoy responded by filing a complaint with the State Commission for Human Rights and, since the subdivision in which he was interested was receiving federal financing, a complaint also was filed with the FHA in accordance with the provision of an executive order signed in 1962 by President Kennedy. It was the FHA complaint which paid off.

Unlike most FHA officials, Warren Thurber, the head of the FHA office in Buffalo, believed in open housing. As a result, a few weeks later Isham Jones, a staff assistant to the FHA regional director, flew to Buffalo and met with Dr. McCoy, the developer and Thurber. Jones told the developer that unless he agreed to sell then and there, the FHA would immediately apply sanctions and he would be unable to get FHA financing again until either he sold the house to the McCoys or an appeal was granted. The developer, who did not like discriminating to begin with, capitulated.

Charles Broadus was not as lucky as Harold Amos or Dr. McCoy. The burden of paving the way for others fell to him.

In 1958 discrimination had forced Broadus to settle for a house in the ghetto. Five years later, his family increased by two sets of twins, Charles and Jean Broadus wanted something better, a new home away from the heart of the city with room enough for their growing family. They had worked hard and saved carefully. The new antidiscrimination laws gave them hope.

Tall and powerfully built, on first acquaintance Broadus appeared to be what he was, a blue-collar worker from a disadvantaged background. Beneath this exterior was an extraordinary man — bright, resourceful, determined — with a tremendous drive to provide a better life for his family. When Jean Broadus quit her job as a nurse's aide to go to school for a year to qualify as a licensed practical nurse, Broadus kept up the family income with a second job and continued to assist with the household work. Although it was circumstance and not design which placed Charles Broadus in a focal position in the battle for open housing, it would have been difficult to have found a better champion.

Finding houses which they liked was no problem for the Broadus family. They read the ads and went to look at the model houses. But buying these houses was a different matter. They tried three different builders, but they could not obtain a sales contract from any of them. In each case they filed a complaint with the State Commission for Human Rights.

For a brief moment it looked as though they might crack the discriminatory barriers they were encountering. The subdivision they liked best was French Lea Estates which was being developed by the Marrano Construction Company. A white couple, members of HOME, went out to French Lea Estates, looked at various houses, and then called the salesman back a few days later to make another appointment. What followed went exactly as planned. The white couple showed great interest in a house identical to that wanted by Mr. and Mrs. Broadus and declared that they were ready to sign a contract and give a deposit. The salesman eagerly prepared the forms while assuring the prospective buyers that he was authorized to execute the sale. Then, at the right moment, the Broaduses appeared, accompanied by an attorney, and the white couple announced that the Broaduses were the people who really wanted the house. Shorn of any excuses and somewhat stunned, the salesman meekly executed a sales contract and accepted the Broaduses' deposit on the house. But Pat Marrano, the head of Marrano Construction, was not so meek. He said Broadus

96

had acted in bad faith and therefore he would not sell to him.

Thus began a long battle of attrition. It was not simply a good guy against a bad guy. Marrano and other members of his family operation honestly believed they had the right to do business with persons of their choosing, and they had a lawyer who held out the hope that such a philosophy might be sustained by the courts.

Racial prejudice on Marrano's part does not appear to have played the dominant role in his determined effort to keep Broadus out of French Lea Estates. During the litigation Marrano urged at a meeting of the Niagara Frontier Builders Association that the group take action which would assist Negroes to obtain housing on the same basis as whites. And several years later Marrano voluntarily rented a house to a Negro family. But in 1964 and 1965, Pat Marrano was not ready to practice equal opportunities.

In some ways Pat Marrano was like Charles Broadus. Behind the ordinary exterior was an extraordinary man. Starting with three years' experience as a carpenter he had, by hard work, skill as a builder, and business acumen, created in fifteen years a business which was building and selling sixty to sixty-five houses a year. All this, in the mind of Pat Marrano, was threatened by Charles Broadus. Marrano believed that if Broadus came to French Lea Estates whites would not buy his houses. So he fought with all his resources, and as he became more and more committed to keeping Broadus out, the litigation became to him a matter of principle just as it always had been for Charles Broadus.

FHA pressure was not effective in helping Broadus because Marrano and other members of his family operated several companies. Consequently, with some legal footwork, the sanctions did not interfere with their overall operation.

The State Commission for Human Rights, as usual, was very slow. But step-by-step the procedure of enforcement was ground out. "Probable cause" was found, but Marrano still refused to sell. When, after a public hearing with all the attendant publicity, the Commission went to court to obtain an order to force him to sell, Marrano's attorney carried the fight to the court — and lost again. Even then Marrano did not give up; a notice of appeal was filed. By now more than twenty months had passed since Charles Broadus had first tried to make a deposit on the house of his choice. He continued to wait patiently, but with such faith in ultimate victory that he resembled a tiger stalking his prey.

The inevitable result also had become clear to Marrano. He was too smart to continue to hope he could win, but too proud to accept defeat. He now felt he had done the wrong thing, that a Negro family in his development would not have cost as much as what he had been through — thousands of dollars in legal expenses, family disagreements, wasted time, emotional strain, identification in the minds of many as a defender of bigotry. But, having done all this, he did not want it to be in vain.

Marrano had already tried to offer Broadus a reasonable alternative to French Lea Estates. With the help of Jack Donovan, the executive vice-president of the Builders Association as well as the Board of Realtors, a search was made for new houses of the type Broadus wanted which were not in subdivisions under development. Two were located and brought to Broadus's attention through an intermediary. Broadus did not like them enough to be willing to buy them. However, his willingness to consider an alternative gave Marrano hope for a new idea. He obtained an option on a lot which was larger and more expensive than lots in French Lea Estates and offered to sell the house the

Broaduses wanted and the lot at the same price that they would cost in French Lea Estates.

The offer was accepted. Marrano built the house well and speedily, sent a gift to a housewarming party to which Broadus invited him. Unlike many long and bitter struggles which end with everyone a loser, here there was an element of victory for all. Although it had cost Marrano dearly, he had achieved his objective of keeping Broadus out of French Lea Estates. Broadus, after his long wait, not only had the house he most wanted, but because of the expensive lot the house was worth at least $3000 more than he paid for it. And for HOME the victory went far beyond assisting Broadus to obtain the home of his choice. Marrano's resistance had provided the type of confrontation which leads to significant gains in the battle for equal rights. The publicity given the case made known that laws against discrimination were being enforced; the price Marrano paid for his recalcitrance broke down builder resistance in the future.

This did not mean that builders stopped discriminating immediately, but when they were caught they gave up relatively quickly. No one wanted to go through the frustrating and costly litigation in which Marrano had engaged. And before long several Negroes had bought homes in new developments without encountering any discrimination.

In Buffalo, as elsewhere in the nation, equality of opportunity is of particular importance in rental housing because most Negroes rent. Unfortunately, voluntary compliance has been poorest and enforcement of the law most difficult in the area of rental housing. The United States has an acute shortage of rental housing and desirable accommodations often are taken in a few hours or filled from waiting lists. This shortage makes discrimination easier to practice and more difficult to overcome.

The tactics used in Buffalo to overcome discrimination were varied to match the situation. Whenever a Negro family was interested in a development where available apartments were filled from waiting lists, a white HOME volunteer who represented himself as having the same family unit as the Negro homeseeker (and whenever possible actually did have the same family size and ages) would apply for a similar apartment. Then, if the checker were offered an apartment prior to the Negro, there was no doubt that the action was discriminatory and that excuses such as "the apartments in that building are only given to families without children" or "we don't like to place unmarried men next door to single girls" were lies to mask discrimination.

When discrimination occurred under these circumstances, a complaint filed with the State Commission for Human Rights usually secured the apartment for the black family immediately. Even when the landlord stalled the Commission and rented the apartment to someone else, other apartments would become available which the Commission could tie up until the case was settled — and, as a result, the case was settled quickly.

A much more difficult problem occurred with a landlord who had only a few rental units. In this case, if the available housing were rented to someone else an acceptable alternative might not become available for many months. And, because the supply of rental housing was tight, it was not difficult to delay the black family long enough to find a white tenant. However, from the experience of many failures came some effective rules.

Negro families were urged to begin apartment hunting as early in the day as possible. A good practice for anyone seeking housing, it is particularly important for a Negro family in order that they have time to counteract a discriminatory turndown. Getting the first edition of the evening paper as soon as it hit the streets downtown often meant the difference between success and failure.

The family was instructed not to reveal that they were Negroes when they telephoned for an appointment. Most blacks, without such instruction, identify their race. Before the days of antidiscrimination laws, racial identification allowed a Negro family to avoid embarrassment and wasting time looking at housing that would not be available. Racial identification also is a matter of honor, a desire not to have the landlord feel that the black represented himself falsely. However, in order that the law be effectively utilized, it is essential that the Negro view the available housing without delay to allow him to decide whether or not he wants it. In fact, when the homeseeker is readily identified as a Negro by voice, it may be desirable to have someone else call to make appointments.

If the homeseeker wants the apartment, a deposit should be made as soon as possible. The longer the delay, the greater the risk that someone else will get the apartment. The advantages of a choice of apartments must be carefully weighed against the risks of delay.

Experience has shown that until discriminatory practices have been essentially eliminated from the community, a Negro homeseeker who has had a deposit declined should suspect discrimination. The records are full of cases involving nice, friendly landlords who lied. Only by the use of a white checker can it be ascertained whether the housing is no longer available or not available to a black family. Since time delays increase the probability that the apartment will be rented, a checker should be immediately available.

For a long time the procedure HOME used when a checker discovered discrimination was to file a complaint immediately with the State Commission and attempt to get a conference as soon as possible. This eventually was abandoned because too often the Negro family did not get the housing they wanted, the delays being so long that the housing was rented before the Commission was able to take action. As a result, when a Negro family definitely wanted the housing and indicated they were willing to file a complaint, it became standard practice for the checker to make a deposit. Then, when a conference was held by the State Commission a few days later, the apartment was available and, if the landlord did not yield, could be kept vacant by the use of a temporary injunction. In almost every instance, the landlord was so stunned by what had happened and troubled by his own guilt that he capitulated at the first conference.

Once these techniques had been developed, most black families working with HOME were able to secure the rental housing of their choice. But it was not only the techniques. Equally important were the determination and the commitment of those involved: the willingness of a checker to drop what she was doing to test an apartment, the willingness of a lawyer to spend several hours at a hearing on short notice.

Still, progress toward voluntary compliance in rentals was slow. In 1968, after three years of relatively effective enforcement on a case-by-case basis, Negroes seeking rentals covered by law were still encountering discrimination about 60 percent of the time. While this represented significant progress, it also was a clear indication that unless those who broke the law were punished, the law would continue to be violated and the great majority of blacks, unwilling to pursue complaints through a public agency, would remain in their ghettos, increasingly resentful of discrimination.

How much can be accomplished by effective and creative enforcement of law, coupled with penalties for those who break the law, is demonstrated by the success in eliminating the practice of blockbusting in New York State. In 1961 the Secretary of State, Caroline K. Simon, issued a regulation which stated:

> No broker or salesman shall solicit the sale, lease or the listing for sale or lease, of residential property on the ground of loss of value due to the present or prospective entry into the neighborhood of a person or persons of another race, religion or ethnic origin, nor shall he distribute materials or make statements designed to induce a residential property owner to sell or lease his property due to change in neighborhood.

After several brokers lost their licenses, violations of the law ceased, but some unscrupulous brokers continued to operate just inside the law. In the Cambria Heights area of Queens in New York City, which contained a 30 percent Negro population, brokers bombarded white homeowners with telephone calls, mailings and door-to-door solicitations offering to sell their houses. However, the brokers avoided violating the law by not directly mentioning race. Faced with the danger that panic selling would start in Cambria Heights, the Department of State quickly adopted a "Cease and Desist Procedure." Homeowners were given a form they could file with the Department of State revoking the otherwise implied invitation to be solicited. These forms were returned by the hundreds; the names were then sent to all brokers operating in Cambria Heights with instructions that if they did not obey the cease and desist order they would be subject to disciplinary action. This greatly decreased solicitations, and Cambria Heights today remains a relatively integrated community.

Unfortunately the related problem of "blockbusting by

attrition" continues. It is the practice of real estate brokers not to take white home buyers to areas with a sizable Negro population. Thus when four Negro families bought on the same block in an all-white area in Buffalo, most real estate brokers did not show other houses for sale on that street to white clients unless the whites explicitly requested to see the house and had been informed that it was in a "racially changing area." On the other hand, Negro clients were quickly ushered there. As a result, this block continued to change racially.

No action could be taken. In 1965, in a similar instance of blockbusting by attrition in Queens Village, the New York Department of State had suspended the licenses of two brokers and a salesman for six months on the basis of well-documented evidence obtained by the Laurelton Fair Housing Council. However, the courts reversed the decision of the Department of State and held that a broker was within his rights to advise prospective purchasers of the racial composition of the community.

Often fine lines separate right from wrong, one man's rights from another man's privileges. But the lines must be drawn by the courts and followed by all if there is to be an ordered society. If blockbusting by attrition cannot be eliminated under the law, it can still be made a relic of the past by organized community action in those neighborhoods which are experiencing significant integration, coupled with open housing efforts in the community at large.

The experiences related in this chapter indicate the requirements for good fair housing legislation and its administration.

Swift and thorough investigations are necessary not only to protect the rights of the complainant but also to be fair to a respondent who has been mistakenly accused of discrimination. The enforcement agency should receive complaints and initiate investigations during evenings and weekends, use white testers as "checkers," and be empowered to issue restraining orders and injunctions to prevent the sale or rental of disputed housing until after a case is settled. While the enforcement agency should clearly represent the interests of the complainant, the agency also must be scrupulously fair to the respondent and, in the rare instances that an innocent respondent suffers a loss, he should receive reasonable damages without having to resort to court action.

An effort should be made to overcome the reluctance of most of those who encounter discrimination to file a complaint. Filing should be made as convenient as possible and should not require corroborative evidence. The enforcement agency should make every effort to minimize the time the complainant must spend in the proceedings, particularly time away from his job. The agency also should be sensitive to transportation problems the complainant may have. It should not always be necessary for the complainant to come to the agency office; the agency should be willing to come to the complainant.

If voluntary compliance is to be achieved, vigorous enforcement must be complemented by sanctions which are well publicized through the community. Without interfering with the right of the aggrieved to resort to court action,[9] the enforcement agency must have and use the power to order a guilty respondent to pay damages for the complainant's inconveniences and humiliation. Awards ranging from $200 to $1000 would seem reasonable.

Punishments for licensed real estate brokers should be more severe. They cannot plead that they were not fully aware of the law. Even for a first offense there should be at least a suspension of license in addition to payment of damages; if a second offense occurs, revocation of license should be mandatory.

However, just as education should not be thought of as an alternative to law, neither should law be regarded as an alternative to education. Both are necessary. They complement and reinforce each other.

The same is true of the relationship between government action and citizen action. They also complement and reinforce each other. The stronger and more visible the fair housing movement, the easier it is for the government to enforce the law with vigor and dispatch. At the same time, forceful action by government strengthens citizen response.

That is the way it should be and must be. The alternative is a vicious cycle of lawlessness by some causing lawlessness by others.

5 / The Fair Housing Group—
Its Strategy and Tactics

How does one succeed in doing something about discrimination in housing? What must be done so that the product of a fair housing organization is not merely a series of meetings and newspaper reports? How do you effect real progress?

Success will be the result of action, not time. Success will come from carrying out programs designed to meet the problems, not from good intentions. Success will depend on the work of an organization which unremittingly seeks open housing, and which serves as a focal point for those willing to help and those who need help.

The group should not be part of another community organization. The advantages of independent activity more than offset the problems of establishing a new organization such as obtaining financial support, establishing an organizational structure, and securing a ruling from the Internal Revenue Service that contributions are tax deductible.[1]

An independent organization maximizes potential support. A fair housing group which is a part of a Protestant Council of Churches cannot expect to get much help from Catholics,

Jews or those with no religious affiliation. Other activities of a parent organization are also apt to drain support. For example, if the fair housing program is made a part of an overall civil rights effort, there will be those who will not lend their support because they are against bussing as a means of integrating schools, or are opposed to the tactics being used to increase employment opportunities, or some other activity unrelated to fair housing.

The multipurpose organization also has the weakness that it leads to conflicts of interest. For example, at one point HOME in Buffalo publicly criticized Governor Rockefeller and his administration for their lack of enforcement of the Metcalf-Baker antidiscrimination law. This action resulted in successes which exceeded expectations and to a large extent reversed the discrimination patterns practiced by real estate brokers. But the tactic was a calculated risk taken only because there was more to gain than lose. Had HOME been part of a larger organization receiving state aid for one of its programs, the decision and results could have been very different.

Finally, most of the benefits which would accrue from being part of an established organization can be acquired by a fledgling fair housing group if an existing organization takes a leadership role in organizing and supporting the fair housing group, but avoids claiming too much credit for accomplishments.

There should be only one fair housing organization for an entire metropolitan area. However, local groups which sponsor meetings and other educational activities are desirable as chapters of this metropolitan organization. Local units increase participation because most people are more motivated to work in their own community than elsewhere. Local groups can handle local problems and provide more effective assistance to homeseekers than can be given by people not familiar with the area. But these advantages for local groups should not becloud the compelling reasons for having fair housing activities organized on a metropolitan basis.

A single metropolitan group allows the most efficient use of human resources, such as managerial, legal and public relations talents; developed resources, such as the knowledge of how fair housing laws and government agencies can best be employed; and purchased resources, such as rented space, telephone answering service and educational literature.

A metropolitan organization greatly increases the chances of establishing good relationships between the fair housing interests and the local press and TV people. Such liaisons lead to improved news coverage of the type which can influence community attitudes. Since fruitful relationships with the mass media result from frequent contacts and mutual interests, fragmented small fair housing groups make such relationships unlikely.

A single metropolitan organization offers the best hope of establishing effective relationships with what sociologists term the "gatekeepers" — people in positions of influence who can directly bring about change. For open housing they include real estate brokers, landlords, builders and bankers. While there are communities such as Denver, Boston and the San Fernando Valley where the gatekeepers have played a constructive role, in most places they have not made any contribution. The support of these groups is not necessary for success; in Buffalo progress came because HOME did not wait for the gatekeepers to help them and, when necessary, fought the gatekeepers. But progress would have been faster had the gatekeepers participated, and their help should always be courted to a sensible extent.

Fund raising also will be greatly aided by the presence of

a metropolitan fair housing organization which is in a good position to approach local business firms and local foundations as well as to submit proposals to government agencies and out-of-town foundations.

A very important advantage of a single metropolitan fair housing group is that it is the most effective means of exerting political influence. This influence will be needed because nowhere are fair housing laws adequately enforced. To stimulate government action, political power is needed.

Probably the most compelling reason for a metropolitan organization involves the relationship of the fair housing movement with the black community. Success in achieving open housing requires active Negro participation.[2] But if there are multiple fair housing groups, the participation will be fragmented and ineffective. Although most Negroes will approve efforts to achieve open housing, few will participate in fair housing activities. It is a matter of priorities. For most blacks who participate in community activities, the pressing problems in the ghetto consume all the time they can give. Open housing is of immediate concern only to the relatively few who seek housing in white areas.

Another advantage of a single metropolitan group relates to those Negroes who need help in obtaining housing. It is difficult for a black family to ask an organization to help them to do something that whites do by themselves. To ask several organizations for help is more difficult, and many will not do it.

Finally, it is important that the open housing effort be made throughout the entire metropolitan area. If the campaign appears to be waged in a limited area, the people in this area will resent being singled out and will have more than the usual fears concerning inundation. Moreover, should a fair housing group succeed only in a relatively small part of a metropolitan area — particularly one with low- or moderate-income housing — the result could be the start of another ghetto.

Several factors contribute to the formation of multiple groups. It is easier to plan and make decisions without consulting and acting in concert with others. Also, it is personally rewarding to be directly involved in decision making, and the more small groups there are, the more people who can participate. However, it usually is less difficult to get fair housing advocates, bound by a common purpose, to work together than to end racial discrimination in housing. Consequently, in metropolitan areas where there are now numerous groups working on fair housing, people would do well to unite; in areas without fair housing groups, the most sensible course of action should be evident: any fair housing activity which is initiated should be on a metropolitan basis.

If a viable fair housing organization is to develop, particular attention must be paid to objectives, tactics, leadership and membership.

The importance that equal opportunities in housing be the broad objective of a fair housing group cannot be overemphasized. Organizations which limit their objective to assisting black families in their search for nonghetto housing will at best make only a minor contribution to ending discrimination. The measure of the success of a fair housing organization should be the degree to which Negro families can secure housing on the same terms as whites, not the number of families who move into previously all white areas. The absence of discriminatory practices is a more difficult criterion to evaluate, but it is the one which counts.

Equal housing opportunities does not mean a goal of a Negro on every block, although probably it is true that if suddenly there were a black family on every block most of

111

the problem of discrimination in housing would disappear. But the objective of the fair housing group must not be achieved at the expense of the black families who come for help. The proper role of the fair housing organization is to obtain the widest possible choice of housing, and, while it is desirable that the fair housing group encourage Negroes to take advantage of their rights, there should never be an attempt to influence the choice of a specific neighborhood or a particular house.

A second critical area of organization policy involves tactics.

If a community organization is to become significant, it must have support. Sometimes support occurs because the group serves the special interests of those who participate, such as a homeowner's association opposing a proposed zoning change. Usually the interest of those who volunteer their services or render financial support is less direct, but as a rule self-interest is a factor. Business contacts, social contacts, prestige and recognition play important roles in motivating people to do good works, and because there are so many opportunities for community service, these personal factors, rather than relative community needs, usually determine which organizations people elect to support.

A newly formed fair housing group cannot compete with well-established community organizations in meeting such self-interests. But the fair housing group has a potential advantage in that it champions a pressing moral issue. To capitalize on this potential, however, the organization must conduct its activities so that it becomes known for its responsible behavior. In particular, care should be taken to guard against rash actions.

In order that operating responsibilities can be exercised rapidly, and also so that meetings can be held to a minimum, the response to tactical situations which are frequently encountered needs to be clearly defined by policy:

(1) Real estate brokers, builders and landlords should not be tested solely to determine that they are obeying the law since such a procedure is an imposition on the time of the person being tested. But if there are indications that discriminatory practices are being followed, a test should be made to determine if there is a violation of the law and, if so, to obtain evidence to support a complaint.

(2) "Straw" buyers (white persons who would buy homes solely for the purpose of reselling them to Negro families) should not be used unless there are very unusual circumstances which suggest that the application of available laws would not obtain the desired housing.

(3) Negroes who suspect they have encountered discrimination should be advised to file complaints only when there is evidence that discrimination has occurred. Otherwise businessmen and homeowners may be unfairly harassed by misunderstandings aggravated by the belief of most blacks that few whites will act honorably with them. However, when there is significant evidence that discrimination has occurred, a complaint or a court action should be filed even if the Negro family is no longer interested in the housing involved. Only through the vigorous prosecution of complaints will voluntary compliance with the law be achieved.

(4) Even though substantial evidence exists to support a charge of discriminatory practices against a broker or landlord, there should not be any public accusations. The fair housing group should not act in judgment, a function which should be left to the courts or the proper government agency. However, after a government agency has ruled that discrimination has occurred, this decision becomes legitimate public information and should be publicized as widely as possible.

The existence of a policy does not preclude an exception

under special circumstances. But if the fair housing group is to become a symbol of responsible moral leadership, care must be taken not to sacrifice this image by a careless reaction to frustration or anger.

Membership and leadership are closely related. When a new fair housing group is formed, the leadership must be given to those who can provide the skilled management required. They must be screened from the heterogeneous group which gathers whenever a new organization for social betterment gets under way. The choice of leadership is a vital step which often makes the difference between success and failure. Organizations do not succeed merely because their cause is just; they succeed because of the drive and judgment of those who lead them.

Good leadership is an ingredient which will build membership. However, neither good leadership nor successful activities will result in a large membership unless a specific effort is directed at membership growth.

The importance of a large membership cannot be overemphasized. Membership dues bring in money which augments income from other sources. A large membership is also a source of volunteers. But the most significant contribution of a large membership is the "community power" which it gives, the ability to influence the actions of government officials and private institutions, and the impact on individuals within the community. When a fair housing organization has many members it is effective partly because it can speak for many people, partly because it is able to communicate with many people, and partly because there are many who, by backing up their belief in open housing with their money, are likely to do something about discrimination in other ways as well.

All elements of the community should be represented in

the membership and leadership. Two groups are particularly important: the power structure and the Negro community.

Every metropolitan area has a power structure made up of those who occupy positions of influence: the business and banking leaders, the political leaders, government officials, the union heads, the executives of the newspapers and TV stations, the heads of community groups, the top people in the educational institutions, the leaders of the clergy. The structure is not a cohesive one that acts in concert: many of its members do not even know other members. But they have a common denominator: they all are people who can get things done, who can transform dreams into programs. They can provide public service announcements on TV, a big feature article in the paper, a church program on open housing, the money to make and distribute a movie, an appointment with the governor to discuss the enforcement of the law. Furthermore, their identification with an organization influences others to volunteer time, give contributions and cooperate.

The support of the power structure should be actively and diligently solicited in the proper way and at the proper time. In Buffalo a Friends of HOME Committee was established so that the names of prominent supporters of the organization could be listed on stationery and brochures. Care was taken in how people were asked and the order in which they were asked. The willingness of a well-known public figure to identify himself with a new fair housing organization is a product of how strongly he supports open housing, his willingness to take risks, and whom he knows already connected with the group. Wherever possible prominent people were contacted by someone whom they knew and respected. Likewise, those who were thought most likely to join were asked first. Thus the Catholic bishop was not approached until after the Episcopal bishop, who was more of a civil rights activist, had joined; it was not until after the Catholic bishop supported HOME that an initial approach was made to John Galvin, a prominent Catholic layman who was one of the most influential business and civic leaders in Buffalo.

Galvin's affiliation with HOME brought to an end a period marked by many frustrations. When HOME was first being organized, almost all the business leaders who were asked to join had refused even though they were those thought most likely to support the organization. The head of a major corporation said he was already on an equal employment opportunity committee and did not want to become known as a civil rights fanatic. A prominent lawyer said he did not trust the leadership. The board chairman of the Council of Churches, the vice-president of a large bank, also said "No."

The approach to the power structure and their response need not always follow the same patterns as in Buffalo. In Chicago the power structure *initiated* the Leadership Council for Metropolitan Open Communities, a professionally-staffed organization to help create open housing. Business and civic leaders not only backed it with their names but with their money, giving $130,000 the first year. While substantial funding and active interest by the power structure are not guarantees of success, money and institutional power are always helpful and ultimately are necessary.

Why did the power structure behave so differently in the two cities? The only real difference was that in Chicago Martin Luther King led open housing marches which threatened to provoke riots.

But the support of the power structure will not accomplish much if the fair housing group does not have significant

Negro membership, a disproportionately high percentage of which participates in policy-making meetings.

The judgment of black members is indispensable, because they will have insights which whites cannot have concerning the fair housing group's relationship with those who come to it for help. The viewpoint of blacks can also be important in making other decisions. For instance, in Buffalo the Negroes in HOME had a much better comprehension than the whites of the lack of cooperation to be expected from the Realtors' and builders' organizations. Black members also correctly cautioned the whites several times that what public officials promised was not necessarily what they would do.

Participation by Negroes in the activities of the fair housing group is the best means by which the black community can quickly learn that the fair housing group can be trusted. In fact, if Negroes do not participate in the planning and decision making from the outset, the fair housing group will appear to be just another paternalistic white man's organization. The Negro members also can show the fair housing group how it can involve itself more intimately with the problems of the black community, thereby developing a better image within that community. Finally, Negroes in the fair housing group, working with whites, will diminish the psychological barriers which often prevent blacks from claiming many of the housing opportunities which could be theirs.

The identity of the black leaders is important. Often the Negroes best known by whites are those who accommodate. They are the Negro men and women who in their relationships with whites tend to say what the whites wish to hear. As a result, these people are held in high regard by whites because they think "right." But to most blacks they are "Uncle Toms." Given leadership positions, they will give the fair housing group poor guidance and project a poor image to blacks. If the accomplishments of the fair housing group are to be significant, the Negro leadership must reflect the black community.

It is impossible to do too much to encourage Negro participation. In Buffalo, it was HOME's policy to hold a disproportionate percentage of meetings in the ghetto area. Although Negroes constituted only about 10 to 15 percent of the paid membership, 25 to 30 percent of both the directors and the friends of HOME were black. Whenever Negroes showed interest in participating in activities, they were encouraged. Letters were sent to two thousand homes in middle-income Negro neighborhoods offering HOME's newsletter free of charge, and door-to-door solicitations for membership were made in middle-income black neighborhoods. All of these helped. But Negro participation still was less than desired, a problem common to fair housing groups throughout the country.

The major activities of the fair housing group fall into two inseparable categories: those which involve housing assistance and those which are educational.

Since a great deal was said about housing assistance in the previous chapter, only two aspects will be discussed here.

Very careful attention must be given to the relationship between the fair housing organization and a Negro seeking assistance. It must be recognized that such relationships are inherently artificial and at best tenuous. The average person does not desire help to do what most others do by themselves since, to a certain extent, it is an admission that "there is something wrong with me." Thus many Negro families seek housing on their own even though they realize that by working with a fair housing group they could exercise a greater choice. With those who do come for help it is essential that the fair housing group operate in a way which is not demeaning.

It is difficult to build a good relationship between an individual and an organization. Since good relationships can be developed more readily between individuals, each Negro homeseeker should have a contact person to act as liaison with the fair housing group. Contacts should be friendly and devoid of paternalism.

The major role of the fair housing group should be to check when discrimination is suspected and, if verified, to remove the barrier. The fair housing group should never directly attempt to influence the area in which a family seeks housing, the sale price or rental it is willing to pay, or the particular housing it selects. Advice on the selection of housing should be limited to information such as general guide lines on the relationship between housing expenditures and family income, the mortgage practices of local banks, and good procedures to follow in buying or renting.

Although black families have the legal right to expect all real estate brokers to give them the same service as received by whites, many Negroes will request the fair housing organization to recommend "cooperative" brokers. If the fair housing group wishes to avoid making the decision as to which brokers to recommend, this can be done by writing all brokers in the area and asking them if they wish to be included on a list of brokers which cooperate with the fair housing group.

Housing assistance means more than just seeing that Negroes get the home of their choice. It also means making certain they can move without incident. Particularly in the early stages of desegregation this may require a considerable effort by the fair housing organization.

An important principle in easing any tensions which may

arise when a Negro family moves into an all-white neighborhood is to involve the residents of the neighborhood in creating an atmosphere of acceptance. The effectiveness of outsiders is limited and may cause harmful resentment.

In Chapter 2 it was pointed out that when a Negro enters a previously all-white neighborhood the opposition begins to disintegrate as soon as a relatively small minority make known that they will accept the new family. Thus the role of the fair housing group is to identify one or more families in the neighborhood who are willing to support the rights of the black family, and to motivate these whites to make known their position to the rest of the neighborhood.

The trick, of course, is to locate as quickly as possible what might be termed the "key person"—the one who will exercise this leadership role. This need is one of the reasons the fair housing group should have a large membership: one or more members may live in the neighborhood. Otherwise the best procedure is to solicit the help of local clergymen.

Although the fair housing group should stay out of the neighborhood, it is important that the key person be supplied with information and literature and be advised on strategy. While there is often little reaction to a Negro family moving to a white neighborhood, at times the key person faces a difficult task and needs to be convinced that what he is doing can succeed, that it represents his long-range self-interest, and that it is right.

Obviously, tactics must be adapted to varying neighborhood situations. But one basic strategy has wide applicability: those who support the right of the Negro family to move into the neighborhood should be as well organized as possible; those who strongly oppose it and represent potential troublemakers are best kept as disorganized as possible. In operation this means that a general meeting for "education" should be avoided since it may serve as a means for opposition to organize. On the other hand, it is desirable that those who support equal opportunities or who are "on the fence" should get together to become better informed, to strengthen their commitment through interaction, and to establish good communications.

The fair housing group differs from most other organizations in that its basic objective is to become obsolete. Its success in achieving this objective depends primarily on the effectiveness of long-range educational programs.

Two public relations tactics appear particularly effective in changing attitudes and achieving a greater acceptance for open housing. The first is to publicize public hearings and court proceedings which show that fair housing laws are being enforced. The other is to publicize success stories (i.e. case histories of what happens in white neighborhoods when Negro families move in).* Such publicity also is important as a means of getting other Negro families to take advantage of the increasing opportunities available to them.

While these appear to be the most effective approaches, there are many others. Information on what happens to property values, the number of Negroes moving into white areas and their distribution, the importance of open housing to the entire community — all of these are important. And, although it has been said many times before, the great moral issue which is involved is worth repeating again and again.

The mass media are the best means of disseminating this type of information. However, even for causes which they strongly support, the media will severely restrict themselves as instruments of propaganda. Therefore the information has to be put in such a way that it becomes significant news.

---

*Success stories should only be publicized with the explicit consent of the families involved. Most black families are willing to have their stories publicized, but some desire privacy.

Speeches at public meetings, testimony at public hearings and the outcome of complaints about discrimination are news. In Buffalo resolutions adopted by the board of directors of HOME usually received good coverage in the newspapers. On one occasion that this did not happen, the resolution was included in a letter which was sent to all real estate brokers in the area and released to the press, which then gave the resolution excellent coverage.

The success of the fair housing group in pursuing such a public relations campaign depends primarily on how well people do their jobs. Releases which are well written fare better with reporters and editors than those which are not. TV news coverage is more frequent if the president and other leaders of the fair housing group are willing to go to the studio to make news statements than when the fair housing people expect the TV people to come and interview them. Meetings get better coverage if newsmen are briefed about what will happen and given requested background material. Sometimes the difference between a good article on a meeting and no coverage at all results from having someone in the fair housing group act as a reporter and telephone the story to the city desk.

Probably the single most important technique for good press coverage is to consistently have something worthwhile to say. A good research program is an essential part of a good public relations effort. The fair housing group must gain a reputation for facts, figures, accurate statements and thoughtful comments rather than inaccuracies, generalizations and accusations.

Patience also may prove to be important in gaining the cooperation of the mass media. Some newspapers, TV stations and radio stations will immediately support the fair housing group and actively attempt to advance its objectives. More often, support will come slowly. The mass media are complicated commercial enterprises, and decisions to support organizations and causes often are made on the basis of business implications. Thus the policy may often be one of "going slow." However, as the concept of open housing becomes better accepted and the fair housing group builds up support among influential people, there will often be a shift toward more active support. Finally, time and patience will allow the fair housing group to cultivate contacts among newsmen.

Good educational programs challenge the imagination. In Buffalo, attitude surveys were used not only to obtain information, but also to provide news stories which gave facts it was felt the public should know. Questions were asked such as "Do you know that there is a law which prevents discrimination in the sale or rental of housing?" "How many Negro families do you think live in the town of   ?" "Would you move if a Negro family moved onto your street?" "Would you initiate action to prevent a Negro family from moving into your neighborhood?"

Public service announcements on TV and radio are another way of reaching large numbers of people.[3] A twenty-second or one-minute spot in the middle of the nine o'clock movie is not going to be shut off by someone just because he is not interested in open housing. Such spot announcements, if repeated often enough, will reach the entire viewing audience.

There are two devices that can be used effectively for widespread impact through the mass media. One is the church-oriented open housing signature campaign, a powerful educational program even without publicity.[4] The other is sponsorship of local or state fair-housing legislation.[5] Even if such legislation does not make a contribution, the campaign can be utilized by fair housing groups to effect widespread dissemination of information on open housing and existing antidiscrimination laws.

Although major emphasis is best placed on those programs which reach large numbers of people, there also is a need to inform in depth those who have an interest in learning more. Publication of a newsletter and distribution of literature to a select mailing list provide future recruits for the fair housing group and create a nucleus of informed people in the community who, by personal contacts, educate others.

A speakers' bureau enables the organization to reach small groups in depth, and, if it is aggressive and imaginative, it can also reach large audiences. In the Buffalo area arrangements were made to present two speakers — one white and one Negro — to high school audiences. The talks, which were attended by all students, had impact because of the availability as the speakers of Ernie Warlick, the Buffalo Bills football star, and Nolan Johannes, a local television personality. As a result many of the students later discussed the program with their families.

Educating people to practice equal opportunities in housing is not easy. But a great deal can be done, and the more that gets done the easier it is to do more. Nothing succeeds like success.

Another concern of the fair housing group is that of neighborhood "stabilization." In Chapter 2 it was shown that in moderate-income areas contiguous to black neighborhoods the high demand for housing by blacks usually leads to racial change. However, in many cities there are such neighborhoods where, because of efforts at stabilization, racial transition is proceeding very slowly if at all.

Hyde Park — Kenwood in Chicago, where for twenty years about half the sixty thousand residents have been black, is probably the best known of these interracial neighborhoods.[6] But there are over a thousand others.[7] A sixteen-block area in Brooklyn, near Sheepshead Bay, about one-third of whose residents are Negro, has been a stable integrated area for fifty years.[8]

The success of stabilizing newly integrated neighborhoods is influenced by the effectiveness of fair housing efforts. If the fair housing organization does its job well, whites will not panic at initial Negro entry, the people in neighborhoods into which blacks move will recognize that what happens in their neighborhood depends on themselves and, perhaps most important of all, blacks will have a variety of neighborhoods from which to choose housing.

However, this is as far as the fair housing group should go. The fundamental objective of a fair housing organization should be that housing be open to all — not that neighborhoods be racially balanced. While the fears of whites everywhere about Negro inundation are increased whenever a single neighborhood shifts from white to black, any effort to discourage Negro families from moving into a changing neighborhood is contrary to the basic principle of fair housing — to maximize the choices that people have as to where they live.

This does not mean that steps should not be taken to prevent integrated neighborhoods from becoming black neighborhoods. However, stable interracial neighborhoods can only be achieved by the efforts of those who live in the neighborhood itself — efforts aimed not at restricting blacks, but at making the area so desirable that whites wish to move there. Most of the success stories are the product of active citizen groups which raised the quality of the schools, kept zoning standards high, instituted neighborhood improvements and, when real estate brokers failed to bring prospective white purchasers or tenants to the area, established their own real estate firms to make certain that housing was affirmatively marketed to whites.[9] The result is that West Mt. Airy in Philadelphia, North Avondale in Cincinnati, Crenshaw in Los Angeles, University City near St. Louis, Park Hill in Denver, Shepherd Park in Washington, the Shaker Communities near Cleveland, just to mention a few, are among the most exciting neighborhoods in America, not merely because they are large interracial areas, but because of the sense of community which has developed.*

Fair housing organizations can make important contributions by influencing government policy and the performance of government officials. The influence of citizen action on agencies which administer fair housing laws was illustrated in Chapter 4. Other government organizations which determine the housing opportunities available to black families include public housing authorities, urban renewal agencies, the Federal Housing Administration, welfare agencies, and zoning and planning boards.

The successful fair housing group will probably go through several distinct phases. Initially it must develop itself as an organization. Developing success stories comes next. After the white community learns that Negroes can move into white neighborhoods without catastrophic results, the reactions to such moves diminish and the fair housing group can direct more and more of its attention toward eliminating acts of discrimination. In its final phase, most of the activity of the fair housing group will be directed at attempting to convince Negroes that they are able to secure housing and live without difficulties outside the ghetto.

The role of the fair housing group also can be viewed in a broader perspective. For whites a fair housing group offers a way that beliefs can be put into practice. For Negroes it of-

---

*Recently an organization known as National Neighbors has been formed to give better unity on a national basis to these neighborhood groups.

fers a means by which a few can secure the housing they want while others watch, gauge the progress, and equate it with hope.

6 / The Church

MORE THAN ANY OTHER GROUP, America's clergymen have been responsible for the progress that has been made toward ending discrimination in housing. Yet, more than any other group, the clergy have neglected their responsibility. For every clergyman who has given effective leadership toward ending discrimination, there have been at least five who did not. That the efforts of a minority have been so effective suggests what could have been done.

Racial discrimination is incompatible with the religious teachings of Protestants, Catholics and Jews. Throughout the Bible there is strong support for the concepts of equality and the brotherhood of man.[1] The spirit of the Bible is embodied in "Have we not all one Father? Has not one God created us?" Ezekiel, talking about aliens, many of whom were black, said, "They shall be to you as native-born sons of Israel. . . . In whatever tribe the alien resides, there you shall assign him his inheritance, says the Lord God." Paul in his letter to the Galatians wrote, "There is neither Jew nor Greek, there is neither slave nor free, there is neither male nor female; for you are all one in Christ Jesus." Jesus urged his followers to love their neighbor as themselves and, in the

Sermon on the Mount, he made it clear that neighbors are not only of one's own race when he said, "If you salute only your brethren, what more are you doing than others?" In the story of the Good Samaritan, Jesus pointed out that a person of another nationality, even a nationality which is looked down upon, should be regarded as a neighbor. Jesus not only preached love, but he urged his believers to transfer love into action. "Truly, I say to you, as you did it to one of the least of these my brethren, you did it to me."

For decades churches did not recognize a responsibility regarding the plight of black Americans. However, by 1955 all major denominations, with the exception of the Southern Baptists, had adopted resolutions supporting equality of opportunity in housing. But these resolutions had little practical effect. As Philip Johnson commented in *Call Me Neighbor, Call Me Friend*, "There have been enough resolutions passed by American church conventions to paper the walls of every courthouse in Dixie. They have their purpose: to run up the flag of the denomination or council so all can see. But it takes more than running up the flag to drive an enemy out of his foxhole. And for many church members, ecclesiastical conventions are 'they' and not 'we'."

Churches have great power to effect social change. Not only can churches influence the actions of their own members, but by the use of church funds, prestige and members' talents they can influence the entire community. However, to serve as an instrument of change, the church cannot merely be favorably inclined, the church must be fully committed. The difference between the two is great, a difference made crucial because the power of the church is exercised even when it does not act. For a church not to decide, is to decide.

Unfortunately, many clergymen have found it difficult to decide what to do about discrimination in housing. In most congregations open housing is a controversial, unpopular subject. When church members argue that "clergy should stick to religion and not concern themselves with social, economic and political questions," it is usually because these church members wish to avoid the discrepancy between their own practices and the tenets of their religion. The obligation of the church to work for justice is not only an indelible part of the scriptures, but a part of the history of the church itself. Countless hospitals, colleges, orphanages and homes for the elderly are evidence of the past response of the church to unmet human needs. And in recent times the Catholics who are outraged by priests and nuns who participate in civil rights demonstrations often are the sons of men who walked side by side with priests in picket lines during the pioneering days of the American labor movement.

However, clergymen must face congregations where, on a national average, almost one-half disapprove of the civil rights movement and many more hesitate about strong church involvement in social issues.[2] Clergymen know that there are pastors who have lost their jobs because they pushed racial justice too hard. Even more frequently, sermons about civil rights have caused diminished contributions. As a result, the response of most clergymen to the discrepancy between church teachings about discrimination in housing and the actions of their parishioners has been either to ignore it or to touch on it lightly — enough to satisfy the conscience of the clergyman, but not enough to cause commotion or change.

There is a certain element of tragedy about the failure of the great majority of churches to function more effectively in ending discrimination in housing. Clergymen, over 90 percent of whom support the civil rights movement,[2] have failed their churches, their communities, the members of their congregations and themselves because they have not understood what they could do. Because some clergymen have encountered serious repercussions as a result of civil rights activities, the majority have not perceived that other churches have given such leadership successfully. These committed churches have lost members, but they also have attracted new people who wanted to be a part of a church which stood for something socially and morally meaningful. While some who left the church were among the largest contributors, church income in some cases has risen as a result of increased giving by many smaller contributors.

Those congregations which have divided over the issue of race usually have not been those which were the most bigoted, but those which were handled the least expertly. It is not easy to provide the type of leadership required without undermining the other missions of the church. More must be learned before most clergymen will be successful, and some clergymen will never be able to handle such a challenge. But it can be done because it has been done.

"Do not neglect routine church tasks" is the most important commandment for clergymen who prefer success to martyrdom. Neglect of duties always brings unfavorable reaction; if neglect occurs because the clergyman is doing something that many in the congregation oppose, the reaction may become protest. In addition, whenever a clergyman has an opportunity to minister to a need, whether that need be counseling on a complex personal problem or helping to organize a bowling party for the junior high group, the clergyman builds support for himself against the day when there is disagreement.

Pastors usually are most successful in causing social change when they limit their direct participation outside of the church community. This does not mean that the clergyman should not participate in public meetings, directly aid Negro families looking for housing, walk in a picket line, or head a fair housing group. Clergymen have done all of these without hurting their relationships with their congregations. However, the pastor should not attempt to exercise personally the church's entire concern for racial justice. His primary role is to be a teacher, to instruct the members of his congregation, to have not one person from the church engaged in social action but ten or one hundred. His personal involvement can be useful both as an experience for himself and as an example to his congregation. But if his personal involvement means that he is constantly out doing good for others and is not available when church members think that he is needed by them, he is going to be in serious trouble with the folks in the pews who do not support the causes with which he is identified.

Another commandment is that a good leader does not get too far out in front. Otherwise people do not follow him. The clergyman must be prepared for changes in attitudes to occur gradually. He must be respectful to those who disagree. His success will be aided by sensitivity to fears and by patience with ignorance.

However, for every clergyman who has gotten too far out front there probably have been twenty who were too cautious and did not go far enough. Moreover, a clergyman can extend his leadership by operating on several levels. If within the church a group is formed of those most sympathetic with the goals of racial justice — whether it be a study group or an action group, whether it be directed at some specific project or at various projects — the clergyman has an opportunity to take more advanced positions on open housing and increase his influence within the church.

Even when a clergyman severely rocks the boat, the results are not always bad. The Reverend George Laurent is a Presbyterian whose interest in open housing has become so great that he has gone from a parish minister to become executive director of the Conference of Religion and Race in Kansas City and then executive director of Baltimore Neighborhoods, a fair housing organization covering the Baltimore area. During his three years as minister of the Federated Church in Saline, Michigan, Laurent's strong preaching and civil rights activities in nearby Ann Arbor earned him the title "nigger lover" and caused three of the twelve members of his church's ruling body, among others, to resign. Nevertheless, during Laurent's ministry contributions went up, not down. However, Laurent prefers to judge his ministry more by the conversation which occurred between a woman who was leaving the church and an elderly farm woman who had never spoken about human relations.

"My husband says George is not spiritual enough," explained the woman who was leaving.

The old farm woman's reply was, "In the last three years under Mr. Laurent there has been more spirituality in this church than in the previous thirty."

How much a church with good leadership can do to aid integration is demonstrated by Hope Lutheran Church in Houston, which is made up of about 280 families living in an area of $10,000 to $17,000 homes into which Negroes began moving several years ago. Well before the church was confronted with the problem of black membership, the Reverend Nolan Sagebiel started preparing the congregation. As a result, there was little reaction when the first Negro came to the church, and now there is increasing Negro participation. The church program is expanding, and some whites who were thinking of moving out of the area have changed their minds.

There are three tactics that churches and church organizations have used effectively in ending discrimination in housing: influencing church members to participate personally in community efforts to end discrimination; initiating and supporting secular organizations aimed at ending discrimination; and directly carrying out a program to decrease discrimination.

When one listens to the men and women who have made significant contributions toward ending discrimination in housing — the leaders of fair housing groups, Realtors who have publicly favored open occupancy, people who have donated substantial sums to fair housing activities, government officials who have done what needed to be done — it is clear that most of them were heavily influenced by a desire to give meaning to their religious principles. But this does not mean, as many mistakenly believe, that if the church teaches what is right, people will do right. Religious institutions have an equally important obligation to give men and women the resolve to do what they believe is right.

The need to reinforce basic values was the problem which confronted Clive Graham, a Realtor in Long Beach, California. Graham, a past president of the California Real Estate Association and a director of the National Association of Real Estate Boards, campaigned on behalf of a fair housing law. But Graham would never have taken this position had not his clergyman, the Reverend Emerson Hangen of the First Congregational Church in Long Beach, spoken out in a sermon and discussed it with Graham afterwards. All of Graham's prior church experience was not enough. "I had to know that I was right and someone whom I respected was for this. . . . I needed that support in the face of all the feeling that existed."

The importance of the church's leadership role is underlined by the religious affiliations of those who have been out front in the battle to end discrimination. Although the teachings of all of the large religious groups are incompatible with racial discrimination and, with the exception of the Southern

Baptists, all have for many years publicly favored open housing, the religious affiliations of those who have been activists is so markedly concentrated in certain denominations that the explanation cannot be confined to socioeconomic, geographic or any other factors unrelated to the church itself.

In 1949, over ten years before the fair housing movement really began, the Hyde Park–Kenwood Community Conference was born in Chicago in a Unitarian Church at a meeting initiated by a Quaker committee and strongly supported by several Jewish temples.[3] Since then many of the thousands of organizations which have been formed to end discrimination and to promote integrated neighborhoods have been initiated, in one way or another, by church organizations. While the seeds thus planted have not always borne fruit, there have been many successes. The Metro Denver Fair Housing Center, the best-funded fair housing group in the nation, was to a large extent an outgrowth of a conference on religion and race held in May 1964. Chicago, Cleveland, Pittsburgh and Atlanta are four of the many other cities where church organizations have played a key role in initiating fair housing organizations which then functioned on their own.

Often church organizations have directly engaged in open housing efforts. For example, the Greater Minneapolis Interfaith Housing Program was an educational effort begun in 1958 which resulted in the publication of considerable material which proved useful not only in Minneapolis, but also in other communities where open housing efforts did not begin until later. In Chicago the Conference of Religion and Race at one time directly assisted Negro homeseekers and, after part of this program was taken over by the newly formed Leadership Council, the Conference's director of housing, Reverend Howard W. Smith, developed an imaginative second mortgage program to assist Negro homeseekers buying homes in white areas. Other cities, such as Milwaukee and San Francisco, have had lesser programs under a Conference of Religion and Race composed of a Protestant-Catholic-Jewish coalition.

The most common type of direct participation by churches, however, has been involvement in open housing signature campaigns. In such campaigns people are asked to sign a statement which indicates their support of open housing and which permits their names to be publicly listed as signatories. Several of the beneficial effects of a signature campaign are:

People learn that there is more support for open housing than they believed existed. Misgivings by whites concerning blacks moving into their neighborhood often are rooted in the fear of how other whites will react. Most whites underestimate the support for open housing. Consequently, many who do not sign the covenant become less fearful when they see the number of whites who commit themselves.

Information about open housing reaches people who are not aware that housing discrimination is against the law or that property values do not necessarily decrease when Negroes move into a neighborhood. Such people do not actively seek information, and probably would not read a feature story in the local newspaper which discussed integration in housing. But if they know they must make a personal decision, there is a reasonable chance they will listen if information is given to them in church.

For the first time many people think through their personal position on open housing and, in so doing, become mentally committed to support, or at least accept, Negro neighbors. This avoids facing such a decision in the emotionally charged atmosphere which may develop when the first Negro family moves into an area. The signature drive permits a decision to be made rationally as to how one would act should there be a practical challenge to one's belief in brotherhood. Many who are not willing to go so far as to sign the pledge, do decide that should Negroes move into their neighborhood they would treat them like any other new neighbors.

One of the most successful signature drives was that conducted by the Greater Kansas City Council on Religion and Race in 1966. The prime mover was the council's executive director, the Reverend George B. Laurent. Laurent came to Kansas City in the spring of 1965 and immediately went to work on the campaign on a full-time basis, with the help of increasing numbers of volunteers.

By the fall of 1965 Laurent and those working with him had formed fifteen fair housing councils which were functioning in different areas. The campaign itself, which was held during a one-month period in February, started with a kickoff meeting to which thirteen hundred people came to hear former Governor David Lawrence of Pennsylvania. The newspapers gave the campaign good coverage, one TV station was particularly supportive, and posters reading "Fair Housing is Fair Play" were placed on taxis and buses. But the major thrust of the drive was carried out by door-to-door volunteers recruited through churches.

The sixteen thousand signatures, which filled three and one-half pages in the Kansas City *Star*,[4] were only the top of the iceberg. For example, in the Westport–Roanoke district four hundred owners of all-white apartment houses were contacted immediately after the campaign. The result: within six months eight black families had moved into eight different buildings, all without incident.

Church organizations and clergymen were responsible for the formation of HOME in Buffalo and have played a vital role in many of its successes. HOME, therefore, is a good example of how churches can effectively contribute to racial justice through the initiation and support of a fair housing organization.

In 1962 the Council of Churches in Buffalo brought together a group of people to discuss how to help Negro families obtain housing outside of the ghetto. By early 1963 this group grew tired of talking and decided to act. The result was the Niagara Frontier Council for Freedom of Choice in Housing, a name which six months later was changed to HOME.

The new organization was hardly representative of Buffalo's civic leadership. A major component came from Buffalo's Unitarian-Universalist Church whose public affairs committee had been concerned with the problem of discrimination in housing before the Council of Churches had initiated the broader group. In fact, five of HOME's first twelve directors were from this church. Quakers also were very much in evidence in the original group, and the Friends Meeting House soon became headquarters for HOME with Friends handling the mail and telephone calls.

But the leaders of the new organization rapidly expanded its base. The first president was a United Church of Christ clergyman, the Reverend Howard Fuller, who through his denominational staff job had become known and trusted by black leaders and was able to get them to join HOME and publicly identify with it. Fuller also stimulated the interest of a prominent United Church layman, Daniel Acker, a Negro who later became president of HOME.

The original group included two Presbyterian ministers who, at a time when the new council had raised only several hundred dollars, persuaded the Presbytery of Western New York to contribute five hundred dollars. The impact of this gift went well beyond providing sufficient funds for initial requirements; it also encouraged people to join and to work.

The two Presbyterian ministers were important in other ways also. The Reverend Herbert White, minister of Covenant-Lebanon Presbyterian Church, a small interracial church in the ghetto, was partly responsible for the membership of three members of his church who later played key roles in HOME. A different contribution was made by the Reverend James Carroll, senior minister of the largest Presbyterian church in western New York. He was instrumental in bringing in other clerical leaders, such as the Right Reverend Lauriston L. Scaife, bishop of the Episcopal Diocese of Western New York, and Dr. Ralph W. Loew, a prominent Lutheran clergyman. Carroll also recruited Kenneth McIlraith, the first important member of Buffalo's business community who publicly identified with HOME, and McIlraith, several years later, persuaded sixty other business leaders to join the organization and support it financially.

The Council of Churches of Buffalo and Erie County also contributed to the growth of HOME. Late in 1963 the council sent a mailing to all Protestant clergymen in the area on behalf of the fair housing group. As a result, many clergymen joined HOME. When HOME's membership reached six hundred, over 10 percent were clergymen and their wives; many others had joined as a direct result of these pastors' efforts.

Clergymen participated in myriad ways. In the first two years, when serious tensions developed in white neighborhoods into which black families had moved, clergymen were effective in calming fears.[5] When John Lomenzo, who as New York's Secretary of State controlled the licensing of real estate brokers, spoke at a HOME meeting, Bishop Scaife, very noticeable in his purple rabat, came to listen and to help establish the good relations which ultimately developed between HOME and Lomenzo's department. And it was clergymen such as Fuller and the Reverend Robert Dady, another HOME board member, who helped the less knowledgeable whites on HOME's board to recognize that it was necessary that the fair housing organization involve itself to a much greater extent in the inner city and the plight of low-income blacks.

In Buffalo, as elsewhere, the greatest participation of churches and their congregations was in open housing signature drives.

According to the *Fair Housing Handbook* published by the American Friends Service Committee and the National Committee Against Discrimination in Housing, the major objective of a covenant campaign is to build the fair housing group by identifying sympathetic people. In Buffalo, however, open housing signature drives were primarily directed at a different, more ambitious goal: to influence that vast majority of people who are reached with greatest difficulty by confronting them with the issue of racial discrimination where they could not avoid it — in church.

Two strategies employed by HOME proved valuable in maximizing the effectiveness of open housing covenant campaigns. The first was to defer the signature drive in each area until there appeared to be enough support so that the impact would reach most of the community and 5 to 10 percent of the adult population would sign the pledge instead of the one to three percent who generally had signed in other areas. The second was to stagger the covenant campaigns in different suburbs in order to time each area's campaign to coincide with local readiness, and to apply lessons learned in each campaign to successive ones. The lessons learned were to be particularly important for the covenant campaign in the city of Buffalo where the largest number of people were involved.

In 1965, in the first covenant campaign in the Buffalo area, twelve hundred residents in the upper middle class suburb of Amherst signed the pledge statement:

> We recognize that it is the right of any citizen to live wherever his taste chooses and his means permit. This right is guaranteed by civil law. We the undersigned wish to indicate our concern for retaining the Town of Amherst as a choice residential community by saying we welcome neighbors into our area regardless of race, creed or ethnic background. We earnestly request the support of all the community in opening our town on an equal basis to all who seek to reside here.

The Amherst signature drive was run by an ad hoc interfaith committee and not by HOME. The role of HOME, in this and all subsequent covenant campaigns, was to initiate local action, act as consultants and provide seed-money financing. This background role was chosen to obtain maximum support for the effort by involving local people to the fullest extent, and by avoiding loss of support because some participants might disagree with other parts of HOME's program.

The campaign in Amherst was not well executed. Most churches did either nothing or very little. Even in the few churches where there was a strong effort, many who believed in open housing refrained from signing the pledge. But still the campaign was encouraging. Although the twelve hundred names listed in a paid advertisement in the Amherst *Bee* were fewer than desired for a community of seventy-five thousand people, the effect was significant on at least two counts. When a Negro family bought a home in Amherst several months later, many of those who were unhappy and apprehensive were saying, "So many people in the neighborhood signed the petitions I guess everything will be all right." Another benefit of the campaign was that many new people joined HOME, including Clayton Stahlka, the head of an award-winning advertising agency whose services were made available to the fair housing group without charge. And while before the campaign some expressed the fear that a covenant drive would produce negative effects, there never was any indication that anyone became more likely to discriminate or react more negatively to a Negro neighbor.

In the next two years, prior to the large campaign planned for Buffalo, five more open housing covenant campaigns were held in suburban communities. In each of these campaigns the proportion of signatures to population was much higher than in Amherst.

One important lesson which had been learned was the great difference between lip service and commitment. If a clergyman merely endorses the open housing pledge and directs attention to the availability of petitions or cards at the back of the church, the results will be very different than if he places the full moral authority of the church behind the signing of the covenant and sees that each person in the congregation is confronted with making a conscious decision about signing the pledge (e.g., by passing pledge cards to everyone in the congregation and then collecting all cards, signed or unsigned).

Another important lesson was to start many months before the actual campaign. The campaign itself was best carried out in three or four weeks — long enough to get the job done, but not so long that people lost interest. The long lead time was necessary to recruit workers, effectively organize, and to enlist the full cooperation of the clergy, many of whom needed time to warm up to the idea. In addition, time was needed for congregations to be prepared. No matter how eloquently a clergyman urges his congregation to sign on the actual day, the covenant will not have the same success as when there have been other sermons on the subject, widespread discussion among leadership in the church, and active committee promotion of the covenant in the church.

Starting the campaign early maximizes the number of well-known people in the community who will allow their names listed as members of a steering committee. During this period of campaign incubation, each time one more well-known person adds his name to the list it becomes easier to obtain others. And often the support of community leaders significantly influences the actions of clergymen. A study of school integration in Little Rock has shown that many clergymen, particularly those with large congregations, were willing to join the action of a minority of clergy provided the effort supporting integration appeared to be going well.[6]

The desirability of having as much community leadership involved as possible should not, however, cause postponement for too long. The suburban Buffalo campaigns were successes even though not one local political leader or prominent businessman publicly supported any of them. In one suburb the clergyman who had taken the lead in organizing the campaign, discouraged by the lack of this type of support, wrote HOME that "our town does not appear to be ready yet." The reply came back, "If your town were 'ready' there would be no need for the campaign."

There was one other lesson of importance which was learned prior to the Buffalo campaign. In Clarence, a suburb with a population of about seventeen thousand, the Reverend Walter O. Kern had been dealing with the race problem periodically from the pulpit of the Nativity of the Blessed Virgin Mary Roman Catholic Church. He organized a committee in the church to assist him with the open housing covenant campaign and preached a strong sermon: "I strongly urge you to commit your signature to where your belief is — in love of neighbor."

Over five hundred of the two thousand Clarence residents in Kern's church signed the pledges. This brought the total signatures to well over a thousand — about 10 percent of the adult population. But more important, it indicated that the greatest potential lay in the large Catholic churches, where the priests seemed to have more influence over their congregations than clergymen of other faiths. That meant that in the city of Buffalo, where well over one-half of the white population were Roman Catholics, the success of an open housing covenant campaign would hinge largely on the actions of the Most Reverend James A. McNulty, Bishop of Buffalo.

Although Bishop McNulty was much more representative of the conservative wing of the Catholic Church than the liberal wing in matters of church policy and urban affairs, his support for open housing had been made clear since 1964 when he issued a letter to be read in the churches which declared: "If a Negro family wishes to move into your neighborhood, the law protects his right to do so. A superior law, the law of God, prescribes something better than toleration. . . . Be then a good neighbor to your new Negro neighbor." Shortly thereafter the bishop joined HOME, and allowed his name to be used publicly as a supporter of the fair housing group. However, he was not directly involved otherwise in the covenant drives in the suburbs.

If Bishop McNulty and other civic leaders were to be of assistance to "Project Good Neighbor," the name given to the open housing signature campaign for the city of Buffalo, it was important that they assume leadership roles. Consequently Dr. Ralph W. Loew, the pastor of the largest Lutheran church in western New York, undertook the responsibility of getting other civic leaders, including Bishop McNulty, to serve as cochairmen. Loew first secured the agreement of Bishop Scaife and Dr. David Cox, the executive director of the Council of Churches, to be cochairmen. Simultaneously he won support for the drive from Brendon Burke, a Buffalo business executive who was chairman of the social concerns committee of the Catholic diocese. Then Loew, accompanied by Burke, went to see Bishop McNulty and obtained his agreement to be a cochairman.

It proved to be more difficult to secure key politicians and business leaders as cochairmen. Two declined invitations and, with very little time left before it would be necessary to announce Project Good Neighbor's principal sponsors, the mayor and county executive continued to avoid invitations to be cochairmen. At that point Dr. Loew went to William Harder, the president of the largest savings bank in Buffalo, and requested that Harder host a luncheon to which Mayor Sedita, County Executive Rath and chief executive officers of the two largest commercial banks be invited. Harder, who talked less and did more than most men, agreed. Then, in the elegant dining room of the Buffalo Savings Bank, men who individually could never have been persuaded to support the campaign, agreed to become cochairmen in the collective security of each other's company.

With seventeen of the most respected people in the city serving as cochairmen, it was relatively easy to secure other civic leaders as members of a sponsoring committee. When Loew sent letters to three hundred prominent citizens — judges, congressmen, school board members, business leaders, community leaders — asking them to become members of

Dad, what would you do if Negroes moved next door?

If you have a youngster, you know how the questions come . . . straight out. No fooling around.

And, there is a slight appraising look in their eyes. Suddenly you are aware that this is one of those times where you don't just toss off some quick answer and disappear behind the newspaper.

I don't know what you told your son. Here's what I told mine.

I said, "Nothing special. Why should I? Black or white, that's not what makes the difference."

The point is obvious to you, but I wanted my son to know that people don't come in blocks or batches like Negroes or Jews or Poles or Italians or Irish.

They come one at a time. And, that's the only way you can decently judge them. Because it's the only fair way you would want to be judged. On your own.

It doesn't make sense that because a man has a black skin he will not take care of his house

anymore than it follows that if our neighbor is a Chinese person he will start a hand laundry in the living room.

It also doesn't make sense that just because Negroes move into a neighborhood, property values will go down. And they don't. That's a fact. The realtors themselves say this.

If Negroes moved next door I'd treat them like anyone else.

Wouldn't *you?*

To: PROJECT GOOD NEIGHBOR
Suite 35
Hotel Statler Hilton
Buffalo, New York 14202

Count me in ! I want to be a good neighbor. You can publish my name as supporting the following Good Neighbor Pledge: As citizens of Buffalo and Erie County, we want to help make it a community of Good Neighbors by welcoming as neighbors all persons, regardless of race, creed or national origin. We support the right — as guaranteed by law — of any person to live where he wishes and his means permit.

Name ....

Address ....

(Contributions to assist publication and other campaign costs are needed and will be gratefully accepted.)

$ ....

Project Good Neighbor

the sponsoring committee, over half joined without further persuasion.

The drive gained momentum. HOME, Catholic Charities, the Presbytery and the Jewish Federation provided over $3,000. A full-time executive secretary was hired to assist the coordinator of the drive, James E. Wallace, a young engineer with the Cornell Aeronautical Laboratories who was given time off by his employer at Dr. Loew's request. Headquarters for the drive was provided without charge by the local chapter of the National Conference of Christians and Jews. Seventy-five thousand copies of a brochure were printed for distribution in churches. Robert Scheu, chief executive officer of the largest commercial bank in western New York, sent a letter requesting contributions to sixty business firms and the $6,000 thus raised made possible publication of a full-page ad in the two daily papers and the two largest weeklies. The ad was headlined "Dad, what would you do if Negroes moved next door?" and won a national award for Stahlka's advertising agency.

The need to maximize the commitment of the churches was the purpose of a May 2 kickoff meeting for the general public and a May 3 meeting of Catholic clergy. Bishop McNulty requested all parish priests in Buffalo to attend both meetings and to reserve the sermons of May 19 and May 26 for the subjects of racial justice and open housing. The Chancery also provided two sample sermons.

The May 2 meeting was a great success. Two thousand people came. While such meetings are often an ordeal which must be suffered to show good faith, the committee in charge of this meeting did not make the mistake of scheduling a battery of speakers. There was a single half-hour talk about the need for open housing. A college band provided music. And, to get across how the open-housing covenant campaign would work and why it was important, the com-

147

mittee relied on a half-hour play written for the occasion. The play was so well received that the following day, at Bishop McNulty's request, it was performed for the meeting of Catholic clergy and, several weeks later, it was performed on local television and radio stations.*

A month after the drive began some twenty thousand adults in the city of Buffalo had signed the pledge and about ten thousand suburbanites and college students also had listed their names. Over twelve thousand of the Buffalo signatures were collected in Catholic churches.

The impact of Project Good Neighbor was by no means uniform. About 7 percent of the white adults in the city signed, but there was virtually no response from the heavily Polish section, and less than one-half of the Catholic parishes actually followed the bishop's instructions. However, there were some pleasant surprises. Over fifteen hundred signatures were obtained in two Catholic churches in a heavily Irish working-class area which, because of its anti-Negro reputation, had fewer Negro residents than there were in most suburban areas.

Project Good Neighbor was probably the most successful effort of its type yet held in the United States. And with the help of the computer facilities of local businesses, the names and addresses of all covenant signers were printed in numerical order by streets. This list of twenty thousand names and addresses was then sent by a mailing service to every resident in the city of Buffalo.

In many ways the efforts to end discrimination by church organizations in Buffalo are representative of efforts elsewhere in the nation.

Potentially no church in America has more to contribute

---

*The text of the play, which was written by Mrs. William Clarkson, is given in the August 1, 1968, issue of *Presbyterian Life*.

to harmonious race relations than the Roman Catholic Church. It is the largest single church. And, as so well stated by John Cardinal Dearden, Archbishop of Detroit, "The Negro-white confrontation in American cities is in greater part a Negro-Catholic confrontation . . . because Catholics traditionally have been concentrated in urban areas."[7]

Cardinal Dearden's archdiocese leads all others in the nation in programs directed toward racial justice. Three staff members at the Chancery have full-time duties in the field of race relations. One of their responsibilities has been Project Commitment, a series of eight meetings designed to bring official church teachings on racial justice through diocesan and parish leadership to worshippers in the pew. Some five thousand priests and Catholic lay leaders have participated in Detroit and the program has been considered such a success that other dioceses are adopting it.

But nationally the Catholic Church has been slow in taking meaningful action toward better race relations and open housing. The same factors which account for past inaction continue to delay bringing Catholic practice in line with Catholic teachings. The background, training and experiences of most Catholic clergymen have not made them sensitive to the issues and problems. Indeed, the great strength of Project Commitment has been its recognition that progress cannot be made until the priests themselves have been properly instructed as to their responsibilities. Another problem is that many Catholics are first- and second-generation Americans who have just made it to middle-class status and feel particularly threatened by black entry into their neighborhoods. Other factors in the lack of attention paid to racial problems include the relatively small number of blacks who are Catholic, and the serious internal problems which occupy the attention of church leaders.

National organizations such as the Christian Family Movement and the National Catholic Conference for Interracial Justice, are leading Roman Catholics in increasing numbers to direct their personal behavior and social action in accordance with their religious belief in the equality of all men. In Chicago, the *New World* has been one of many diocesan weeklies which have strongly supported fair housing efforts. In Denver the diocese is giving $10,000 per year to the fair housing center. In Missouri all of the Roman Catholic bishops supported the brief filed by the National Catholic Conference for Interracial Justice in behalf of the petitioners in the *Jones* v. *Meyer* case. In Baltimore, Lawrence Cardinal Sheehan urged the City Council to pass a fair housing law which he termed a "moral responsibility."

There are three ways the Catholic Church can assume greater responsibility for racial justice: by internal transformation as a result of programs ordered from the top by men like Cardinal Dearden; by a changing of the guard, the replacement of a generation rooted in old traditions; and by the influence of non-Catholics. But for the present the Catholic Church resembles a sleeping giant which shows some signs of awakening. In a few dioceses, such as Detroit, there has been some motion; in others, such as Philadelphia and Los Angeles, the giant is still in a deep sleep.

The effect that one religious group can have on others is most clearly demonstrated by the Society of Friends. There are only a hundred and twenty thousand Quakers in the United States, yet the Friends have probably done at least as much as any other church group in behalf of open housing.

The fair housing movement is an outgrowth of Quaker pioneering to a considerable extent. The American Friends Service Committee, one of several national organizations run by Friends in behalf of social justice, receives about $2,000-000 per year from Quakers (along with $5,500,000 from other sources). It was the AFSC which in the early 1950's sponsored several interracial developments for the purpose of demonstrating that whites and Negroes could live in the same neighborhoods. In the early 1960's AFSC staff workers helped organize fair housing groups in New York, San Francisco, Washington and Chicago which not only were responsible for many of the pioneering moves in those areas, but laid the groundwork for more effective organizations. And AFSC staff have set an example by their cooperation with other fair housing workers.[8]

The influence of AFSC activities has gone beyond the geographic areas in which they were carried out. The listing service concept used by the AFSC groups (i.e. finding whites who were willing to sell and matching them with blacks who were interested in buying) became a standard procedure with most fair housing groups, at times a major part of their program. Literature published by the AFSC, or jointly by the AFSC with the National Committee Against Discrimination in Housing, has guided many initial efforts in fair housing across the nation.

Quaker commitment to open housing also has been exercised through the actions of Meetings and individuals. The first fair housing group probably was one formed by the Friends Meeting in Syracuse in 1954.[9] In 1958 Quakers not only provided much of the initiative but $2,000 of the $11,000 needed for funding a housing opportunities program in Hartford. Quaker money provided a third of the financing for Concord Park, Morris Milgram's first interracial development. In 1956 Quakers in the Philadelphia area organized Friends Suburban Fair Housing (now known as Suburban Fair Housing to indicate a broader base of support), a real estate firm which deals only with open housing listings in the suburbs and which, since 1956, has resulted in the integration of over one hundred neighborhoods.

The work of the Friends has only scratched the surface. But it has been a remarkable accomplishment for a group which comprises less than one tenth of one percent of the population. The Quakers have set an example for others out of a religious concern for putting the preachments about the brotherhood of man into practice.

Because most Unitarians are social liberals, and their churches encourage social action, they have rather naturally played a key role in the fair housing movement. The membership and leadership of fair housing groups usually have representation from this small denomination which is ten to one hundred times that which would be expected on the basis of the percentage of Unitarians in the population. Some groups, such as CHOOSE (Clearing Housing for Open Occupancy Selections) in Pittsburgh and Community Interests, Inc., in Rochester began as the product of Unitarian social action groups.

Many Jews have been in the forefront of the battle to end discrimination in housing and, at the national level, Jewish organizations, such as the Anti-Defamation League of B'nai B'rith, the American Jewish Congress and the American Jewish Committee, appear to have played a more important role than any national denominational group other than the AFSC. The major direction of the Jewish agencies has been to combat prejudice by education and to support government action to end discrimination. In addition, the Anti-Defamation League, through its twenty-eight regional offices in the United States, has provided assistance to the fair housing movement at the community level by making available literature and films and, at times, tactical guidance.

It is also evident that Jews have been more willing than most others to sell to Negroes. In cities such as Baltimore, Cincinnati, Denver, Houston and St. Louis, many of the bet-

ter black neighborhoods were formerly Jewish neighborhoods. The first blacks could not have entered these areas
had some Jews not practiced open housing. While the fact
that other Jews then "pulled out" shows that many Jews
share the racial fears of the other whites, Jewish liberalism
toward integrated housing is well demonstrated by the disproportionate number of Jews generally found in stable interracial neighborhoods.

However, while there are many exceptions, Jews have
not engaged in open housing activities to an extent consistent
with their high educational achievements and their tra-
dition of participation in community affairs. Such involvement by Jewish groups and individual Jews has been greatly
limited by the priority given to assistance for Israel and Jewish refugees.

There is considerable variance in the contributions to
open housing efforts by the six largest Protestant denominations. Presbyterian and United Church of Christ churches
seem to have the best overall record; Episcopal and Lutheran churches in general have done less; Methodists, with
rare exceptions, have shown no inclination to go beyond
pious statements, and Baptists usually have not even done
that.[10]

In part these differences arise from the sociological class
makeup of the various denominations. Communicants of
Methodist, Baptist and Lutheran churches tend to be lower
on the socioeconomic scale and to have less education than
those in Presbyterian and United Churches. But by this criterion the Episcopalian Church should be leading the group.
Relevant here is the important influence of such liberal theo-
logical schools as Chicago, Harvard, Union, and Yale. The
Presbyterian and United Church clergymen who attended
these schools have been in the vanguard individually and
have influenced others in their denominations.

Paradoxically, although congregations dampen the activities of many clergymen in behalf of racial justice,[11] most of the active pastors have come from congregational churches where they were less insulated from direct pressures than the clergy in churches with an episcopal structure. However, as long as churches with an episcopal structure continue to base clerical promotions largely on a clergyman's ability to raise money, these churches will not realize their great potential to effect social change.

Despite a growing, affluent population, the financial contributions to many churches and church organizations have decreased because of the activities of churches in controversial social action projects.[12]

Consider the anatomy of one such loss. Early in 1968 Bishop McNulty agreed to sell a tract of land, owned by the Diocese of Buffalo in an all-white area in the city of Lackawanna, to a nonprofit Negro group planning to build single-family homes of comparable or higher price than nearby housing. When this became known, the City Council responded to the fears and anger of their constituents, the great majority of whom are Roman Catholics, by voting four to one to rezone the land to recreation and parks.*

Lackawanna's residents did not confine their protests to their elected representatives. On one Sunday 260 of 1,000 offertory envelopes handed in at Our Lady of Victory Parish were empty. A greater vengeance was reserved for the 1969 Catholic Charities Drive. In Lackawanna an estimated eleven hundred did not contribute and collections decreased from $65,000 to $55,000; in nearby South Buffalo, where many Lackawanna residents have relatives, contributions also were decreased. The overall charities drive for the

---

*This legislation later was repealed after the diocese, supported by the U.S. Department of Justice, challenged the action in court.

diocese, which normally went several percent over its goal, barely fulfilled its quota of $3,100,000.

However, these events do not mean that vigorous church leadership aimed at racial justice must result in a loss of funds. Under normal circumstances the substantial liberal element throughout the diocese might have increased its contribution, but at the time the liberals were unhappy about unrelated matters of church policy. More significantly, the backlash directed at the church in Lackawanna was a penalty the diocese paid for having failed to properly instruct its Lackawanna parishioners about their Christian responsibilities and the realities of racial integration. The people in Lackawanna believed that their church was going to bring delinquency and filth to their midst, that their church had let them down.

Leading a congregation into new ideas is not the easiest of tasks, but there is evidence that income losses can be negligible when this is done properly. For example, when Father Kern studied the impact on contributions of his forceful support of the open housing signature drive in Clarence, he found no evidence that any contributions had been cut and, over a two-year period, collections rose a normal 5 percent.

Many churches report good experience with the use of special funds, rather than church funds, for controversial projects. The First Congregational Church in the St. Louis suburb of Webster Groves has an Urban Challenge Committee which involves about 10 percent of the congregation in ghetto-related projects. The money for their work has come from specific contributions, several of which have been one thousand dollars, and special offerings. Thus anyone who does not wish to support the endeavor need not do so.

It may be significant that in 1968 the only conference of the United Church of Christ which did not have a decrease in contributions was Massachusetts. Yet the United Churches in Massachusetts had one of the most aggressive programs of social action. People in Massachusetts may be more liberal on the race issue than elsewhere, but this cannot also be said of Detroit. Yet when Cardinal Dearden diverted over one million dollars into core-area projects largely controlled by blacks, the diocese raised more than expected. Detroit is an exciting preview of what churches can do when they face up to the problem.

However, if the churches are going to face up to social responsibilities, it would seem that major changes are needed in the training clergymen receive and in the entire structure of the institutional church. For example, why not have many more clergymen who do not serve a single church, but rather minister to a specific need for a group of churches.

One step toward change was taken in suburban Chicago by the First Presbyterian Church of Oak Park. After much agonizing about what the church and its clergy should or should not do, a committee was formed to determine priorities. Its report, which was overwhelmingly adopted by the fourteen-hundred-member congregation in April of 1968, explicitly stated that the first priority was to act in the community. It said "We acknowledge that the church helps man discover his individual relationship with God and provides guidance and strength to each of us as we try to exemplify the Christian life through our daily actions. The challenge to the Church now is to learn how to act corporately in responding to the realities of the world."

The report stated that the corporate action should manifest itself "through the use of our resources, both finances and talent, in the most efficient ways we can speak the word of Christ to the community," and the congregation voted to hire a third clergyman to free the senior minister to devote more time to this first priority. While this church has been

losing one to two percent of its membership each year, all
of the Protestant churches in Oak Park have been decreasing in membership because of an increasing Catholic population. Individual contributions to First Presbyterian have been
increasing an average of 10 percent per year.

In some ways the role of the church in the world of today
is a shrinking one. Science, not theology, now explains the
physical world, and social agencies with trained counselors
and psychologists are supplanting pastors in helping people
cope with personal problems.

Yet never before have churches been in a better position
to contribute to the well-being of mankind. The complexi-
ties of modern life increase the need for the church to inter-
pret how basic values which have been developed over cen-
turies can be applied to improve the quality of life. And
modern technology, with its capability of producing an abun-
dance of material goods, raises the hope that basic religious
principles may ultimately take priority over narrow self-interest and not be savagely cast aside as in the past.

There are many who believe that the health of the church
will best be served if religious organizations continue to be
inactive on social issues, and there is good evidence that
many Americans are satisfied with a church which serves as
a place where people can meet others like themselves, enjoy
each other, and have interesting things happen to them. On
the other hand, others believe that, unless it changes, the
institutional church will not survive, and they document
their position with statistics showing an alarming decrease
in church membership among those in the twenty to thirty
age bracket.

The important question, however, is not how the church
can best flourish as an institution. It is whether the church
is to be relevant.

7 / A Promise Kept

HELPING A BLACK MAN to purchase a house is the most important thing that Samuel H. Liberman II has ever done. In fact, his attempt to get Joseph Lee Jones and his wife Barbara Jo the home they wanted in Paddock Woods, a subdivision in a St. Louis suburb, may well be the most important thing he ever will do.

In 1965 Sam Liberman, a 1959 graduate of the Harvard Law School, was vice-president of Freedom of Residence, a fair housing organization serving the Greater St. Louis area. He also functioned as chief attorney, which means that he handled much of FOR's legal work without a fee.

At that time the fair housing activists in St. Louis had no legal means to overcome discriminatory acts. Nevertheless, a viable organization had developed, primarily as a result of the efforts of the organization's executive secretary, Mrs. Ruth Porter, a Negro woman in her mid-forties with boundless energy and the ability to motivate others. In fact, had it not been for Ruth Porter there would have been no *Jones* v. *Mayer*, a Supreme Court decision which may be one of the most important of the twentieth century.

One of Mrs. Porter's contributions was to motivate Liberman to use a Reconstruction era law to give St. Louis's Negroes a better chance to get the housing of their choice. For years lawyers throughout the country had talked about attempting to use Section 1982 of the 1866 Civil Rights Act as a fair housing law. This act declared that "citizens, of every race and color . . . shall have the same right, in every state and territory . . . to lease, sell, hold, and convey real and personal property . . . as is enjoyed by white citizens." In an 1883 Supreme Court decision, Section 1982 was interpreted as applying only to state action (i.e. discrimination by state agencies or officials) and had become regarded as merely a ban on "black codes" — local laws which prevented Negroes from such rights as the purchase or rental of property. However, with the growth of the civil rights movement an increasing number of lawyers began to believe that, given a case, the courts would rule that the sale of houses in a new subdivision constituted state action because there was so much state involvement in the building and operation of such developments. A very few civil rights advocates dared to go further, to believe that a winning legal argument could be made that Section 1982 also applied to the actions of private persons. One such advocate was Samuel Liberman.

Ruth Porter's second contribution was to find a case which was perfect for the circumstances. When the Joneses went to Paddock Woods to look at model houses, they were ignored by the salesmen; when Mr. Jones told a salesman he was interested in purchasing a house, the man replied, "We are not selling to Negroes." Thus when a suit was filed against the developer, Alfred H. Mayer, there were no side issues to becloud the basic question of whether discrimination was legal. And unlike most families in a similar situation, the Joneses had no hesitation about bringing a suit which might receive a lot of publicity. They even advanced a considerable sum of their own money to help pay expenses.

Jones v. *Mayer* was filed in the United States District Court on September 2, 1965. Arthur Allen Leff, a Washington University Law School professor who had been a college classmate of Liberman, collaborated in the brief. Another Washington University Law School professor, Daniel R. Mandelker, also participated at the beginning of the case. Mandelker's discussions at a conference sponsored by the National Committee Against Discrimination in Housing helped reinforce the decision of bringing suit, and students working with Mandelker under a Ford Foundation grant helped provide necessary research.

It was not easy to arrive at the basic strategy to be followed in presenting the case. Liberman believed that, taken with the Thirteenth Amendment (which abolished slavery), Section 1982 could be shown to apply to the actions of private persons, thereby making racial discrimination unlawful in the sale or rental of any housing. However, Leff and others who were consulted thought the best hope of success was to relate the discriminatory act to state action, thereby making the discriminatory act a violation of plaintiff's rights under the Fourteenth Amendment which reads in part: "No State shall make or enforce any law which shall abridge the privileges or immunities of citizens of the United States . . . nor deny to any person within its jurisdiction the equal protection of the laws." Liberman agreed that this argument was more likely to prevail, at least in the lower courts. Consequently, although references were made to Section 1982 and the Thirteenth Amendment, the thrust of the argument in the District Court was that Mayer had been granted the right to build and regulate a small community as if it were a political subdivision, and the discrimination which had occurred constituted state action.

The District Court dismissed the complaint, finding insufficient state involvement to support the charge under the

160

Fourteenth Amendment and that Section 1982 applied only to government action. The case then was brought to the Court of Appeals and Liberman began soliciting national organizations for financial backing for the battle ahead. One of these was the National Committee Against Discrimination in Housing (NCDH).

Liberman's request for funds was referred to Sol Rabkin, chairman of NCDH's legal committee, who recommended financial support because *Jones* v. *Mayer* was precisely the type of suit which he had been seeking as a test case. But this recommendation was only the beginning of Rabkin's contribution. A long-time civil rights lawyer who was the director of the Law Department of the Anti-Defamation League of B'nai B'rith, Rabkin believed that a winning case could be based on the so-called statutory argument — that Section 1982 could be applied to private actions. Energetic and dedicated, Rabkin wrote an *amicus* brief which was filed in his name and that of NCDH's general counsel, Joseph B. Robison, the Director of the Commission on Law and Social Action of the American Jewish Congress and one of those who had proposed the possible use of the statutory argument. This brief, unlike Liberman's, used as its main thrust the statutory argument that Section 1982 was applicable "without regard to the presence of any indicia of state action."

The petitioners lost again. But the decision of the Court of Appeals gave hope. It declared that the Supreme Court might assert that Section 1982, because of its derivation from the Thirteenth Amendment, was not dependent upon state involvement. The Court of Appeals added, "If we are wrong in this conclusion, the Supreme Court will tell us so and in so doing will categorize and limit those of its prior decisions, cited herein, which we feel are restrictive upon us."

From the very beginning Liberman had planned to go to

the Supreme Court if necessary. The wording of the decision of the Court of Appeals was hardly likely to change his mind.

But now the hurdles were higher. The first was to persuade the Supreme Court to hear the case. Neither Liberman nor Leff was admitted to practice before the Court, so by mutual agreement Rabkin filed the petition for a writ of *certiorari* (i.e. review of the case) with Liberman, Leff, Robison and Robert L. Carter of the NAACP.

An extremely important development then occurred: the Department of Justice submitted a Memorandum *Amicus* asking the Supreme Court to hear the case. The decision of Attorney General Ramsey Clark to take this unusual step probably was an important factor in the Court's decision to accept the *Jones* v. *Mayer* case for review. The action emphasized the importance of the case and made clear to the Court that hearing the case would not constitute a conflict with the Johnson Administration over closely related legislation pending in Congress.

Meanwhile things were not proceeding smoothly between St. Louis and New York. The problem: who was to argue the case and reap the benefits to career and self-esteem that would come with victory. Liberman had always intended that he would present the case to the Supreme Court. It was his case, and the fact that it might become a history-making decision made him want to do it all the more. However, because he needed the money and the other help which he could obtain from NCDH, he had not made this clear. The result was that Rabkin and the NCDH staff came to believe what they wanted to believe: that Rabkin would present the case.

Had Liberman and Rabkin been the only ones involved it is possible that they might have reached agreement. Both are men who on other occasions have demonstrated a willingness to put belief in principle above self-interest. But less altruistic men also were involved. The National Committee Against Discrimination in Housing, constantly in need of funds, had a strong organizational interest in having its lawyer present the case. With this incentive NCDH easily rationalized that the best qualified attorney should present the oral argument, even though, as most recognize, the quality of advocacy before the Supreme Court usually matters less than the case and the brief. As a result, Edward Rutledge, one of the executive directors of NCDH, wired Liberman that unless NCDH's attorneys handled the case, NCDH would not contribute any funds for the brief.

Thus at a time when energies should have been concentrated on presenting the strongest possible case to the Court, they were dissipated by infighting. Tired of the bickering, Liberman and Loff decided that if necessary they would personally absorb costs beyond those they could raise from other sources and that they, along with a friend who was admitted to practice before the Supreme Court, would represent the Joneses.*

NCDH made one last effort to gain control. Without consulting Rabkin, Jack Wood, NCDH's other executive codirector traveled to St. Louis to persuade Joseph Lee Jones to replace Liberman as his attorney. Wood argued that Liberman might lose the case because of his lack of experience. But Jones had confidence in the young attorney and refused to make a switch. As a result, NCDH was relegated to submitting an *amicus* brief which served NCDH's fund-raising interests by providing an opportunity to claim a disproportionate share of the subsequent triumph.

The case was argued before the Supreme Court on April 1 and 2, 1968. This time the brief submitted by Liberman,

*Ultimately the American Civil Liberties Union and Freedom of Residence paid all costs.

Leff and Samuel A. Chaitovitz stressed the statutory argument based on the Thirteenth Amendment. Rabkin's influence and the response of the Court of Appeals to Rabkin's *amicus* brief ended any doubts that otherwise might have existed about the strategy of using the statutory argument. This approach, naturally, also dominated the *amicus* brief jointly filed by NCDH, the NAACP, the Anti-Defamation League and the American Jewish Congress, with Robert L. Carter of the NAACP and Arnold Forster of ADL joining Rabkin and Robison as attorneys for *Amici*.

As it turned out, Liberman did not argue alone for the petitioners. He was joined by Ramsey Clark who again showed his great concern by personally presenting the government's case as an *amicus curiae*, his only appearance before the Supreme Court during his tenure as Attorney General, an appearance made all the more unusual because it was for a private suit in which the United States was not a party. Clark felt very strongly about the case. He believed it was the government's responsibility to press forward on all fronts as far and fast as possible in ending the segregation in housing which lay at the root of many other problems of race.

Although the government's brief dealt with both the statutory argument based on the Thirteenth Amendment and the state action argument based on the Fourteenth Amendment, by agreement with Liberman, Clark confined his oral argument to state action. This also was the argument in most of the dozen or more other *amicus* briefs presented by a wide variety of organizations ranging from the American Federation of Teachers to the National Catholic Conference for Interracial Justice. While these briefs made no legal contribution to the ultimate decision, the concern expressed by such a large number of important organizations may have been taken into consideration by some of the Justices.

In a decision that brought criticism from many and surprised almost all, the Supreme Court, by a 7 to 2 vote, with Harlan and White dissenting, agreed with Liberman, Rabkin and their associates and declared "Section 1982 bars *all* racial discrimination, private as well as public, in the sale or rental of property, and that the statute, thus construed, is a valid exercise of the power of Congress to enforce the Thirteenth Amendment." In the decision, written by Justice Potter Stewart, the Court stated, "When racial discrimination herds men into ghettos and makes their ability to buy property turn on the color of their skin, then it too is a relic of slavery." The Court concluded:

> Negro citizens, North and South, who saw in the Thirteenth Amendment a promise of freedom — freedom to "go and come at pleasure" and "buy and sell when they please" — would be left with "a mere paper guarantee" if Congress were powerless to assure that a dollar in the hands of a Negro will purchase the same thing as a dollar in the hands of a white man. At the very least, the freedom that Congress is empowered to secure under the Thirteenth Amendment includes the freedom to buy whatever a white man can buy, the right to live wherever a white man can live. If Congress cannot say that being a free man means at least this much, then the Thirteenth Amendment made a promise the Nation cannot keep.

Perhaps the most important reason that the *Jones* v. *Mayer* decision met considerable instant criticism was that just two months earlier Congress had passed Title VIII of the 1968 Civil Rights Act, a fair housing law covering most dwellings. This act complicated the determination to be made by the Court concerning the meaning of the related law passed in 1866 (Section 1982), but the Court justified its decision in the wake of the recent Congressional action by the argument: ". . . [there are] vast differences between, on the one hand, a general statute applicable only to racial discrimination in the rental and sale of property and enforceable only by private parties acting on their own initiative, and, on the other hand, a detailed housing law, applicable to a broad range of discriminatory practices and enforceable by a complete arsenal of federal authority."

Another concern of the Court was to show that in 1866 Congress had intended Section 1982 to be a fair housing law. The legislative history in the excellent Department of Justice brief* was of particular help in making this clear, but the Court itself added much material not presented in the briefs. In its decision, the Court clearly documented that in 1866 many members of the 39th Congress viewed Section 1982 as an all-encompassing fair housing bill, and that the majority rather obviously meant it to be more than a prohibition of "Black Codes."

There is also substantial evidence that many in the 39th Congress who voted for Section 1982 did not intend it to have the interpretation given by the Supreme Court in *Jones* v. *Mayer*. But it is precisely because the Court did not follow its usual policy — deciding a case in an area where Congress had acted on the narrowest possible grounds — that *Jones* v. *Mayer* is an exceptional decision. Rather than render what was legally most defensible, the Court instead acted as part of the political fabric of the country. The evidence of its wisdom is clear: the decision could in effect have been reversed by Congressional repeal of Section 1982, yet no such action has even been initiated.

*The principal architect of the brief was Louis F. Claibourne, a deputy solicitor general.

The opportunity presented to the Supreme Court in *Jones* v. *Mayer* was the result of a willingness by many people to do something about their belief in open housing, including paradoxically the builder, Alfred H. Mayer. In principle, he believed in housing equality and had contributed money in support of this belief. However, like most people, he was reluctant to allow his beliefs to interfere with his income.

Unlike other builders in St. Louis, Mayer had tried an open housing policy in his developments. He found it made little difference in his overall sales, but he did experience difficulty selling houses directly adjacent to Negroes. Eventually he sold all such houses, but in some cases it took as long as a year. One house had to be sold twelve times; each time the buyer was told that a Negro family was going to be next door, the deal fell through. One potential buyer was a clergyman who said, "If they were living down the block I wouldn't mind, but next door . . ."

Mayer had hoped that, because he was a large builder with an annual sales volume of seven hundred to eight hundred homes, other builders would follow his example. When he contributed $1,000 to Freedom of Residence, Mayer was only one of about a half dozen builders in the St. Louis area who had given a substantial sum to the fair housing organization. These builders felt that something ought to be done about open housing and that Freedom of Residence was an appropriate mechanism. But other builders were afraid to sell to blacks, and when Mayer found himself at a competitive disadvantage he reverted to a discriminatory policy.

Mayer's honesty, however, was not limited. Because it was against the law to discriminate in developments receiving financing from the FHA, Mayer stopped obtaining preconstruction commitments for FHA financing, a move which he felt would result in less loss than the problems related to Negro entry since his houses were in a price range where few buyers used FHA financing anyway. It was also his policy to tell Negro buyers that sales were restricted. Unlike most builders, Mayer had the sensitivity to realize that the anguish of discriminatory encounters was only compounded by the hypocrisy practiced by most whites.

The candor with which he admitted discrimination to all, thereby allowing the plaintiffs to base their suit on a principle of law rather than proof of discrimination, was one of several ways that Mayer made the Supreme Court decision possible. While Mayer did not believe that the Joneses would win, he felt the case should be resolved in the courts because of its significance. On at least one occasion he stated publicly that he hoped that he would lose.[1] Indeed, had Mayer not been sympathetic, he and the former Rhodes Scholar who served as his attorney probably could have found some way to terminate the case at a cost considerably less than the $15,000 Mayer spent fighting the suit.

An account of *Jones* v. *Mayer* would not be complete without further mention of Mr. and Mrs. Joseph Lee Jones. They too were exceptional. Very few Negro families are willing to engage in a public court fight since blacks, like whites, often tend to overestimate the hazards of standing up for equal opportunity. But the Joneses' only concern was the limited amount of money they could put into the suit and, as things turned out, that was the only concern they needed to have. The adverse reaction they experienced amounted to a total of two telephone calls. Moreover, there were some fruits of victory beyond being participants in an historic decision of the Supreme Court. In an out-of-court settlement, Mayer compensated the Joneses for the expenses they had incurred. And Mr. Jones's business as a bail bondsman increased. People looked up to him.

One triumph was denied. The Joneses did not get the house they wanted in Paddock Woods. Before the case was settled, they bought another home. Three years was too long to wait.

It is still too early to judge history's verdict on *Jones* v. *Mayer*. Because the decision bars racial discrimination by private parties in the making of contracts and the purchase and rental of personal as well as real property, it has significant implications beyond the field of housing. The ruling has neither the sweep nor the trailblazing quality of *Brown* v. *Board of Education*, the 1954 school decision which struck down the doctrine of "separate but equal," but *Jones* v. *Mayer* eventually may become one of the most significant decisions of the Supreme Court for other reasons: the ease with which it can be implemented and its immediate effect on the nation's real estate industry.

Almost overnight the *Jones* v. *Mayer* decision converted fair housing's greatest enemy to what, at least at an institutional level, is now an ally. In an article which appeared two weeks after the decision in *Realtor's Headlines*, the official publication of the National Association of Real Estate Boards (NAREB), Eugene P. Conser, NAREB's Executive Vice-President commented, "The Negro in America henceforth is a free man. This is the message that every Realtor should now know and understand. Yes, every citizen — whatever his attitude toward racial prejudice. Those who oppose that view should now understand that their position is forever negated."

In another article in *Realtor's Headlines* published several weeks later, Conser wrote, "Local boards of Realtors can do much to forestall punitive legislation by publicly announcing adherence to 'the law of the land' — now a fact, irretrievable. If Realtors adhere to the law and by their professional skill assist the property owners in not running afoul of it, there will be no need for punitive legislation."

169

Many state and local boards have responded to Conser's message by making genuine efforts to encourage brokers to cease discriminatory practices and to promote nondiscriminatory attitudes in the community. The California Real Estate Association, which fought so hard and effectively against fair housing legislation[2] spent $50,000 to make a twenty-five-minute documentary motion picture entitled *A House to Live In*. This serious attempt to dispel fears about racial integration has been shown on television and to almost all of the 176 local boards in the state.

The real estate industry responded so positively to the *Jones* v. *Mayer* decision for several reasons. Many real estate brokers had been troubled by the immorality of discrimination. And the fight to continue discrimination had been a losing cause which drained the industry's money and energies and damaged the personal reputations of real estate brokers with those who believed in equal opportunities. The action of the Supreme Court gave the Realtors a chance to disengage honorably from a battle they no longer wished to fight.

There was another factor which prompted the brokers to accept the sweeping decision of the Supreme Court. Among the many compromises which had been required to pass the 1968 fair housing bill was the exclusion from coverage of single-family homes not sold by a broker. Thus the self-interest of the real estate industry was well served by the Supreme Court decision which then brought all housing under the law. NAREB's Executive Vice-President observed:

Sellers and lessors of property — all kinds of property — have every reason now to place representation of their property in the hands of experts — experts who are prepared to conduct their business in conformity with the law. For example, the homeowner cannot af-

170

ford to sell "on his own." An advertisement or a "for sale" sign is an invitation to inspection. And any refusal to show, if the applicant is of a different race, is an invitation to a lawsuit in the federal courts.

The significance of the reaction of the real estate industry to the *Jones* v. *Mayer* decision goes far beyond the impact of the educational programs which were undertaken by some boards. Historically Realtors have served as the nucleus for opposition, making open housing a controversial political issue and serving as a restraint on the support that open housing received from most public and private institutions, including even those charged with enforcing the law. Now that opposition is gone

The ease with which the *Jones* v. *Mayer* decision can be implemented gives fair housing organizations their ultimate weapon. If "checkers" can be mustered to obtain evidence and lawyers to handle the cases, racial discrimination in housing can be effectively countered in any community, regardless of local laws or their enforcement, by filing suit in Federal Court. There an injunction may be obtained quickly to prevent the loss of the housing desired by the black family. Usually such cases never even reach the judge; in St. Louis and San Francisco, where this tactic was used energetically during the first six months following the *Jones* v. *Mayer* decision, the discriminating party quickly capitulated in 80 to 90 percent of the cases when faced with a lawsuit.

The most potent use that fair housing groups can make of the Supreme Court decision is to see that those who discriminate are sued for damages and to use this deterrent to bring to an end discriminatory acts. The *Jones* v. *Mayer* decision itself makes no mention of damages because it was not an issue before the Court. However, Federal District Courts have awarded both compensatory and punitive damages to plaintiffs. In Boston in July 1969, an award of $1,052, which included $400 for emotional distress and $350 for the services of their lawyer,[3] was given a biracial couple by Judge A. Arthur Garrity, Jr. Federal courts in Chicago, Cincinnati and San Francisco are among others which have awarded damages ranging from $430 to over $1,000. These awards have been influenced by the provision in the 1968 Civil Rights Act for punitive damages up to $1,000 as well as greater recognition that discriminatory acts cause psychological damage.

A few court suits resulting in damages will not, by themselves, end discrimination in a community. But when there is a fair housing organization which effectively makes blacks aware of their rights and makes whites realize that those who discriminate often will pay for their unlawful acts — then discrimination in housing will be nearing its end.

8 / The Employer

"I'M NOT GOING TO TAKE this crap . . . I'm tired of being humilated."

Claibourne Smith was having second thoughts about working for Du Pont. Since arriving in Wilmington, Delaware, at the beginning of the week he had visited ten suitable apartment complexes. All had claimed that they were filled and would not have any vacancies in the near future. His wife, Hazel, who accompanied him househunting, felt they should leave the area and Du Pont.

Racial discrimination was not a new experience for Claibourne Smith. He was twenty-six years old, and as long as he could remember he had suffered indignities because he was black. But he had come a long way since he was thirteen — working every day from 6:00 A.M. to 10:00 P.M. during the hot summer in Memphis as a "carry-out boy" in a supermarket, working long hours after school during the rest of the year, being told by his bosses that he should get used to carrying groceries and mopping floors.

In a way that was what made him so angry now. He had overcome the obstacles. He had gone to college, earned a Ph.D. in organic chemistry and secured a high-prestige job as a research chemist with E. I. du Pont de Nemours & Company. He had attained a position where he once had thought he would be given the same chance as others, and now he saw that belief had been an illusion.

The Du Pont Company did not want to lose Claibourne Smith. During the first week all that had been done was to have Dr. Smith's immediate superior accompany the couple in their search for housing — partly as a guide, but primarily to avoid unpleasant incidents and increase their chances of getting a place. Stronger action clearly was needed.

Robert M. Joyce, Director of Research for the Central Research Department, took on the task. Joyce, a man who knew how to get things done, decided to approach the manager of one of the more desirable developments rather than contact the rental agent with whom Dr. Smith had dealt. Before calling, he carefully planned his arguments. However, the preparation was not necessary. The manager told Dr. Joyce that he did not discriminate and that Dr. Smith should reapply. The next day, at Dr. Joyce's suggestion, Smith checked back at what will be called the Shamrock Apartments where previously he had been told there would be no vacancies for at least two months. Shortly thereafter the Smiths moved into an apartment in the Shamrock which had been vacant for two months.

Claibourne Smith went to Wilmington in 1965. Early in 1968 the Smiths started looking for a house, but they gave up after continually encountering discrimination. They recognized that it probably was possible for them to get a house of the type they wanted if they made a sufficient effort, but they decided that it just was not worth the anguish. Their decision was difficult for them to explain, and difficult to understand for someone who has never experienced discrimination.

While Dr. Smith appreciates the role that Du Pont played

in helping him obtain his apartment, he thinks the company failed him by not doing enough about discrimination to allow him to buy a home in the same way as his white colleagues. His beliefs in this respect are shared by many other blacks who work for Du Pont in the Wilmington area. Discrimination, and the housing problems it creates, may have influenced several Negro employees to leave Du Pont for other jobs.

Black employees are not the only people critical of Du Pont. Several proposals aimed at open housing have been presented to the company without success by the Fair Housing Council of Northern Delaware (which covers the Greater Wilmington area) and by other civil rights workers. Some of the civil rights activists are disappointed; others are sharply critical.

The difficulties with housing discrimination which confront the world's largest chemical company typify problems which almost all large employers in America face today. The failure of employers to take aggressive action to end discrimination in housing has become a handicap in recruiting Negroes, a factor in losing them, and perhaps most important, a very negative influence on their attitude toward their employer. If an employer is not already aware of these reactions to inaction, it is probably because his communication with black employees is poor. With a few exceptions, such as IBM, private corporations have not developed a favorable image among blacks.

Du Pont's record in helping its employees obtain equal access to housing is better than that of most other private corporations. Since 1959, when the company officially adopted a nondiscriminatory policy in hiring, there have been increasing efforts to end housing discrimination against employees. At first such efforts were on the level of the assistance provided to Claibourne Smith. It soon became evident that this was inadequate, that more had to be done to prevent black employees from being humiliated. Consequently, in 1966 a company representative visited thirty owners of apartment houses in the Wilmington area to express Du Pont's desire that all its employees be given equal opportunity in housing. That was all that was said, but fifteen of the thirty agreed that they would not discriminate against any Du Pont employee.

Because this suggestion was sufficient to accommodate new employees coming to Wilmington, no attempt was made to go further. A list of "open" developments was given to the supervisor of the new black employee. The supervisor would then take the employee only to those developments known to be open. Since these provided a wide choice of good housing, everything usually was satisfactory at first. Unfortunately, the system made no provision for the housing needs of families of increased size and incomes who wanted to buy a house, or for those who looked for an apartment on their own. Thus the frustrations of Claibourne Smith were experienced by many others.

There were less direct ways by which Du Pont attempted to promote open occupancy. In 1967 the company and eight other major Delaware firms jointly endorsed open housing legislation. Early in 1968 Du Pont's president, Charles B. McCoy, restated the company's support for open housing in the lead article of a newsletter sent to all supervisory and management personnel. McCoy declared, "We can no more turn our backs on urban and community problems . . . than we can ignore production or sales problems. . . . Personally, I would be delighted if there were a sharp rise in the number of corporate employees in the midst of community affairs." Later in 1968 the company quietly adopted a policy that whenever Du Pont sold or rented real estate the listing

176

agreement with the broker must include a provision indicating the property was to be offered on a nondiscriminatory basis.

Du Pont employees, acting as individuals, often made important contributions to fair housing efforts in their communities. For example, Dr. Clyde Davis, the director of a large research laboratory in southern New Jersey, was not only a cofounder of the Gloucester County Fair Housing Council, but provided free office services for the group in the same way that similar help was made available to the Boy Scouts and the United Fund. The fair housing efforts of Dr. Davis and other Du Pont employees could not have occurred without a favorable climate within the company.

Unfortunately, these activities have not made much difference to most blacks trying to find housing in Wilmington. Negroes still have limited access to housing outside of the ghetto area and several all-black suburban developments. There are several suburban subdivisions built for mixed occupancy which have continued as interracial developments, but they are all small. Also, many new houses are available as a result of an agreement by members of the Builders Association to sell on an open occupancy basis, a pledge honored by some and avoided by others. Some resale housing in white areas has been available through listings given by sympathetic people to Charles Foreman, a black real estate broker whose firm deals almost exclusively in white areas. But discrimination remains the rule followed by most landlords, real estate brokers and homeowners.

The fair housing movement in Wilmington has attracted a few people of substance and ability. But the Fair Housing Council has not prospered, and paid memberships have declined from a high of about two hundred. The absence of any applicable fair housing law until 1968 limited its effectiveness. The Council has also lacked sustained effective leader-

177

ship. The people involved have not had the time to make it a success. However, they recognized that if money were available to hire staff — or if a suitable person could devote six to twelve months to fund raising, then they could mount an effective program. And in Wilmington when people think of resources such as money and people, they think of Du Pont.

They also thought of Du Pont's power. They felt that if Du Pont really wanted to end discrimination, it could. The stories of Claibourne Smith and others who had been helped by the company showed what the exercise of a small amount of influence could do. But Du Pont used neither its men nor its money nor its power.

Power in a large corporation such as Du Pont is scattered. The mechanism by which the corporation takes new directions is basically conservative — many people are consulted and strong objection by a minority is often sufficient to prevent action.

A new Du Pont policy, aimed at the promotion of open housing and the assistance of Du Pont employees who encountered discrimination, would probably have to satisfy many interests: the Employee Relations Department, the Real Estate Division, the Legal Department, the Public Relations Department and the Community Affairs Committee. Before anyone would present an open housing proposal to the ten-man Executive Committee, whose approval is required for corporate policy, they would want to have the support of at least most of the concerned groups.

Thus the failure of Du Pont to respond more aggressively is in part a result of the system. The system requires that someone in a position to act effectively must negotiate an acceptable policy and shepherd it to a decision. Unfortunately, those in such a position have not had the exposure required to recognize the problem, and those who have recognized the problem have not been able to reach the people who could do something about it. The Fair Housing Council would have had a better chance of success if, instead of writing President McCoy, they had first tried to involve some of Du Pont's middle management and, perhaps at the same time, attempted to obtain support from established community leaders, such as church leaders, with whom Du Pont's top management often dealt in community affairs.

If a suitable open housing policy proposal were to develop, it almost certainly would receive good support from the most influential of people within Du Pont. Charles Brelsford McCoy, the fifty-nine-year-old president, is a thoughtful man known as a good listener. In his short time as chief executive, he has demonstrated a willingness to allow the company to extend its role in public affairs — not because he believes that past actions of Du Pont were inadequate, but because he feels that new policies are needed in today's world. As McCoy puts it, "We used to be able to say 'that's the Mayor's job. . . . If I do my job well and he does his job well, it will all come out rosy.' Today it isn't that simple." In addition, McCoy feels that Du Pont has an important responsibility in providing equal opportunity in employment, and he recognizes that equality of opportunity in jobs cannot be separated from an employee's right to equal access to housing.

The problem is to develop a suitable policy, one that is meaningful but still observes appropriate restraints. One such restraint is to avoid excessive use of corporate power. "We want to pull our weight, not throw it around," is McCoy's way of saying it. Indeed, many who criticize corporations for not doing something about housing discrimination would be among the first to scream if corporate power were focused on certain other issues.

Another restraint has to do with the limitations in the skills which a company such as Du Pont can bring to a community problem. McCoy believes that private industry should participate only where it has competence, and therefore cannot be expected to provide a panacea for urban problems. "We don't have the insight in social work and housing problems that we have in polymer chemistry."

Finally, there is the relationship between the corporation and the people who work for it. It is Du Pont's policy to avoid influencing the personal lives of employees. Since the line between helpful assistance to an employee and paternalism is a narrow one, Du Pont at times is cautious lest it cross it.

While there are limitations to what corporations can do to aid their Negro employees obtain suitable housing, these limitations have been only part of the problem.

Fear of reaction by company employees or by customers is probably the most important single explanation why corporations have done so little to combat housing discrimination. Corporate executives have been carefully trained to consider the negative consequences of a decision. These men are being influenced by such questions as "What effect would this have on our Southern plants?" and "If somebody reads in the paper that we are helping a Negro get a house in a white neighborhood, will he buy our toaster?"

Bigotry is also a factor. The power in most American corporations is concentrated in a generation less sympathetic to racial equality than that of the younger people who work for them. And, as we have already mentioned, the workings of a corporation are such that a minority with strong feelings can often block action.

Two additional reasons for corporate inaction are closely related. First, executives do not recognize the extent to which black employees encounter discrimination; secondly, they do not connect the problem with a corporate responsibility.

The lack of recognition of discrimination is illustrated by the comment recently made by a General Motors spokesman that "We are not aware of any occasion wherein a professional employee recruited by the corporation has encountered discrimination when seeking housing." A statement such as this about a corporation employing over one-half million people means that the atmosphere in General Motors is such that blacks who encounter discrimination do not complain to their superiors or, if they do, the incidents are not considered sufficiently important to be communicated to higher echelons of management.

General Motors is only one of a number of large companies which have made such statements. Most executives do not understand how discrimination affects their black employees. For example, late in 1967, as part of an effort to increase recruitment of black professionals at a General Electric plant employing fifteen thousand in Cincinnati, detailed discussions were held with black employees to obtain their views as to what needed to be done. Much to their surprise, GE's managers became aware, for the first time, that many of the blacks already employed were unhappy with the housing they had been able to obtain. GE's management also discovered that dissatisfaction with housing may have contributed to some black employees leaving for other jobs.

A black man usually does not initiate a complaint to white bosses about discrimination in housing. If the bosses want to know, they are going to have to ask him to tell it like it is. If they have not heard the story before, they ought to listen

The availability of housing for black employees on the same basis as whites can be justified as a corporate objective beyond its obvious importance in the recruiting and keeping of black employees. Without equal opportunity in housing there cannot be equal opportunity in employment.

Increasingly, employment opportunities are shifting to suburban locations distant from black communities. For example, employment in Philadelphia in the central city decreased from 770,000 to 720,000 between 1951 and 1965, but during this period jobs in the suburbs increased from 370,000 to 590,000. During this same fourteen-year period jobs in the city of Baltimore stayed at about 345,000, but suburban jobs went from 86,000 to 172,000.[1] The pattern is similar in every metropolitan area in the United States.[2]

One reason that Peter G. Peterson, the board chairman of Bell and Howell, has actively participated in a fair housing organization was his discovery that many of his black employees were forced to travel over two hours each day between Chicago's ghetto in the southern part of the city and Bell and Howell's plant in a northern suburb. Such a situation has serious disadvantages for both the employer and the employee. The employee is more likely to be fatigued, is apt to have a higher rate of absenteeism, and may not be available when unexpected emergencies develop. From the employee's viewpoint it places him at a disadvantage in the competition for a better job, decreases the time he has for recreation or further education, and decreases his net income by disproportionate transportation expenses.

Housing discrimination against black employees may limit their transferability, a limitation which has obvious negatives for both the employer and the employee. When in 1966 the Bell Laboratories were shifting a group from Murray Hill, New Jersey, to Naperville, Illinois, two Negro scientists could not obtain satisfactory housing because of discrimination. As a result, the two black employees remained at Murray Hill. A 1967 survey by the Fair Housing Council of Delaware Valley indicated that it took over a year for most black professional employees transferring into the Philadelphia area to get permanently settled.

These are the more obvious ways that housing discrimination interrelates with corporate responsibilities. In addition, there is some evidence that the ability of Negroes to obtain jobs at all may be adversely affected by housing segregation. Based on elaborate statistical analysis, John F. Kain, a Harvard economist, has estimated that Chicago Negroes may lose as many as twenty-five thousand jobs because of segregation; in Detroit, which is smaller and less segregated, the loss of jobs was estimated to be between four thousand and nine thousand.[3]

Even less obvious, and admittedly less defined, is the effect that housing discrimination may have on how a black employee feels about his employer and his job, and the impact of these feelings on his job performance and his development in the company. It is doubtful that a man who is forced to live in a ghetto, apart from the people with whom he works, can think of himself as just another employee with the same opportunity as everyone else.

Although most large private corporations have made an excellent start in providing job opportunities, none has taken a proper *leadership* role in combating housing discrimination directed at its black employees. If many of these corporations have not received the criticism which has been directed at Du Pont, it is only because few had the potential to influence a city to the extent Du Pont could effect change in Wilmington.

A large number of corporations have supported open housing legislation in the past few years. Many others have not. A few companies have undertaken specific affirmative action programs at specific locations. Hardly any companies — perhaps none — have yet faced up to the problem of adopting as corporate policy an affirmative action program.

Some companies have even been guilty of maintaining segregated company-owned housing until forced by government action to end the practice. In 1968 the Department of Labor charged Bethlehem Steel, the Scott Paper Company and the American Can Company with violating the equal opportunity clauses of their government contract by maintaining segregated housing for employees. Until Bethlehem, under the pressure of losing its federal contracts, changed its rental practices, the housing assigned to whites at their Sparrows Point plant in Baltimore was of standard quality, that assigned to blacks was in a separate area and of lesser quality. Such action does not necessarily reflect a high level of racism by management; in 1968 Bethlehem, in concert with other firms in the area, contributed money in Buffalo to two different programs related to equal opportunities in housing.

Private corporations are not the only employers who have been remiss. Even federal agencies which are publicly committed to open housing have completely neglected their responsibility by failing to implement their open housing policy. For example, the Atomic Energy Commission does not appear to have directly assisted a single black family in the past ten years. AEC's headquarters are in Germantown, Maryland, an all-white community over twenty miles from Washington's ghettos.

Another laggard federal agency is the Manned Space Center of the National Aeronautics and Space Administration (NASA). About 6 percent of the forty-five hundred employees who man the nerve center of America's space program are black. Many people at the Center believe that the reason almost all these Negro employees live over twenty miles away in Houston is that most of them are in the lower pay grades, and housing in the area near the Center is expensive. While a shortage of moderate-priced housing in the "NASA area" undoubtedly is a factor, it does not explain why the housing pattern of blacks is significantly different from that of the whites who are in the same pay grades.

Discrimination is the reason, and the blacks are quick to tell anyone who makes the effort to ask them. Some have tried to obtain housing near the Space Center but were unable to do so. Others have never tried, but would have lived nearer their work "if conditions were different." However, they do not want to be pioneers.

Joseph Atkinson, who runs the incentives awards program at the Center, is an articulate Negro with a master's degree from the Harvard Business School. He was one who tried to buy a home close to the Center when he came to NASA five years ago, but was unable to do so. As a result, he lives in a predominantly black neighborhood in Houston and spends about eighty minutes a day driving the twenty miles each way to and from work. Recently a colleague told him about a house in the NASA area which he thought Atkinson would be able to buy and said, "Why don't you grab it?" But by now Atkinson, his wife and four children have established ties in the neighborhood in which they have been living and have become accustomed to the cost of a second automobile which gets heavy usage. However, Atkinson, along with the other blacks at the Center, wants to feel that he could move into the NASA area if he wished and live there comfortably. He believes that the management of the Center should have done more.

The man who has been in the best position to have accomplished something is Wesley L. Hjornevik, Associate Director of the Manned Space Center. Hjornevik is a perceptive, intelligent man with a far better understanding of the problem of housing discrimination than most business executives or government officials. He has raised the issue of housing with developers and has had assurances that it would be open, but he knows that as a practical matter it is not. He has talked to the people in the Chamber of Commerce, but has been unable to generate support because "the community is not interested in having the Negroes come." He has discussed his concern with bankers who have said that if there were a group of Negroes who wanted housing, they would build homes in a Negro area. And he candidly sums up his efforts as "informal, gentle and ineffective."

Hjornevik understands the use of institutional power as an instrument of social change and has used NASA's power to help end discrimination in public accommodations in the NASA area. On one occasion a large dinner was canceled at 4:00 **P.M.** on the day it was scheduled because the place where it was to be held would not serve Negroes. But open housing is a more sensitive issue than public accommodations.

Because of the housing situation, a man whose technical skills were needed refused a job offer. However, the senior managers of the Center have viewed this as a smaller loss than the potential danger of involving the Center in a controversy that might bring sharp reactions from the community — a controversy they wished to avoid because the task of putting a man on the moon was consuming all of their energies.

The NASA program has been one of the most spectacular achievements of man. Fantastic dreams have become realities in a relatively few years by adopting a long-range plan of step-by-step progress, coupled with a national commitment for the necessary resources of people and money. But there are questions that must be raised. Have not our past priorities — brilliantly and faithfully executed by men like Wesley Hjornevik — placed too much emphasis on getting a man to the moon and too little on raising the quality of life for those on earth? Could not comparable planning, backed up by the commitment of appropriate resources, be used to make real other dreams?

But there has been one federal agency which has viewed equality of housing opportunity as a priority which could not be ignored. On July 1, 1967, Defense Secretary Robert S. McNamara imposed sanctions which banned new rentals by military personnel in apartment developments near bases in Maryland and metropolitan Washington containing five or more units whose landlords did not agree to rent without regard to race. Faced with the prospect of renting to all servicemen or to no servicemen, many landlords agreed to drop their discriminatory policies. By September 1, the number of units available to Negro servicemen in Maryland had increased from five thousand to ten thousand; in metropolitan Washington the increase was from ten thousand to twenty-eight thousand.

With this pilot program a success, the Department of Defense extended it to the entire United States. Since some landlords might agree to rent to all servicemen and then continue to discriminate against blacks, a complaint system was instituted and, if a complaint was found valid, sanctions were imposed. And, with the advent of national fair housing legislation, procedures were modified so that legal action was taken when appropriate.

The direct impact of this program has been limited to rental developments near military installations, a small part of the total housing market, and in some areas post commanders have not followed up properly. Still, many black servicemen have obtained desirable housing which previously they were denied. The technique of making the equal opportunities program part of a new housing referral system which benefited all military personnel was instrumental in preventing serious reactions from whites. Many officers who once felt the program could never be successfully accomplished were saying less than two years later, "Why didn't we do it earlier?"

The affirmative action taken by the Department of Defense contains many lessons. McNamara's concern about housing discrimination against servicemen did not start in 1967 but in 1962. At that time McNamara issued a directive which requested military commanders to organize *voluntary* programs to eliminate housing discrimination in the communities surrounding their bases. This directive incorporated recommendations of a committee headed by a well-known attorney, Gerhard A. Gesell, commissioned by McNamara to study progress towards equal opportunity in the armed forces. However, when seventeen thousand families of Negro servicemen were surveyed four years later it was clear that the voluntary program had failed. In his book, *"The Essence of Security,"* McNamara analyzed this failure:

> It lacked sufficient leadership from the top, starting with me, and going right down through the senior echelon of the Defense Department; and it lacked appropriately stiff sanctions for violation of our anti-discrimination policy.

Affirmative action has also been taken by many universities and colleges to meet the housing needs of their black students and faculty. The housing offices of such institutions usually insisted that all listings be nondiscriminatory long before such action was required by law. They have also taken other steps. Early in 1968 the directors of the Stanford Linear Accelerator Center (SLAC), at the urging of the Center's Director, Dr. Wolfgang Panofski, adopted a fair housing policy which explicitly urged employees to report to SLAC if they encountered housing discrimination so that the personnel office could investigate and prepare "necessary documents for the use of appropriate authorities in taking legal action." The housing policy also provided that SLAC's position be made well known within SLAC and throughout the community.

The Fair Housing Policy adopted by SLAC encompasses only several of the methods an employer can use to assist black employees. A course of action which will comfortably suit one employer may conflict with established ways of doing things in another organization. However, there are certain essentials to which all employers should adhere. The organization should have a formal policy which supports the right of its employees to equal access in housing. At the very least, if an employee encounters discrimination he should be able to take time off from work to assert his legal rights, under the same conditions that would prevail for some other personal problem beyond his control. Also, the policy of equal opportunity in housing should be brought to the attention of all employees in a manner that insures they are aware of it and understand it. It is doubtful that this can be accomplished without at least one meeting where employees discuss the equal opportunity program with their immediate superior or, in the case of a new employee, with the personnel officer who handles his recruitment.

Employers should work with responsible fair housing organizations. One form of cooperation is to publicize the services offered by the fair housing group to those employees who might be able to use them. This can be done by posters on bulletin boards, by articles in company publications, and by seeing that personnel people and union stewards are well informed.

Cooperation by the employer should include participation in financing fair housing activities. There have been a few cities where business has made moderate contributions. Chicago has about a hundred corporate contributors with gifts as high as $7,500 per year. In Pittsburgh, U.S. Steel's $5,000 per year is the largest of a number of corporate contributions to the Urban League's "Operation Equality Program"; about eight other Pittsburgh firms are giving $1,000 or more per year to this program. Housing Opportunities Made Equal (HOME)* in Cincinnati has received "service contracts" from two of Cincinnati's large employers, General Electric and Procter and Gamble. The Procter and Gamble contract gives HOME $125 for each employee who is provided any assistance and guarantees a minimum of $1,000 per year. Both companies entered into these arrangements as a means of improving their ability to recruit black employees from outside the Cincinnati area by offering them more effective assistance in getting housing. The service contract was preferred over a contribution because it was felt to be a justified payment of funds for a service the corporation was utilizing and because the contract required less consultation and approval by management. However, most employers have preferred to give financial assistance as a contribution. One of the most generous grants to date has been $1,500 from Minneapolis-Honeywell to Metro Denver Fair Housing, an annual contribution of one dollar for each Honeywell employee in the Denver area.

Most corporate financial support has come either when there was someone in the corporation whose interest in fair housing gave strong internal support or when there was

*This organization had no relationship to HOME in Buffalo.

enough business support already in hand so that other business leaders followed. Fair housing groups have seldom been successful when they approached upper management from the outside. In Cincinnati, Donald Roberts, the Chairman of HOME's board of directors, is a manager in GE's Aircraft Engine Group and played an important part in giving GE confidence that the proposed contract would work out satisfactorily. At Procter and Gamble, James Percival, who heads the company's equal opportunity program, is a committed member of HOME who has chosen to live in an integrated area in the North Avondale section of the city.

Civil rights advocates in the past have often urged employers not to locate new plants or other facilities in communities which did not provide satisfactory assurances of open housing. The most famous example was the losing fight to prevent the location of a high-energy accelerator for the AEC in Weston, Illinois. Now that there are federal open housing laws, this criterion for plant location is outdated.* In fact, since equal opportunity in housing for all employees should be regarded as a corporate responsibility, locating a plant in an area where housing is not yet open to blacks can provide a stimulus which greatly decreases housing discrimination.

When Armour and Company transferred nearly two hundred employees, including forty-one Negroes, to a newly built slaughterhouse in Worthington, Minnesota, a Bible-belt town with ten thousand whites and no blacks, it appeared at first that serious difficulties might develop. Dr. James Stern, a University of Wisconsin economics professor who had been retained by the Armour Automation Fund Committee

---

*However, the availability of moderate and low-income housing near a plant should be a consideration in plant-site selection since it improves the availability of all labor and, unless such housing is available, few Negroes will live in the area.

to handle the relocation of the black workers, met a stone wall when he attempted to obtain cooperation from the Worthington Chamber of Commerce. To all the usual fears that accompany black entry in white neighborhoods was added the rumor that Worthington was going to become an experimental community to test integration. But Stern, at the suggestion of a friend who knew the community, went to James Vance, editor of the Worthington *Daily Globe*, and Vance provided the leadership so badly needed by setting up a series of meetings with other local leaders during a one-day visit by members of the Automation Committee, including high-ranking Armour executives and union officials. After this there was sufficient support in the community, coupled with excellent press coverage in the *Globe* so that the Automation Committee staff could successfully relocate all the families who were transferring to Worthington.

In June 1968, a black employee who worked at IBM's typewriter plant in Lexington, Kentucky, was making no progress in finding a house after two weeks of searching. However, the discrimination he was encountering from real estate brokers was about to diminish.

IBM, Lexington's largest employer, guarantees the sale of employees' homes when they are transferred. As a result, in 1967 IBM was responsible for the sale of $4,000,000 worth of real estate in the Lexington area. These sales were distributed to members of the Lexington Real Estate Board's multiple listing service by the First Security National Bank & Trust Company acting as the company's agent. Consequently, when Clair F. Vough, IBM's vice-president for manufacturing, reacted to the Supreme Court decision which declared housing discrimination unlawful by writing a letter to the president of the bank which said, "IBM's policy is to utilize only those Realtors who provide their services to prospective purchasers without discrimination . . . because of race," it was predictable that this was going to make a difference.

Within two days the black IBM employee who had been making no progress had received nine phone calls from brokers.[4]

It was not the first time that IBM had done something such as this. Managers in the giant business-machine company, one of the first large companies to recruit blacks for professional positions, recognized that Negro employees troubled by housing problems would not produce at top efficiency. Consequently, in the early 1960's IBM in Poughkeepsie and several other locations quietly put the same type of pressure on local real estate brokers that they later exercised in Lexington. In Poughkeepsie a nondiscriminatory policy was made a prerequisite for rental housing listed with IBM's rental service. These actions have been part of an overall equal opportunity program which has given IBM an image among blacks as one of the best private corporations in the nation. However, it should also be recognized that certain factors tended to help IBM achieve this position. IBM's business is such that it did not need to fear adverse consumer reaction, and their labor force consists more of professional and highly skilled workers than in most companies. In addition, there is a general corporate personnel policy to take care of employee problems, a policy which critics have termed too paternalistic.

To require that real estate brokers and landlords not discriminate in order to receive listings or referrals is a powerful lever in creating open housing. However, corporate action of this type can be effectively used only by large employers and it does not influence builders, individual home owners, or others not engaged in business dealings with the company.

The most effective assistance that any employer can give his employees is to deal with the problem directly: to encourage employees to assert their legal rights and to provide employees with the means to do it. All housing discrimination is against the law, and there is no better way to break the barriers of discrimination than by the use of the law.

Because of the laxity with which fair housing laws are enforced in most communities, a private lawsuit is often the best response to a discriminatory act. When this is the case, the support of the employer may be critical. Very few employees will initiate such an action on their own.

The employee, without expense to himself, should have the services of a competent attorney. Legal services can be provided either directly by a company attorney or by a lawyer retained for this purpose by the company. In either case legal fees usually can be recovered as part of the settlement for damages. Another alternative is to use a fair housing organization which is capable of supplying legal services.

The merits of reacting to housing discrimination by the assertion of legal rights are well demonstrated by the story of Doyle Willis, a drill press operator with Bell and Howell.

When Willis encountered discrimination in Chicago, it never occurred to him to go to Bell and Howell. He was only one of four thousand hourly workers at the large plant. Instead, Mrs. Willis called Mrs. Robert A. Cleland, the chairman of the Fair Housing Committee of the Wilmette Human Relations Committee. Mrs. Cleland was someone she felt she could trust and who might be able to help.

Jean Cleland spoke to several people including her friend Susie Stein, the wife of Bell and Howell's vice-president of finance. "Why doesn't Bell and Howell do something?" she asked.

Mrs. Cleland really did not expect what happened. Herman Stein, briefed by his wife, discussed the problem with Roland ("Riff") Finkelman, the corporate director of industrial relations, and Peter G. Peterson, Senator Charles Percy's successor as board chairman. Peterson told Finkelman to see what he could do.

Finkelman, a tall, prematurely gray man of forty with a patch over one eye, a strong believer in equal opportunities who knew that Peterson would back him up if he took justifiable action, got the facts from Willis. When he could not reach the offending landlord he phoned the landlord's attorney. He told him that Bell and Howell was prepared to support their employee and to make company attorneys available to advise him of his rights.

A lawsuit was not necessary. Doyle Willis had his apartment. The other lawyer said, "Mr. Finkelman, I get your point . . ."

An example of what vigorous corporate leadership can do effectively and swiftly is the current training of hard-core unemployed. The leadership came from the top, from the President of the United States to top business leaders to corporation presidents and then down the line. Having decided to work together, business leaders did not let fears of adverse reaction deter them, and as often happens not much objection was raised. No man was more identified in the public eye with this program than Henry Ford II, board chairman of the Ford Motor Company. While it is true that as a result of his activities and the activities of his company some individuals wrote that they would not buy Ford products, Ford's marketing research office has found no evidence that sales have been affected one way or the other.

It seems reasonable to assume that the support of employees' legal rights to equal opportunity in housing would bring no more reaction than the preferential hiring and training of unemployed blacks.

Emory University in Atlanta provides some interesting data on the extent of reaction to antidiscrimination measures. The university runs a housing service to help faculty and students who live off campus find suitable housing. The service also is available to others, such as employees of the Communicable Disease Center of the United States Public Health Service which is located near the Emory campus.* In 1967 the university inserted a nondiscrimination clause in the listing form used for off-campus housing, all of which was in the all-white area surrounding the university. As a result of this action, only eleven of 445 listings were withdrawn from Emory's service — less than a 3 percent loss in a Southern city which had no fair housing legislation and essentially no integration.

Affirmative action programs by employers also have an important secondary effect in that they influence the private actions of employees. Those employees who favor equal opportunities will be more apt to participate in fair housing efforts; those employees who have fears about integration are less apt to engage in discriminatory practices.

In considering their role in effecting equal opportunities in housing, businessmen should remember that equal opportunities for their employees are not their only stake.

The health of business is inexorably tied in with the health of the nation. Racial discord severely damages both. If

---

*The housing office at Emory does not have any records of the percentage of its clients who are black, but it is under 10 percent and probably much less.

people stay away from work, a window is smashed or a building is burned, there is an economic loss — a significant part of which must come from profits.

In addition, the corporations which most effectively help black employees obtain equal access to housing can gain a competitive advantage in recruiting other blacks. Skilled employees are always in demand by business, and in the future there will be more and more trained black people who can fill vital needs.

The recruitment of white employees also may be aided by corporate action to bring about equal housing opportunities. The students emerging from college today not only strongly believe in equal opportunities, but they want their careers to have meaning beyond the pursuit of corporate profits. They are most apt to go where they believe they best can satisfy this career interest.

There are times that short-term business needs may appear to conflict with an equal opportunity program. But from a long-range viewpoint, employer self-interest should not allow day-by-day pressures to encroach on equal opportunity responsibilities.

9 / The Black Side

THE BOMB TORE A HOLE in the pavement where it exploded outside the front bedroom. The impact shattered windows and drove nails through the walls. Although it was 1:00 A.M., there was a crowd of two hundred in the streets within two minutes, sullen and hostile, not a single white man or woman among them offering assistance or even sympathy to the two black people who were in the house. When a Negro motorist attracted by the noise of the explosion drove onto the street, some members of the crowd attempted to attack him.

The police had been called immediately. Twenty-five minutes later a patrol car arrived. When asked if they would provide protection, one officer replied, "I ain't got time to stay around watching."

This happened fourteen years ago in Atlanta, Georgia. As a result, a Negro family who had moved into a white neighborhood moved out.[1]

Not many black Americans are acquainted with this particular incident, but every Negro in the United States indirectly has been the victim of terrorism directed against blacks who moved into white areas. A nagging fear of violence is an important reason why, even in the absence of discrimination, most Negroes do not move to white areas. Past terrorism also is a partial explanation of why blacks have a distorted idea of what it would be like for them to live in a white neighborhood. When a Negro family moves into a white area there are problems which few whites appreciate, but these problems usually are far less than the blacks anticipated.

Most acts of terrorism have been in the South where, until recently, such actions received scant attention from police and at times took place in collusion with law enforcement officials. For example, during a thirteen-month period starting in March 1949, seven houses were bombed in Birmingham without a single arrest. In one case a bombing occurred at 11:00 P.M., but was not investigated until the following day.[2]

Acts of terrorism and physical violence also have a long history outside of the South. In 1925, shortly after Dr. Ossian Sweet and his wife Gladys moved into a house in a white neighborhood in Detroit, a shouting, cursing mob of over five hundred people started flinging rocks at the house without any interference from the police. Inside the besieged house the Sweets, with several relatives and friends, were terrified. Remembering the thousands of Negroes who had been murdered and lynched, Dr. Sweet's brother, Henry, fired a rifle at the crowd. This dispersed the mob, but a man was killed and all of those inside the house were arrested and charged with murder. After two trials they were acquitted, but only as the result of a brilliant defense by Clarence Darrow.[3]

America has come a long way since then. During the past five years most police forces have attempted to prevent acts of terrorism and investigated them when they occurred. When there have been bombings or acts of arson, it generally has been clear that they were perpetrated by only a few and that most of the community was repelled. Nevertheless acts of terrorism have continued. Here is a sample of articles from the *New York Times*:

Warren, Ohio, Feb. 15 (1964) — The home of a Negro, located in a formerly all-white neighborhood, was damaged by fire today when Molotov cocktails were thrown through the living room and garage windows. . . . Firemen who put out the flames estimated damage at $5,000.

Bloomington, Ind., July 22 (1964) — A home in an all-white neighborhood was destroyed by fire early today several hours before a Negro family was to move in. Authorities termed it arson.

Philadelphia, June 18 (1965) — A crowd of several hundred white persons demonstrated last night outside a northeast Philadelphia home reportedly purchased by a Negro couple. Rocks, bottles and garbage were thrown through the windows. A gate was ripped loose and a fence smashed.

Lakewood, N.J., Oct. 11 (1965) — This pleasant resort in the piney woods of Ocean County reacted angrily today to the apparent deliberate burning early Sunday of two homes being built for Negro families in a predominantly all-white section of town. The Lakewood Township Council held an emergency meeting and announced the start of a community fund to help restore the property damage.

Chicago, Nov. 11 (1965) — Bricks and fire bombs were thrown last night at a South Side house into which a Negro family of six moved Saturday. The neighborhood is white.

Cleveland, Sept. 24 (1966) — A house purchased recently by a Negro minister in a wealthy Cleveland suburb was swept by fire today. Arson was suspected. The police in the community of Westlake, joined by State arson investigators, searched the area around the ranch-style house.

Chicago, Nov. 5 (1966) — A dynamite bomb exploded today near the home of a Negro family in a largely white area on the West Side. . . . Members of the family escaped injury. Three white persons . . . were slightly injured.

Youngstown, Ohio, Oct. 3 (1967) — The authorities investigated today a "deliberately set" fire, the second in three days in a home being built for a Negro in an all-white section of suburban Campbell.

Oceanside, L.I., Nov. 24 (1967) — Community leaders and residents have failed to persuade one of the few Negro homeowners here not to sell his home after a bomb was hurled through his dining room window. . . . "I haven't been able to conduct my business because I've been so tense," he continued. "On some nights I've been getting up at three and staying up until five just looking and listening at the windows."

The reluctance to move into white areas, even when the opportunity exists, is partly the heritage of this past. Even the most sensitive of white Americans are just now beginning to understand how rough it has been on their black countrymen. Probably Martin Luther King said it best when he wrote:[4]

When you have seen vicious mobs lynch your mothers and fathers at will and drown your sisters and brothers at whim: when you have seen hate-filled policemen curse, kick and even kill your black brothers and sisters with impunity; when you see the vast majority of your 20 million Negro brothers smothering in an affluent society; when you suddenly find your

201

tongue twisted as you seek to explain to your six-year-old daughter why she can't go to the public amusement park that has just been advertised on television, and see tears welling up when she is told that Funtown is closed to colored children, and see ominous clouds of inferiority beginning to form in her little mental sky, and see her beginning to distort her personality by unconsciously developing a bitterness toward white people; when you have to concoct an answer for a five-year-old son asking, "Daddy, why do white people treat colored people so mean?"; when you take a cross-country drive and find it necessary to sleep night after night in the uncomfortable corners of your automobile because no motel will accept you; when you are humiliated day in and day out by nagging signs reading "white" and "colored"; when your first name becomes "nigger," your middle name becomes "boy" (however old you are) and your last name becomes "John," and your wife and mother are never given the respected title "Mrs."; when you are harried by day and haunted by night by the fact that you are a Negro, never quite knowing what to expect next, and are plagued with inner fears and outer resentments; when you are forever fighting a degenerating sense of "nobodiness" — then you will understand.

Rejected by much of American society, most black people have retreated into their own world. Virtually every American Negro has personally been hurt or deprived by some white person's categorical racial discrimination. Experience has taught that contacts with whites are often unpleasant and sometimes dangerous, that comfort and safety lie in minimizing involvement with whites.

The alienation and isolation of America's blacks is not

new.[5] What is new is that whites have become more aware
of this alienation as a result of the recent efforts by blacks
to improve their living conditions and to achieve independence from white domination. The barriers which exist
between the two races also have resulted in some reverse
prejudices. Many Negroes believe that white people do not
know how to relax or have fun. Because of the deceit blacks
have experienced from whites, Negroes also believe that
whites are deceitful in all dealings and are unable to speak
forthrightly even among themselves.[6]

But the reluctance of blacks to move to white areas after
barriers of discrimination have been lowered is not only a
legacy of the past.

While terrorism and mob action have in the past five
years involved only about one in a thousand families of
those who have broken the color line outside of the South,
individual incidents of harassment have occurred much
more frequently: from as low as one percent in some communities to as high as 15 percent in others. The probability of harassment also depends on the particular neighborhood. There appears to be general agreement that an incident is more likely in a working-class neighborhood than
among upper middle class professional people, more likely
in an area where no blacks are nearby, more likely when
there is no fair housing activity. And incidents are less
likely to happen in the future. But there still are no white
areas into which a Negro family can move with assurance
that they will not encounter harassment.

In the Buffalo area, where over five hundred Negro families moved into previously all-white neighborhoods, six
incidents of harassment were reported from 1963 through
1969. Five were isolated acts in working-class neighborhoods: KKK signs and derogatory slogans on houses
being constructed, broken windows of occupied homes,

and the ignition of kerosene poured on the lawn in the shape of a cross. The only case of prolonged harassment occurred when Dr. Frank Cole, a cancer-research scientist, rented an apartment in a middle-income suburban development. He and his wife received telephone calls at night, as late as 2 or 3 A.M., calls that would end as soon as he picked up the receiver. One day a florist phoned to confirm an order to send $35 worth of roses to a ghetto address, an order Dr. Cole had never placed. The anonymous harasser entered magazine subscriptions in the Coles's name, sent a TV repairman to their apartment, and placed an ad in the paper which offered baby-sitter services and listed the Coles's phone number. The end came when a moving van showed up with instructions to move the Coles. Furious at the loss he was going to take because of a prank, the mover called the police. A neighbor, disgusted by what was happening, gave the police the name of a suspect who was questioned. No arrest was made, but the harassment ended.

While the incident rate of about one percent in the Buffalo area was less than in most communities, such occurrences have been relatively infrequent throughout the country. For example, only one to 2 percent of the three hundred black families who have moved into white areas in the San Fernando Valley have experienced harassment, which reflects, at least in part, the effectiveness of the fair housing movement there. An extensive study made over ten years ago in Connecticut of 219 Negro families who moved into white areas indicated serious incidents occurred in about 5 percent of the cases.[7] A 1964 report on Seattle indicated a frequency of 5 to 15 percent.[8]

There have been times when those who harassed accomplished their purpose: forcing the black family to leave. The first Negro family to enter the middle-class Chicago suburb of Deerfield moved out of their rented apartment after windows were broken and excrement was smeared on the front walls of the house.

Dearborn, Michigan, an all-white Detroit suburb of over one hundred thousand people, also proved too much for its first Negro family. The family moved out in June 1968, after two and one-half years during which the community made it obvious that they were not welcome. When it was announced that they were leaving Mayor Orville Hubbard said, "Of course, most people like to live in a neighborhood where they are accepted. You can't force people to like each other."

One of the worst cases of harassment took place in the Philadelphia suburb of Folcroft, when a black family moved into the Delmar Village development in the summer of 1963. Crowds gathered outside their home shouting insults and hurling rocks, and a two week campaign of threatening phone calls and letters followed. The family's home and automobile were damaged by vandals, and boycotts were directed against businesses that dealt with them. Neighborhood children called the husband by his first name and asked, "When you moving?" After over two years of this, during which the husband suffered a nervous breakdown, the family left.

The wife of another black family forced to move out of a white neighborhood told an interviewer, "It is wonderful to be able at last to wheel my baby carriage in front of my house without fear my baby will be spat upon."[9]

Yet most black families who have encountered harassment in white neighborhoods have stayed, especially when some of their white neighbors made clear their support. But because some black families have had KKK signs painted on houses, rocks thrown through windows, fences erected by neighbors (occasionally painted black on the side facing the home of the Negro family), motorists shouting,

"Nigger, get out," garbage thrown on lawns and crosses burned at night — the ranks of blacks who otherwise might have wanted to move to white areas have been decimated.

The decision of a Negro family to live in a white neighborhood involves more than taking a risk of suffering terrorism or harassment. Other hardships are almost inevitable.

These other hardships seldom are recognized by whites. As an example, a research group, which made a study of the experiences of Negro families who moved into white areas in New York City between 1964 and 1966, has reported that over 80 percent had not experienced any racial problems after moving.[10] However, the results were based on a questionnaire, filled out by the black families. Conclusions from this work and similar studies must be interpreted in the light of an article by Mel Watkins,[11] a Negro staff member of the *New York Times*, which pointed out: "Even though these two families initially maintained that they had experienced no racial prejudice in the suburbs, as they talked it turned out they were not really telling it like it is."

If we are going to tell it "like it is," we have to recognize that all neighborhoods contain some people who are prejudiced and show it. Often bigotry takes the form of a cold stare — "as if I was contaminated," was the way one Negro put it. Such hostility is not pleasant, even if practiced by only a few. Neither are other slights, such as tradesmen who ask the Negro housewife if they may see the lady of the house.

Because children depend even more than their parents on neighborhood reactions, they sometimes have worse problems. It hurts a little boy to see a white child head the other way or, as often happens, be led away by a parent. It hurts even when there are nineteen other children who treat him just as they would anyone else.

Then there is the name calling. Even if only one person does it, it hurts. As one suburban New York mother told Mel Watkins, "She's five, she didn't even know what a nigger was. One of the kids called her that and she said she wasn't a nigger, she was a Catholic. But still, now she knows. And it's hurt her. You can see the difference."

In some ways these are small incidents. But so was the one described in Countee Cullen's poem:[12]

> *Once riding in Old Baltimore,*
> *Heart filled, head filled with glee,*
> *I saw a Baltimorean*
> *Staring straight at me.*
>
> *Now I was eight and very small,*
> *And he was no whit bigger*
> *And so I smiled, but he*
> *Stuck out his tongue and called me nigger.*
>
> *I saw the whole of Baltimore*
> *From May until November.*
> *Of all the things that happened there —*
> *That's all that I remember.*

A black family moving into a white neighborhood must face problems of isolation as well as hostility.

It is human to feel uncomfortable when with a group of people who have a common denominator which you alone do not share. For a black person living in an all-white neighborhood, this discomfort is intensified by the mixed feelings black people have toward whites. A black family may also feel on display, being watched and judged by the neighbors.

Contrary to the impression of many whites and even some

blacks, most Negroes who move into white areas do not do so to "integrate," to shed their past and become a part of the white world of the majority. In fact, when they "move out" they usually go to some length to maintain contact with the black community. Negroes wish to enjoy the cultural pluralism practiced by other ethnic groups.[13] Even such well assimilated groups as Americans of German ancestry have maintained social and cultural organizations.

In Buffalo, 80 percent of Protestant Negro families who moved to the suburbs remained active in their ghetto churches even though they had been invited to join at least one local church.[14] In addition, all families continued fraternal connections and social friendships. The amount of travel necessary to maintain these contacts, and to continue to patronize such services as black beauty shops, was a cause of complaint. A national study by the Opinion Research Corporation indicates that in large metropolitan areas, where travel times from the suburbs are longer than in metropolitan Buffalo, many black suburbanites do attend suburban churches, but that very few blacks living in white areas of the city go to the white churches nearby.[15]

Residing in a white neighborhood generally complicates living for blacks. The teenage daughters of pioneer families often have very few dates. If the neighbors are aloof the problems are much worse. Every family needs to have people nearby to turn to in an emergency for a ride to the hospital with an injured child or merely for the loan of a quarter pound of butter for unexpected dinner guests.

Although not as apparent, a black family which moves into an all-white area also risks more than geographical isolation from the black community. Black people today have strong feelings about unity and self-help, and in today's environment the family that leaves the ghetto is judged by some to have "sold out."

When these factors are added to the many difficulties any family encounters when moving to a new area, it is no wonder there are relatively few blacks who are taking advantage of housing which is more open. Many consider moving, but most are stopped by asking themselves, "If we ever get the house, would we enjoy it?"

Yet of the five hundred Negro families who have moved into previously all-white neighborhoods in the Buffalo area since 1964, none are known to have moved back to the ghetto. About fifty of these families, including most of those who experienced unpleasant incidents, were interviewed in some depth. All were glad they had made the move. All would do it again.

At least four other studies have been published which have surveyed how Negro pioneers felt about living in white areas. In all of these studies the results were basically the same: the great majority were glad they had made the move.

The explanation is that the advantages outweighed the disadvantages. The principal advantages were those which were clearly evident and had caused the families to take the risk: better neighborhoods, larger and better quality housing, better schools. Unanticipated advantages often were found after the family moved:

"We don't feel the tension . . . [In the ghetto] there were so many problems; it always seemed that a police car was chasing something."

"It's good not to be bothered by door-to-door peddlers."

"[In the ghetto] the children were always fighting; here they don't."

Most of the families who moved found something else they had not anticipated, a warm welcome by some of their new neighbors. Fair housing groups throughout the nation report that black families moving into white neighborhoods usually had more friendly calls of welcome than did white families who moved into the same neighborhoods. Having six neighbors call, with many bringing gifts, was quite common. Whereas a new white family might be visited by some of the immediate neighbors, black families often received calls not only from those close by, but also from families several blocks away.

This overcompensation is desirable provided the visits are meaningful and not merely perfunctory. Such visits create a climate which minimizes racial slurs and incidents by those who are not happy to see a black family in the neighborhood, and they help to sustain the Negro family during a difficult transition for them.

When black families have encountered hostility, community reaction almost always has improved with time. One author observed "the crisis of the entry stage seemed to end within a few weeks."[8] The chairman of a group formed in Levittown, Pennsylvania, to "restore our entire white community" was quoted seven years later as saying, "Integration has worked out far better than we anticipated." The Connecticut Civil Rights Commission study previously cited found that many whites who were annoyed when Negroes first moved to their neighborhood later changed their minds.[7] When asked why, the answers ranged from "They don't bother anyone" to "We realized our earlier attitude was silly."

When Paul D. Coombs, an oiler at a smelting and refining plant, moved into a white neighborhood in East Baltimore, his family probably experienced more initial difficulties than any of the hundreds of other black families who made similar moves in Maryland's chief city. During the first week their windows were shattered by rocks and firecrackers, and they were picketed by eleven members of

210

the National States Rights party who carried signs with such slogans as "White Power" as they marched in front of the Coombs's $10,000 two-story brick row house. Eighteen months later, while most of the neighbors still were not friendly, only one remained openly hostile, and four had demonstrated friendship and support. The Coombses were glad they had moved and viewed the new neighborhood as a better environment for their four children than the area from which they had come.

The potential for change in white attitudes is demonstrated by a suburban-Buffalo woman who did not call on the Negro family who had moved next door until after several months. She brought with her a valuable family heirloom.

"You shouldn't give us something so precious," the surprised recipient said.

The reply, because of its honesty, was even more of a surprise. "We wanted you to have it, to make up for how we felt when you first came here."

Sometimes it takes a small act of kindness to destroy the barriers. A Seattle family which led the neighborhood opposition to a recently arrived black family had a spastic child. One day the child fell in the road near the Negroes' garage. When the black family picked up the fallen child, the opposition was gone forever.[8]

Whether or not a family moves into a neighborhood depends less on what that neighborhood is really like than what the family thinks it is like. Almost all blacks who have moved into white areas, even many of those who have experienced unpleasant incidents, have been surprised at how well the move ultimately worked out. As one black housewife commented, "We expected the worst, but it never came."

There is a great difference between reality and the image which most blacks have of how they would fare if they moved into a white neighborhood. Not many years ago physical violence, even murder, was the community response to black people in the South, and parts of the North, who dared to break the color line; only in the past decade have Negroes desiring housing in white areas received significant assistance from whites or white-controlled institutions. When there is a racial incident involving a black family who moves into a white area, it is widely publicized by newspapers and TV; when a black family moves into a white area without incident, it is not news. In the black community racial incidents frequently are exaggerated; successful integration usually receives little notice.

Probably the greatest concern of a black family considering a move to a white neighborhood is the effect it will have on their children. The fear is that the youngsters will have a shortage of playmates, will be left out of activities, will suffer much mental and some physical punishment. The reality is that the children are generally accepted immediately by most of the other children and often receive special acts of kindness.

The number of black families who move into white areas is limited in another way: many blacks do not realize that they can get housing in white areas until long after barriers have come down. A Negro college president once compared this problem with the case of a lion locked for years in a cage. At first the lion leaped against the walls in an effort to get out, but after many futile and painful attempts, the lion abandoned his effort to escape. When the lock on the cage was removed, the lion would not attempt to open the fragile barrier separating him from freedom.

Thus it is essential not only to end discriminatory practices, but also to make certain that black people know that substantial change is taking place. The result of such dissemination of information will be quickly evident. For example, in the summer of 1965 the Connecticut Human Rights Commission contacted four thousand Negro and Puerto Rican families in a door-to-door campaign and informed them in detail about the services and law enforcement powers of the Commission. The result was a dramatic increase in complaint activity.

Whenever the black community has been informed of progress there has been an increase in the number of those taking advantage of the progress. But a vast communication gap remains, and substantial resources must be committed in imaginative ways to bridge it. Such efforts to communicate change do succeed: attitude surveys by Louis Harris indicate that whereas in 1963 the majority of blacks condemned white hotels and motels, movie theaters and bus lines as "obstructionist" toward equal rights, by 1966 these same institutions were being praised by 70 to 80 percent of Negroes as helpful to their cause.[16]

While communication of change is an essential component of an effective program aimed at equal opportunities in housing, it only becomes relevant when substantial progress has been made. At the heart of the reasons why blacks do not move into white areas are the racist attitudes and practices of many white Americans. Until these are largely destroyed, many blacks will feel more comfortable walking along a crime-ridden ghetto street than living in a white suburb.

The nature of the real estate business also tends to perpetuate and extend ghettos. Negro families looking for housing frequently contact only black brokers since these are the only ones known to them. Negro brokers, with rare exceptions, follow the same practices employed by white brokers to maximize profits: in order to avoid sharing commissions they market their own listings most aggressively and, should none of these prove suitable, they minimize travel time and expense by affirmatively marketing only properties reasonably close to their offices. As a result, until there are large real estate firms which maintain offices in both the ghetto and other neighborhoods, many black home-seekers will not be shown housing other than in the ghetto and fringe areas.

Of increasing significance in recent years is the belief by many blacks that their interests are best served at present by living in a predominantly black community. Black people still want to end discrimination, and there are virtually no exceptions to that, but the emphasis today is on building strong, viable black communities.

Part of this change is a reaction to not being accepted: "You don't want me. Okay, well let me tell you, I don't want you, your food or nothin' to do with you."[17] But viable black communities also represent a strategy for economic, social and political improvement. Large black communities will elect officials who must answer to black people, and therefore will be responsive to their needs and values; large black communities, which are controlled by black people, will encourage blacks to have pride in their heritage and experience; large black communities will permit black-owned businesses to find markets quickly.

The desire to build strong black communities is not a trend away from integration as a long-range objective. While some vocal blacks believe in racial separation as the ultimate goal, they appear to be a minority of less than 10 percent. A University of Michigan survey in 1968 of five thousand blacks in fifteen cities showed only 8 percent had strong separatist leanings.[13] Similar results were obtained in more recent studies by the Opinion Research Corporation and *Newsweek*.[18]

Many Negroes feel that only by exercising "black power" can they make sufficient improvements in their education, economic wealth and political influence so that at a later date they can join with the majority group on an equal basis. They do not wish integration at the expense of accepting en-masse everything that is white. A greater concern for human beings than they believe currently exists in white society is one value which black Americans are particularly reluctant to surrender.

But integration in housing, as we shall see, is the only realistic way that black Americans can achieve economic parity; it offers Negroes a chance to contribute in a proportionate way to the leadership of the nation; and it offers all Americans a chance to overcome psychological barriers which restrict the nation's ability to provide world leadership.

A close relationship exists between racial integration and the ability of blacks to advance in the large organizations which, to an increasing extent, are providing most of the better-paying jobs in the nation. Those who succeed and move up in these organizations do so for a number of reasons. A very important one is to be able to function effectively within the organization.

Competent teachers can give a student the skills to set up a computer program, design electronic components or perform complex chemical syntheses. These are technical skills which result in good jobs. But most of the better jobs require something in addition, the ability to get things done and be able to influence others.

This ability to be effective is a skill for which there are no tests other than performance. Those who are successful in corporate organizations and government services have many different characteristics, but they seldom have large cultural differences between themselves and their superiors. People are most influenced by those who "talk their language," those similar in their manner of speech, dress and social conventions.

As a result, a Negro who has lived all his life in a black ghetto will be at a disadvantage in a white organization because he is culturally different. It is more difficult for him to be assimilated into the organization than if he were raised in an integrated environment.

Differences in background are a handicap at all levels. For example, a research scientist working in industry, a man whose success is much more dependent than most others on his own technical skills and what he can do himself, will impair his performance if he does not relate well to the organization. He depends on designers and craftsmen to make the equipment he needs; therefore he must be able to communicate his priorities in such a way that these priorities are accepted. As part of his work he may need to collaborate with someone whose experience in a highly technical area can avoid costly efforts aimed at "rediscovering the wheel"; thus he must find this person and influence him to collaborate. At other times the research scientist must effectively persuade his superiors that he needs an expensive piece of apparatus, that the timetable of his program should be changed, or that there has been a discovery which ought to be pursued by others in the organization.

Men with excellent university records sometimes have limited success because of their failure to relate to the organization. This is evidenced by what has happened to foreign scientists who have migrated to this country. Although far above average in technical ability, as a group they have not done as well as those who were raised in the United States. Additional evidence is that relatively few of those raised in America's ethnic ghettos successfully climb organizational ladders, and of those who succeeded, most assimilated culturally.

It is a fantasy to think of black-dominated corporations manufacturing automobiles, computers or steel. Only through integrated schools and interracial social contacts can talented, well-trained blacks be as well prepared as whites to assimilate and to succeed in the white-dominated organizations where most blacks must earn their livelihood.

In fact, given the chance black Americans may well provide more than their share of leaders for all Americans. Their potential is enhanced by a heritage of ambition to succeed and strong social motivation. But if this potential is to be realized, it must be done not as an ethnic triumph but as the harvest of integration.

Perhaps the most important benefit which the United States may eventually derive from racial integration will be the alteration of attitudes which at present destroy the nation's ability to solve other problems. Integration cannot be achieved if it depends on black people becoming white any more than the United States can provide world leader ship toward peace by insisting that everything be based on American standards, American values and American customs. Rather, ways must be found for people to interact so that they learn to appreciate and assimilate each other's strengths.

Similarly, those with ambition may still need a helping hand. Integration will not be achieved in an atmosphere of "We worked for ours and you have to work for yours," any more than peace will come in a world where there is great want, and some groups hungrily covet that which belongs to their neighbor. Rather, the haves must learn to invest a share of their affluence to create opportunities for the have-nots.

White Americans must learn some lessons. The incentive of peace at home may someday help to bring peace abroad.

10 / The Activists

THOSE WHO ATTEMPT to combat discrimination often fail, but change never comes until people try. Even what one person does can make an important difference

Large meetings seldom move people to take significant action. But there are exceptions. In 1964 five hundred civic leaders in Hartford attended a "town meeting" to discuss the problems of the ghetto. One of them was a wealthy automobile dealer who, because of his desire for anonymity, we shall call Thomas Williams. After the meeting Williams told his attorney, George Ritter, the deputy mayor, "Let's do something about this; I'm willing to put my money into it."

This was the birth of the Robert Littleton Corporation — a pseudonym signifying only the acceptability in New England of an Anglo-Saxon name. A plan emerged from discussions for a nonprofit corporation which would buy houses in white areas and sell or lease them to black families. Recognizing that many Negroes would be reluctant to pioneer integration of all-white areas, it was decided to price the housing attractively and to use imaginative financing ideas from the automobile business.

Pat Ritter, the deputy mayor's wife, went to work for the Robert Littleton Corporation as a part-time employee on a small salary, turning all her commissions over to the corporation. In the first year she bought thirty houses in white areas around Hartford. Twenty families rented, and ten others bought with assistance on their down payments. As the program progressed, the ratio of home buyers to renters increased. Another success came with time: the corporation was able to obtain mortgages. At first the banks had refused mortgages for the rental houses and the entire purchase price of each house had to be put up by Williams.

Williams supplied money and involved himself in all of the planning, but his participation was known to only a few people. The public identification was assumed by the Ritters. On them alone was focused all the wrath and resistance which, in most other communities, was diffused among many. There were angry phone calls saying, "You'll never get any more business here." There were vicious remarks from real estate brokers. And there was one frightening incident. Once, after Mrs. Ritter had shown a house to a Negro family, people from the neighborhood blocked her car as she attempted to leave, rocked the car, and threatened her. But none of this deterred George and Pat Ritter, a couple who were deeply committed by their Quaker faith to the cause of social justice. They had experienced and ignored even greater threats to themselves and their children when George, as a councilman, had led an investigation into organized gambling.

By the end of three years the Robert Littleton Corporation had demonstrated what could be done. One hundred and five houses, well dispersed in white areas, were now occupied by blacks. Of these families, forty-six were renting and fifty-nine, including nine who originally had leased, had bought houses with the help of the unique second mortgage program that had evolved. This success had been made possible by Thomas Williams's personal investment of $550,000. Operating losses during these three years were about $100,000 and were made up by contributions from Williams and a few friends.

The work of the Robert Littleton Corporation is being continued by a new, nonprofit corporation, the Connecticut Housing Investment Fund, which is including the entire state in its program. Not by coincidence, its director, Howard Chamberlain, is married to Pat Ritter's cousin. Chamberlain, an engineer with a master's degree from the Harvard Business School, was a success in the business world as manager of administration of Kerr-McGee's Nuclear Division when he was thirty-two years old. But he wanted "a career that wasn't just piling up money in a bank."

By 1970, after two years, everything had gone smoothly. Local contributions, including one donation of $50,000 to help get the program rolling, were augmented by a $218,000 grant from the Ford Foundation for administrative expenses until the business became self-sustaining. Hartford's business and philanthropic community responded to the appeal for loans of $3,300,000 for a revolving fund to provide second mortgages to 1,000 Negro families in the next three years. The program is structured so that administrative expenses eventually should be met by real estate commissions and a small differential between the interest paid to the revolving fund's subscribers and the interest paid by the home buyers.

The Connecticut Housing Investment Fund has limitations. It makes no provision for the many Negroes who are either too poor to buy their own home or who prefer to rent. Nevertheless, the fund is an exciting experiment from which other programs should evolve.

Until ten years ago not many people tried to do anything

about discrimination in housing. In 1960 there were only eighteen fair housing groups in the entire United States, and these were small and impotent.[1]

In the past decade the fair housing movement has experienced tremendous growth. Today between fifteen hundred and two thousand independent organizations are actively working on fair housing. Most of these groups are local committees which cover a small part of a large urban area and which work in varying degrees of harmony with each other and with one or more metropolitan fair housing organizations. As discussed on pages 108 to 111, the effectiveness of local organizations is limited.

The multiplicity of fair housing organizations probably is related to the motives people have for becoming active in them. It is an oversimplification to say that fair housing activity is purely the result of a commitment to racial equality. People become involved to fulfill personal needs: helping others, accomplishing a difficult task, participating in decision making, meeting new and interesting people, getting away from other problems, or maybe a desire for fame and recognition or an opportunity to develop new skills. Organizations proliferate because multiple groups allow more people a chance to make decisions and hold positions of prominence. And when there is a conflict between fair housing progress and personal satisfactions, interest in racial equality usually loses.

Organizations also tend to commit money or staff to meet their own needs rather than to where the resources might do the most good. Many groups undertake feeble housing programs rather than combine with others who share similar objectives. A survey made in Rochester, New York, which is only the forty-fifth largest city in the United States, showed that there were at least fifty different organizations concerned with housing. At best the result of duplicating efforts is inefficiency in the utilization of people and money; occasionally there is destructive competition between organizations with similar objectives as they compete for funds and glory.

As also is true of many other organizations, most fair housing volunteers come from a relatively narrow socioeconomic band. Fair housing organizations are composed mainly of professional people and their wives, but are relatively devoid of the wealthy, prominent people who are the backbone of the boards of hospitals, symphony orchestras, private schools and colleges.

The typical member of a fair housing group makes a financial contribution, but is relatively inactive. However, some are very dedicated. For example, Mrs. Lucie Buchbinder in San Francisco and Mrs. Mary Larsen in Los Angeles have performed on a volunteer basis full-time executive jobs with fair housing groups. The number of volunteers who work ten to twenty hours per week must be in the hundreds.

Witnessing discrimination and seeing the hurt has been the most frequent reason that the most active fair housing workers have been motivated. Usually direct experiences have done even more than increase commitment. Many fair housing workers originally believed their role should be one of educating the community, to motivate others to do the right thing. Their experience made it clear that education had to be augmented by forceful action.

Listening to black homeseekers played an important role in motivating a young lawyer with one of Buffalo's most prestigious firms. Anthony Dutton started out handling an occasional complaint, but before long he was spending as much as twenty hours a week providing the nucleus of the legal work that contributed so much to HOME's success in Buffalo.

Mel Johnson, a production manager with Minneapolis-Honeywell in Denver, had never had any contact with the housing problems of blacks until he was given the responsibility for the equal opportunity in employment program at the plant. As a result of this exposure he became a board member of Metro Denver Fair Housing and eventually was responsible for obtaining a sizable contribution from his company for the fair housing organization.

James E. Wallace, a young engineer, was exposed to discrimination before he joined a fair housing group. When Wallace and his wife came to Buffalo in 1962, they told prospective landlords they intended to entertain Negro friends. The result: they were turned down in white areas on the basis that they would cause trouble with the neighbors. More than anything they could ever learn in a meeting or a book, these experiences enabled Jim and Julia Wallace to understand what it was like to encounter discrimination. And there was one final lesson. The apartment the Wallaces eventually rented in the ghetto was offered to them by the white landlord at $55 per month, $20 less than the rent paid by the Negro family which previously occupied it.

Interviews with fair housing activists throughout the nation indicate that most have experienced far less negative reaction that they anticipated. Some received anonymous letters with advice ranging from "Why not have those black bastards on *your* block?" to a suggestion to emigrate to Africa, China, Israel or Hell. There were also anonymous telephone calls in the middle of the night. But from one to five poison-pen letters, from one to ten nuisance telephone calls, were usually all that even well publicized fair housing activists experienced over a period of several years.

While fair housing activity is certainly not supported by most Americans, election results indicate that in many places it is tolerated by a majority. The thousands of legislators at the national, state and local level who have voted for fair housing legislation provide evidence that such support is not inconsistent with political success. Mayor Thomas G. Currigan of Denver, who won an election after allocating $20,000 of city funds to launch Metro Denver Fair Housing, assessed the political impact of his support of fair housing as, "There were people who were opposed, but they had never supported me to begin with." In suburban Chicago, Edward I. Rothschild was re-elected to the Highland Park school board while his wife was serving very visibly as the vice-chairman of the Highland Park Fair Housing committee. And in suburban Buffalo, Nolan Johannes, a local TV personality, won election as president of the local civic association even though both he and his wife held leadership positions in HOME, and Mrs. Johannes's work as head of HOME's rental committee often had been mentioned in the press.

To an increasing extent the task of ending discrimination in housing is being assumed by full-time professional staff. Volunteers cannot always be available when needed, and the effectiveness of the organization is related to the quality of research, planning, and coordination, tasks that frequently require professional skills.

Funds for staff have come to organizations across the country in a variety of ways. In New York City, Operation Open City supports a staff of nearly fifty, primarily with money from the city's antipoverty agency. Most of the money for Metro Denver Fair Housing, with the same size staff, comes from grants by the Office of Economic Opportunity and the Ford Foundation, but sizable contributions also come from the city, the state, the Catholic diocese and donations by private citizens. The Office of Economic Opportunity provides funds for a large fair housing center in Los Angeles and a small one in Akron; the Ford Foundation has given large grants to Washington, D.C., and the state of Connecticut. Until recently in St. Louis, Freedom of Residence barely supported an executive director and a secretary through private contributions, but from 1969 to 1972, Freedom of Residence has an additional $50,000 per year from the Danforth Foundation. Business contributions set up the Leadership Council in Chicago which has since obtained additional funds from HUD. Cleveland, Miami, Philadelphia, Pittsburgh, Rochester, St. Louis and Seattle have Operation Equality programs financed primarily by a grant given by the Ford Foundation to the National Urban League, but augmented by local funds. In Philadelphia the Housing Association of the Delaware Valley supports a staff of five with a grant from the United Fund. Fair Housing, Inc. of Boston pays fourteen workers from local foundation grants and individual contributions.

A large staff does not insure success because low salaries and lack of security increase the difficulty of getting good people and because the presence of staff usually decreases volunteer efforts. While it is more efficient to use a few full-time staff people than a large number of part-time volunteers, the participation of volunteers has advantages which cannot afford to be lost: greater impact on community attitudes, and increased influence with public and private institutions. The challenge is to structure programs so that broad participation is maintained as staff is increased.

New York City enacted the first fair housing law in the nation, and today the New York City Commission on Human Rights is one of the best such agencies in the nation* — not

*Philadelphia, Pittsburgh, Colorado and New Jersey also have antidiscrimination agencies which appear to have won the respect of most civil rights activists.

as good as the fair housing people in New York City would like, but effective enough so that complaints are always filed with the City Commission rather than the State Division of Human Rights.

Operation Open City, New York's professionally staffed fair housing organization which receives almost $400,000 a year from the city's antipoverty agency, also is one of the best in the nation. Its executive director, Mrs. Paul Hoeber, the wife of a well-known publisher of medical books, was a diligent volunteer worker in the fair housing movement before becoming the first director of the organization she helped to found in 1964.

The most pressing problem for Operation Open City has been insufficient staff to handle the nearly one thousand new applicants for housing each month. When the organization was first set up there was an extensive campaign to publicize its services by sending speakers to meetings, furnishing news stories to the Negro press, and getting radio announcements. Now very little of this is done. Word of mouth brings in more than can be properly handled.

A great strength of the Operation Open City program is the information given people who come for assistance. Each registrant gets a kit with an assortment of factual material of great help to any homeseeker, black or white. This includes forty "neighborhood spotlights," which give detailed information on desirable areas throughout the city, and a "homeseeker's guide" with suggestions on how to use the classified ads. Also included is a simple presentation of the rights of the homeseeker under the law and how Open City can be used to fight discrimination.

Aggressive action against discrimination has become a distinctive feature of the Open City operation. When it was found that volunteer "checkers" often responded too slowly to get apartments in the fast-moving New York market, col-

227

lege students and others were hired at $2.00 per hour to make certain that someone would always be immediately available. Also, Open City initiated action which caused the revocation or suspension of the licenses of a number of real estate brokers who discriminated.

Still another activity has been the needling of government officials to do more. Betty Hoeber and her assistant, Eileen Lee, played a significant role in getting the City Commission to charge the Metropolitan Life Insurance Company with discrimination in the rental of apartments in Parkchester, the nation's largest completed apartment complex. This development, which included over twelve thousand rent-controlled apartments at $100 to $165 per month, had less than 0.5 percent non-white occupancy. In the face of the charges, Metropolitan Life in 1968 agreed to two significant changes. One was to drop the practice of giving preference to the relatives of tenants, thereby enabling them to avoid the three to five year wait normally required to get an apartment. The other was to allocate some vacancies each month to Negro and Puerto Rican applicants who wanted to transfer to Parkchester from another Metropolitan project in Harlem. As a result of this agreement, over twenty black and Puerto Rican families have been moving into Parkchester each month.

A confrontation technique, made possible by the close cooperation between Open City and the City Commission on Human Rights, has been used to overcome discrimination and obtain apartments speedily. If a black family is unable to see or rent an apartment, a checker applies and, if accepted, gives a deposit and makes a date to sign a lease a few days later. This appointment is kept by the checker, accompanied by the complainant and an investigator from the Commission who informs the landlord of the charges against him. Caught red-handed in this manner, the landlord is usually confused and dismayed, torn between anger and guilt.

Often he capitulates. If he refuses to rent to the complainant, the Commission can immediately "post" the apartment, tacking a large sign on the door which states that the apartment is involved in an investigation on charges of discrimination and warns innocent parties against attempting to rent it.

The need for extremely fast response has tended to diminish the use of volunteers in favor of paid checkers and Open City's overtaxed staff has not taken time to involve volunteers in long-range programs. As a result, the volunteer fair housing groups have deteriorated badly and activities aimed at changing attitudes in the white community have been reduced. Consequently, Open City's excellent record on law enforcement has not had the impact it should have had on ending discriminatory practices. However, Open City has provided an important demonstration of success: in its first three years of operation, some twenty-five hundred families were directly assisted in obtaining housing, and countless others were aided indirectly by the vigor with which Open City confronted those who disobeyed the law.

Open housing activities in Chicago are probably more varied and more exciting than anywhere else in the nation. Racists in Chicago avoid the hypocrisy of talking about equality and then practicing discrimination. Even clergymen have publicly stated their opposition to integration. The speeches have been supported by mob action, violence and the ballot. This resistance to housing integration is partly Midwestern conservatism, but it also is a consequence of the large number of descendants of Eastern European immigrants who live in the Chicago area in ethnically homogeneous neighborhoods and display great fear and hostility toward black entry.

The enforcement of Chicago's fair housing law has been

relatively ineffective. According to information supplied by the Chicago Commission on Human Relations, housing has been secured in about one complaint in ten, and this includes cases in changing neighborhoods where landlords tend to give up easily. When landlords have resisted, they have easily stalled Negro families for so many months that the blacks usually were forced to make other housing arrangements. It is not worth reciting the procedural regulations of Chicago's Commission which result in such delays between the filing of a complaint and the issuance of an order to stop discrimination. What is more relevant is that Mayor Daley has shown no interest in seeing that Chicago's fair housing law is properly enforced.

The Leadership Council for Metropolitan Open Communities, the fair housing organization for the metropolitan Chicago area, has had more people of real influence on its board of directors than the other two thousand fair housing groups in the United States combined, and its contributions from Chicago's business community are greater than the business support which has gone to the rest of the fair housing movement in the entire nation. Among the heavyweights who have served on the board, most of whom are still members, are Thomas G. Ayers, President of Commonwealth Edison; John Cardinal Cody, Archbishop of Chicago; James W. Cook, President of Illinois Bell Telephone; Ben W. Heineman, Board Chairman of the Chicago and North Western Railway; Robert S. Ingersoll, Chairman of the Board of Borg-Warner; David M. Kennedy, the former Board Chairman of the Continental Illinois National Bank & Trust Company who is now Secretary of the Treasury; C. Virgil Martin, President of Carson, Pirie, Scott; the Right Reverend James W. Montgomery, Bishop Coadjutor of the Episcopal Diocese; and Peter G. Peterson, the Board Chairman of Bell and Howell. That this array of power, supported by money, has not been

approached anywhere else stems from the historical fact that
the Leadership Council came into being not as the response
of farsighted citizens uniting to meet a critical need, but
as the bargained concession of a frightened establishment to
get Martin Luther King off the streets of Chicago!

Heading the Leadership Council's staff of twenty-two is
Edward L. Holmgren, a man with a long record of service
to the cause of open housing who can deal successfully with
the business leaders he serves. Under Holmgren's leadership
the Council has turned out some of the best public relations
material in the fair housing movement, and has expanded its
operation with a $167,000 per-year contract with HUD and
two grants from the state of Illinois.

But the Council also has run into some very serious difficulties. Because it has failed to get the city to enforce
the fair housing laws, the number of black families using its
services has been disappointingly small and the fair housing
activists have screamed for aggressive action to end discrimination. Workshops, brochures and newspaper ads are
important auxiliaries in combating discriminatory practices,
but a black family looking for an apartment wants someone
who will go down the line to get the law enforced. In fact,
there are only two ways that fair housing organizations make
a good impression on black communities. One is to fight discrimination aggressively; the other is to supply assistance to
blacks who are taking action on their own. Until Chicago's
Negroes see the Leadership Council engaged in these activities, many will continue to view it with suspicion as
another honkey gimmick.

In many ways the problems of the Leadership Council
reflect the frustrating dissonance of the urban crisis. Even
if the Leadership Council used its full influence to get the
city administration to enforce the law vigorously, it might not
succeed. Mayor Daley would find it politically difficult to ig-

nore the fears of the majority, particularly since many of
those whites who hail him as Chicago's greatest mayor do
so not because he has done a good job in physically rede-
veloping the city, but because they credit him with keeping
blacks out of their neighborhoods. In addition, it would be
difficult for the Leadership Council to commit its full potential to such a struggle since the powerful men who serve
on the board have other causes they must represent at City
Hall.

In 1969 the Leadership Council took a step which may allow it to fulfill its excellent potential. A series of lawsuits
was initiated under the 1866 Civil Rights Act which seeks
damages for discriminatory acts.[2] By February 1970, thirty-
six separate suits had been filed of which eleven resulted in
cash awards and many others resulted in making apartments
available. This tactic gives the Leadership Council an opportunity to fight discrimination aggressively without taking
on City Hall. However, if a good bridge is to be built to the
black community, not only must this strategy be vigorously
pursued, but the board of the Leadership Council must recognize the importance of broadening its own base to include more blacks and some of the leaders of the fair
housing organizations. If this were done, the powerful institutional support would still be there, but added to it would
be people with a better knowledge of the black community.

The Leadership Council is not the only organization in
Chicago working for open housing and racial integration on
a metropolitan basis. Of particular importance is the Home
Investments Fund program sponsored by the Chicago Conference on Religion and Race with the assistance of a grant
from the Ford Foundation. Home Investments Fund is very
similar to the Connecticut Housing Investment Fund;[3] one
slightly different feature is that the Chicago program guarantees resale at 98 percent of purchase price as an encourage-

ment to Negro families who might otherwise hesitate to move for fear of being trapped in a hostile neighborhood. Although the Chicago program was set up late in 1968, the Home Investments Fund already has gained more acceptance in the black community than the Leadership Council.

The fair housing movement in Chicago's suburbs has been built up by a combination of the great need for such organizations, the availability of competent leadership and the failure of the Illinois legislature to pass a fair housing law. In the absence of a state law most of the higher-income communities have enacted local antidiscrimination ordinances after battles of varying intensity which served to identify and unite those who actively favored open housing. Once the fair housing activists had banded together, they continued as an organization.

One of the most effective of the more than fifty suburban groups is the Oak Park–River Forest Citizens Committee for Human Rights. Its chairman, Mrs. Lawrence A. Cervini, the wife of an IBM marketing manager and mother of two small children, spends more time carrying out her fair housing responsibilities than many people do earning a living. But Donna Cervini is only the most active of a well-organized group which was a going organization before she moved to Oak Park. Membership exceeds six hundred in this politically conservative area of seventy-five thousand, and activities range from working with church groups to gathering evidence of discrimination and demanding enforcement of the law. There also have been creative attempts to build bridges with the black community, such as holding a benefit in which the attraction was an evening of music and drama by black groups. Although the event was held in River Forest, almost half the audience was black as a result of aggressive ticket selling by black community organizations and the performers themselves.

233

The greatest progress in ending discrimination in Chicago's suburbs probably has been in Park Forest, an upper middle class community whose twenty-five-mile distance from Chicago's ghettos helped further allay fears of inundation. But what happened in Park Forest would not have occurred were it not for Harry Teshima, a structural engineer with an abhorrence of racial prejudice derived from his own experience as an American of Japanese ancestry. When the U.S. entered World War II, Teshima was forced into a detention camp until his loyalty was established, after which he served in the army. When he left the service he had trouble buying a home in Park Forest because he was an Oriental.

"The way to have integration is to integrate," has been Harry Teshima's philosophy. Since 1959, when the first Negro family came to live in Park Forest, this philosophy has been his modus operandi. Teshima knew a young Negro university professor who had tried unsuccessfully for six months to buy a home in Park Forest. He also knew a couple who were planning to move and who he thought might sell to a Negro. Consequently, he invited both to a party at his home. He reasoned that the white couple would then no longer be able to reject a Negro not wanted by some of their neighbors; they would have to reject a family they knew. Whether this tactic was necessary is uncertain, but it brought the desired result. And when the black family lacked $2,000 of a $5,000 down payment, Teshima loaned it from his modest savings.

This type of effort enabled Teshima, with just a few others helping, to bring many black families to Park Forest. By keeping close watch on FHA repossessions (which by federal regulations had to be sold on a nondiscriminatory basis) and by personal contacts, they found available housing and steered Negro families to it. After about eighty black families had settled in Park Forest (almost one percent of the population), such assistance was no longer needed since real estate brokers began to serve Negroes rather than lose commissions. Today the black population in Park Forest, about 2 percent, is well dispersed, and housing is relatively open.

Some strong fair housing groups have also developed in the city. There is far more demand by blacks for city housing than for housing in the suburbs. But because of the danger of inundation, the whites in the city feel even more threatened by integration than the whites in the suburbs and attempts at integration can quickly result in white fears becoming hatred. The challenges presented by this situation were what led Carl A. Van Kast in 1968 to resign as a ghetto schoolteacher and, at a financial sacrifice, to take a less demanding job so that he would have more time to devote to his duties as president of the Committee for an Equal Opportunity Community, an organization of northwest Chicago citizens whose major objective was to open their essentially all-white area to some of Chicago's one million ghetto residents. The CEOC and North Equal Housing, which operates in the Lakeview area to the east, are aggressive fair housing groups which have responded to the frustrations of poor law enforcement with increased determination and, more than other fair housing groups, have criticized the cautious tactics of the Leadership Council.

In Chicago the battle to end racial discrimination in housing is being fought very much in the open with large numbers of people participating. The evidence of racism still is very clear. The suburbs of Cicero and Berwyn are only the best known of many large areas which have no Negro residents. But there is visible evidence of progress toward an integrated society. The Hyde Park–Kenwood area in the city has been the most stable, racially integrated neighborhood in the nation; Park Forest is essentially open; Prairie Shores is the best known of a number of well-integrated apartment complexes; a federal court has ordered the Chicago Housing Authority to build 75 percent of all new public housing in white areas of the city and suburbs; and business and church leaders are strongly supporting open housing.

Denver has the best-funded fair housing program in America. It leads all other cities in institutional support for fair housing, and is one of the cities with the least discrimination in America. In Denver open housing not only has the strong support of the churches, but also receives active support from the Board of Realtors, the Denver *Post,* and the political leaders of both parties. But Denver also serves as an example of how difficult it is to achieve racial integration, and to demonstrate that money and institutional support alone are not sufficient.

The institutional support and relative lack of racial discrimination are, in part, a consequence of the fact that Denver is more of a middle class city than most as judged by the education and income of its inhabitants. Denver does not contain the concentrations of second-generation ethnic groups which provide so much of the resistance to open housing in many other Northern cities and the fifty thousand Negroes average a twelfth-grade education. In fact, it is not the blacks but the eighty thousand Hispanos (i.e. those with Spanish surnames) who are at the bottom of the socioeconomic ladder.

It probably was these sociological factors more than anything else which led Colorado in 1959 to become the first state to put into operation a fair housing law and to implement this law with a properly staffed, efficient Civil Rights Commission. The sociological makeup of Denver also was of assistance in obtaining large grants from the Office of Economic Opportunity and the Ford Foundation. This money was given not only to help the people of Denver, but to demonstrate to the nation that problems of discrimination and integration could be solved.

However, Denver would not have gotten these grants if people had not made a major effort to secure funding. More than anyone else, the man responsible was Richard E. Young. When Young came to Denver in 1960 from the University of Michigan Law School, he had no previous involvement in open housing. However, when he started looking for a house and people told him "Don't go to Park Hill; there are Negroes moving in there," Young and his wife decided to live in Park Hill. An energetic, take-charge man, he was soon chairman of the Park Hill Action Committee, an organization concerned with stabilizing the area. In 1963 Mayor Thomas G. Currigan appointed him as head of the Community Relations Commission.

The stage was set. Young did most of the work to develop a plan for Denver as part of an Office of Economic Opportunity study by the National Committee Against Discrimination in Housing to develop programs to improve the housing of low-income people. When Young's plan was judged the best of those submitted from four cities, the decision was made to try to implement it by seeking funding to expand Denver's all-volunteer fair housing center.

With Richard Young first serving as finance chairman, then as chairman, proposals were submitted to both the Office of Economic Opportunity and the Ford Foundation. Eventually both were approved. It is possible, however, that neither would have been funded had Young not first gotten Mayor Currigan to give $20,000. The significance of this grant went well beyond demonstrating the support of the city administration: the grant allowed the Center to hire, as a full-time executive director, the Reverend Robinson G. Lapp who resigned as the minister of his church in suburban Denver to take the job. Lapp not only bolstered the fund-raising effort, but provided assurance to the O.E.O. people that their grant money would be administered in ways relevant to the poor.

Denver's half million dollars a year are the envy of fair housing organizations throughout the nation. It is unlikely these grants would have been given were it not for the time Richard Young devoted to Metro Denver Fair Housing business during a twenty-nine-month period: sixty-four working days out of town, two thousand additional hours of normal office working time on fair housing business, and two hundred and fifty-five meetings during the evenings or on weekends.

The support in Denver by the Board of Realtors of the enforcement of fair housing legislation was largely due to John I. Hasselblad. As the vice-president of Van Schaack & Co., Denver's largest real estate firm, a former president of the Denver Board of Realtors, and a director of both the Colorado and National Associations of Real Estate Boards, Hasselblad was in a good position to be effective.

Prior to his appointment in 1964 to a committee to rewrite Colorado's fair housing law, Hasselblad had never been involved with the issue of open housing. He believed discrimination was wrong, but he also felt that a seller should have the right to discriminate. However, his involvement changed his views. One person in particular who caused him to rethink his position was Rabbi Samuel Adelman, a man who was particularly effective because of the gracious manner with which he listened and reacted to the ideas of others. As a result of this involvement, it was Hasselblad more than anyone else who influenced the Board of Realtors to adopt a policy supporting enforcement of the law. Then, when he saw how well the new law worked, Hasselblad's conversion became complete and he has since spoken throughout the country on the fairness of open housing laws.

As indicated earlier, Denver's program has some serious weaknesses. One of these is that the fair housing movement is relatively complacent. Although considerable discrimination still occurs, particularly in rentals, there has been no attempt to impose negative sanctions on those who discriminate. When discrimination occurs and is reported, the smooth working Civil Rights Commission usually gets the housing. But the fact that Denver still experiences as much discrimination as it does suggests that if this case-by-case approach continues to be followed, discrimination will persist for a long time.

Another weakness is that there is not enough citizen participation. Because of the large staff, it is not necessary for people to volunteer to do things in Denver — and so they do not.

But the greatest weakness of Denver's program to date has been that the large available resources of staff and money have not yet really been focused on strategies which will break ghetto patterns and result in large-scale racial integration. The statistics from Denver are more impressive than the social changes they have created. In 1968 the Center served over two thousand families, 80 percent of whom had low incomes, and of these families 510 made what was termed an "integrative" move. However, an integrative move was defined as where the family went from an area where their ethnic group dominated to one where they were a minority. Also, about 50 percent of the registrants at the Center were Hispanos whose problems of poverty and poor education were much more significant than those of discrimination, and only 20 percent of the registrants were black.

The staff at the Center are dedicated and have become involved in many activities which might be judged either as the province of other agencies or the responsibility of the clients themselves. These "welfare-type" activities may eventually be turned to advantage: no fair housing organization in the country can legitimately claim to be better known or have a better image in the black community it serves than does Metro Denver. Now the task would appear to be to connect this link with large supplies of available housing, a task which will require much more involvement by the business community. With a program still very young, Metro Denver may yet provide a dramatic demonstration of how to achieve racial integration in an urban area.

The most intense fight ever waged over fair housing legislation was in California concerning the 1964 vote on Proposition 14, an amendment to the state constitution which in effect prevented fair housing legislation. Specifically, Proposition 14 forbade the legislature from enacting any law that "shall deny, limit or abridge, directly or indirectly, the right of any person . . . to decline to sell, lease or rent such property to such person or persons as he, in his absolute discretion, chooses." In addition, it prohibited the courts from creating legal remedies for those who were hurt by discriminatory actions.

The powerful organized support for Proposition 14 came almost entirely from the California Real Estate Association (CREA). California is a state with a very mobile population and, as a result, almost 20 percent of the Realtors in the United States are in California and the membership of CREA is nearly 50,000. Against the CREA, in a fight which assumed the proportions of a major political campaign, were almost all organized Protestant and Jewish groups, five Roman Catholic bishops, the California Labor Federation, the League of Women Voters of California, the State Bar of California, the State PTA, the California Teachers Association, the Greater San Francisco Chamber of Commerce, most large newspapers, the Democratic State Central Committee and a number of other groups.

Proposition 14 posed complex issues. But for the average voter these issues were reduced to the simple question of whether he wanted blacks to be able to move into white neighborhoods. In the privacy of a voting booth, fear and prejudice were more influential than massive institutional support. Proposition 14 passed by about two to one.

The Realtors and other backers did not have long to enjoy their victory. The United States Supreme Court declared Proposition 14 unconstitutional. But there was no way to rescind this additional evidence to California's Negroes that they lived in a racist society.

Proposition 14 crystallized support for open housing and many of the fair housing groups which were active then continue their work today. In the San Francisco area these groups, several of which now have staff, tie in closely with the Council for Civic Unity which coordinates activities. A similar function is performed in the Los Angeles area by a more recently funded Housing Opportunities Center under the sponsorship of the Community Relations Conference of Southern California.

There has been progress toward ending discrimination in the San Francisco Bay area as a result of a combination of community education programs, the aggressive pursuit of complaints, and the relatively liberal social attitudes of much of the population. But the future does not look promising for integration. The housing shortage in the Bay Area is one of the most critical in the nation and a tight housing market both encourages discrimination and makes it easier to practice. The limited business support once given to the Council of Civic Unity has decreased substantially, mainly as a result of controversial positions taken by the Council in matters not related to housing discrimination, but also because the few business leaders who had shown interest in minority housing problems appear now to be focusing that interest on ghetto rebuilding programs. Finally, a HUD grant in 1969 for a demonstration program aimed at integration in the Bay Area bypassed the Council of Civic Unity and set up a new organization, thereby splintering the fair housing effort.

The pride of the fair housing movement in the Los Angeles area is the Fair Housing Council of the San Fernando Valley. This group, which covers an area with well over a million people, is one of the most successful fair housing organizations in the nation. The $12,000 yearly budget, which maintains a paid staff of one and a half, represents the contributions of about one thousand families plus a $1,000 corporate gift.

The San Fernando Council is one of the few fair housing groups that has been able to work cooperatively with a local Board of Realtors, an option which never existed in most communities, and was muffed in others. Shortly after its organization in 1960 the Council entered into discussions with the local Board of Realtors which, following the leadership of its president, Clare Short, decided that it would be better to act than to react. The eventual result was not only a public statement in support of open housing, but even before there was a law a number of brokers gave service to Negro clients by showing listings not explicitly restricted by the owner. The latter category turned out to be less than one percent.

Significantly aided by this Realtor cooperation, about three hundred Negro families have moved into previously all-white areas in the valley. One of the first, a physicist, encountered severe harassment. Rocks were thrown at his home and, very late one night, a hearse pulled up to the house "to pick up the body." But this was the only really serious incident, and the overall experience of the black families since then has been among the best anywhere in the nation. At present an important component of the Council's education program is to picture Negroes and whites together in advertisements to strengthen attitudes favorable to integration in both the black and white communities.

The impact of the San Fernando Council has extended beyond the valley. Members of this group provided most of the effort which in 1968 created the Housing Opportunities Center for the Metropolitan Los Angeles area. A member of this group, Mrs. Carol Schiller, later headed the fair housing portion of the Center's program. In working with landlord associations, Mrs. Schiller emphasized the policy of the Center to bring lawsuits against those who break the law, and the necessity of explicitly instructing employees not to discriminate, since otherwise employees might do so assuming this is what their employers want. Her efforts were aided by the example set by a large property management firm which has required every employee to sign a statement acknowledging compliance with the policy that "every prospect has to be shown the same courtesy, with no discrimination. . . ."

Although in Los Angeles fair housing efforts are well coordinated and comparatively well funded, the future of integration does not look any better than in San Francisco. While Los Angeles is helped by a County Human Relations Commission which has engaged in constructive educational programs and works closely with the Housing Opportunities Center, in conservative Los Angeles the institutional support is weaker than in San Francisco. For example, until 1970 the Catholic archdiocese was headed by a cleric who would not even speak against Proposition 14.

The housing opportunities for the millions of Negroes who live in the South has followed a different pattern from elsewhere in the nation.

In one respect the past has been the same as in the North: some housing was for blacks and some was for whites. But in other respects there were differences. In some cities, particularly before the Supreme Court decision on school desegregation, Negro areas were more dispersed. Often white leaders negotiated with black leaders about which areas would be made available to a growing black community. On the other hand, it has been much rarer in the South than in the North for a black family to pioneer a white neighborhood, even one only a block or two away from a black neighborhood. The response to such attempts has frequently been terrorism.

While housing in the South has been more clearly segregated than elsewhere, in other respects housing opportunities have been better. The fine homes where Atlanta's wealthy blacks live are only one example that quality housing has been obtainable for those who could afford it. Between 1945 and 1956 Atlanta's growing black population acquired over ten thousand additional units, of which about 80 percent were new houses.[4] Unlike the Negroes who migrated to the North, those in Southern communities have not been confined to old decaying areas in the city.

Ironically, housing segregation, Southern style, has been less difficult for blacks than housing segregation, Northern style. The Southern system robbed Negroes of their dignity and a chance to be better assimilated into the mainstream. But that happened in the North also. In the South, the Negro had a better housing supply available, paid less of a "color tax" (i.e. the difference in price between identical housing for a white and black family), and, because he knew where he stood, experienced less frustrations.

White Southerners have paid a high price for the total segregation they have practiced. When areas have gone from
white to black, the change has been very rapid. While in the
North a previously white area in the path of an expanding
ghetto might become 70 to 95 percent black over a period of
five to ten years, in the South it frequently has become 100
percent black in less than a year. So great is the pressure on
whites to move, a pressure often skillfully magnified by real
estate brokers who specialize in the transition-area market,
that people sell their homes before they look for another.
Many then discover too late that they do not have the money
to get anything comparable to what they have just abandoned.

Although racial discrimination in housing has had a different history in the South, it can be decreased in the same
ways, and as speedily, as in other parts of the country. What
has been done with public accommodations in the South can
be done with housing.

In many ways open housing in large Southern cities stands
where it was five to ten years ago in Northern cities. For
example, in the past few years in Houston and Atlanta a
few Negro families — probably less than ten in each city —
have moved without incident into housing in all-white areas.
However, as of this writing there has not been a single black
family in either city who has used the power of the law to
obtain housing. In fact, in both cities fair housing activity
only started in 1968. As was often the case in Northern cities, such activity was preceded by attempts to stabilize areas
in transition, such as the South MacGregor area of Houston
and the Cascade Heights area in Atlanta. Both of these efforts were supported by the press and both have slowed
down transition.

Because it is not part of the Deep South, one might expect Houston to move toward racial integration more rapidly

than Atlanta. The Houston Council on Human Relations has fifteen hundred members, including many influential people. But the Council did not publicly support open housing until 1968 and still does not appear close to undertaking the type of program which would bring about change. Apart from the Council, no significant institutional support has developed on behalf of fair housing. There are many community leaders who believe that discriminatory practices should be ended, but as long as these people feel open housing is unacceptable in Houston it will, of course, remain so.

The situation is very different in Atlanta. Churches for the first time are beginning to speak up and, after much debate and some loss of support, the Christian Council of Metropolitan Atlanta publicly supported an open housing conference early in 1969. Women's groups such as the League of Women Voters, the YWCA and Church Women United also have given their support. The press gave extensive coverage and strong editorial support to the efforts of SWAP (Southwest Atlantans for Progress) to stabilize Cascade Heights. In the long run the most significant support of all may come from the Chamber of Commerce which, guided by the realization that for the community to progress there must be a favorable racial climate, has often provided more leadership than the churches on racial issues.

Over a half dozen fair housing councils have been formed in upper middle class areas. A Negro family moving into a white neighborhood today would be unlikely to encounter anything like what happened in 1965 to Samuel L. Adams, a distinguished Negro journalist.

I remember the first night — the sound of gunshots fired above the house, the sight of cherry bombs and Molotov cocktails tossed on the lawn. I remember re-

246

turning home with my wife and two children after a short trip to the city to find windows broken and streams of toilet paper decorating the front yard. I remember the sight of my trembling teenage daughter telling her mother and me of an attempt by a white teenage motorist to run her down as she walked along the road from school. I remember the words of my six-year-old son telling us of being chased by larger white boys. "I wish I was white so they wouldn't do it."[5]

The question, of course, is whether the developing institutional support will crystallize into a meaningful fair housing program that can change the status quo in a Southern city. The problems range from the almost certain lack of support from the Baptist churches, to which a majority of the white inhabitants belong, to how the members of the black community can be encouraged to seek housing in nontraditional areas after being even more thoroughly conditioned to a dual housing market than in the North. The latter is particularly serious because the paucity of blacks willing to move into white areas at present may cause the whites interested in fair housing to direct their civic interest to other problems.

If Atlanta does succeed in providing leadership in the South toward racial integration of housing, it will be largely because of the leadership provided by its mayor, Ivan Allen, Jr. He has supported open housing personally, advocated national fair housing legislation, and strongly backed the City of Atlanta Community Relations Commission which is actively working for open housing. He has been able to integrate all but the smallest of five previously all-white public housing projects, the blacks currently ranging from 5 to slightly more than 50 percent. However, the greatest contribution that Ivan Allen has made to open housing probably was something which did not have a direct bearing on housing: his support of a national civil rights act which, when it finally passed in 1964, was instrumental in bringing about a rapid end in Atlanta to segregation in public accommodations.

In 1963 President Kennedy badly needed additional support if he was to get his civil rights bill through Congress. Not a single Southern political leader was publicly supporting it. However, the President knew that Allen, who only six years earlier had publicly talked of "preserving our Southern way of life" and who freely admitted he had "developed a social conscience late in life," was privately in favor of such a law. Consequently Kennedy first sent an emissary to talk to Allen in Atlanta and then personally urged that he come to Washington to testify on behalf of the bill. This courtship posed a difficult decision for the Mayor. Allen knew there were very few whites in Atlanta who felt the way that he did and he believed that if he were to support the Civil Rights Act he would be certain of defeat if he ran again in 1965. But Allen went to Washington. One important influence was that he was a wealthy man who did not need to be mayor to live well. Another was his wife, Louise, who told him, "You won't be able to live with yourself if you don't."

Before he testified, Allen informed a group of twenty-four Negro leaders what he was going to do. Twenty asked him to reconsider because he was needed as mayor and would not be re-elected. Yet in 1965 Allen won a smashing re-election victory with 70 percent of the vote, including a majority of the white vote. This victory would not have occurred had Allen not been a first-class mayor who had spurred economic growth and brought major league sports to the city. However, people had neither forgotten nor approved of what he had done on the civil rights issue. They voted for him anyway, partly because of his other accomplishments, partly because they respected him for doing what he thought was right.

Providence and Seattle are two cities where notable accomplishments have been made largely as a result of the efforts of a single individual.

In the Providence area, Irving Jay Fain, the wealthy head of several Rhode Island industrial and mercantile concerns, purchased rental properties in white areas, usually two or three family dwellings. When a vacancy occurred in a house which did not contain a Negro family, every effort was made to rent it to one; when a vacancy occured in a house that already had a black family, it was preferentially marketed to whites.

Fain began his program in the spring of 1905 with the help of the real estate firm of Rotkin and Sydney, which purchased the properties. By early 1968 Fain had forty-seven houses occupied by 115 families, of which twenty-five were non-white. Neighborhood reaction was helped by purchasing houses that were as good or better than others on the block. In addition, Fain improved many of the houses he purchased. No serious adverse reactions resulted from any of the integrative moves, and in the following two years Fain purchased over sixty more apartment units.

In Seattle, Sidney Gerber, a retired businessman and former chairman of the Washington State Board Against Discrimination, raised $100,000 in working capital, using some of his own, money from friends, and a substantial bank loan. This was enough to launch Harmony Homes [6]

Serving without salary as president and general manager of Harmony Homes, Gerber purchased lots in white areas, built twenty-five houses, and sold twenty-two of them to Negro families and three to whites. Two of these were preferentially marketed to whites because they were next door to houses just sold to Negroes.[7]

Gerber also organized a fair housing listing service for the Seattle area and functioned as a broker without fee, making a great effort to make certain that Negroes found homes they really liked. He insisted that each family inspect at least a dozen houses and become fully informed about the advantages and disadvantages of each. Through this service more than one hundred black families obtained housing.[6]

Gerber was killed in 1965 in an airplane accident, but his work provided a foundation for Seattle's Operation Equality program, one of the best fair housing programs in the United States.[8]

As one looks across the nation at what has been accomplished in ending housing discrimination and starting toward racial integration, the contrast between metropolitan areas is striking. It also is very unpredictable. With the exception of the South, the extent of integration has not been so much a matter of the liberalism or conservatism of the area, or whether the black population was large or small, but rather whether people were willing to do what was necessary.

A dearth of people willing to act accounts for the lack of progress in most of the smaller cities and towns throughout the country. Although such communities tend to be "conservative," this is a relatively minor factor. In fact, probably nowhere in America has the transition from closed housing to open housing been as rapid as in Worthington, Minnesota.[9] But in Worthington local leadership did what was required once it had been activated by the Armour Automation Fund Committee.

There is no formula which spells out what is necessary. But there is what might be termed a "critical mass." One housewife, one clergyman, even one millionaire cannot do it alone. And while this "critical mass" is less in a small community, the probability that it will form is very much less. For one thing, the critical mass is not proportional to the size of the community; in a smaller community a greater proportion will be needed. More important, the probability of someone being willing to play an active role in promoting social change is much less in a small community than a large one. It is very difficult to isolate oneself from the world in which one lives and, at times, it is an economic impossibility. In a large community those who give leadership to open housing usually already are part of a society which is largely supportive. Moreover, any lost social and business contacts can be readily replaced with new ones. In a small town, however, social and business contacts necessarily extend over a much wider spectrum of the community.

Thus it is probable that open housing will not be achieved as soon in most small towns as in most large cities. But this time lag will not be long if public and private institutions are willing to recognize a responsibility to the often forgotten black minorities in small communities and attempt to reach into these communities to stimulate change.

As individuals and through the institutions that they control, white Americans are now taking action with increasing effectiveness to end discrimination and to effect racial integration. This is as it should be. White racism remains the primary reason we continue as two societies, separate and unequal.

However, whites cannot do the job alone. In fact, progress will depend more on what blacks do than whites. We would not have progressed as far as we have if it were not for the Joseph Lee Joneses in St. Louis, the Charles Broaduses in Buffalo, the William Meyers in Levittown, the Percy Julians in Chicago, and all the others like them.

Black activists insisting on their rights have been the key to progress toward racial equality ever since a black lady in Montgomery refused to go to the back of the bus.

11 / *The Hopes and the Challenges*

I STARTED TO CRY when my husband told me we were to live here. I cried for three weeks. I didn't want to come and live here where there were so many colored people. I didn't want to bring my children up with colored children but we had to come; there was no place else to go. . . . Well, all that's changed. I've really come to like it. I see they're just as human as we are. They have nice apartments, they keep their children clean, and they're friendly. I've come to like them a great deal. I'm no longer scared of them. I'd just as soon live near a colored person as a white; it makes no difference to me.[1]

This statement by a woman living in an integrated public housing project gives the most important single reason to hope for racial integration in housing: it has worked — not only in middle-class neighborhoods where pioneer families have moved, and in planned interracial developments, but also where the chances of success would seem to be least —

in public housing projects where the number of Negro and white families was about equal, and where they lived in integrated housing of necessity, not choice.

Repeated research studies have shown that racial integration usually leads to improved attitudes about people of other races.[2] For example, a study by Deutsch and Collins showed that the attitudes of whites toward Negroes were greatly improved when the whites lived in integrated public housing projects. Sixty percent of the whites in these projects indicated that they had raised their opinion of Negroes, and only 5 percent had lowered their opinion. Similar interviews with a control group from public housing projects where whites lived in areas separate from the blacks indicated that only 22 percent had improved their attitudes about Negroes, while 10 percent had an unfavorable change.

What social scientists have learned by research studies, others have learned by watching. Their observations were summarized in the words of W. Max Moore, a Denver Realtor whom no one has ever called a civil rights activist: "The most effective education is experience. You find out the world doesn't come to an end. People begin to say, 'What the hell is so bad about that?' "

Even where the climate for integration has been the most unfavorable, a start can be made. Lackawanna, New York, is a bleak, begrimed steel town to the south of Buffalo with a population of almost thirty thousand. Three thousand of these people are blacks and Puerto Ricans who live in an isolated ghetto in the first ward under the smoke pall of the Bethlehem Steel plant. The remainder of Lackawanna's inhabitants are mostly working-class descendants of Eastern European immigrants who probably are as resistant to the entry of blacks into their neighborhoods as people anywhere in the United States outside of some areas in the South.

When Frederick L. Perry, a "steel pourer" at the Bethlehem plant, who also ran a TV repair business, decided to move out of the rented tenement in which he had lived for twenty-six years and build his own house, it was not surprising that he had trouble acquiring land in Lackawanna. However, with the help of Buffalo's HOME and the State Commission for Human Rights, he was able to buy a suitable lot. He then started to build a $50,000 two-family dwelling, the most expensive house in the neighborhood.

When several anonymous telephone callers threatened his life, Perry obtained an unlisted number. As the house neared completion, vandals struck. Perry notified the police, but within a week there were two more incidents of vandalism. Nazi swastikas and KKK's were burned into brick walls.

HOME offered a $500 reward for information leading to the apprehension of the vandals and requested that the Federal Justice Department provide protection for Perry in the light of the demonstrated failure of the local police to act with sufficient vigilance. The reward was quickly raised to over $1,000 as a result of the response of private citizens to the newspaper and television coverage, and the FBI questioned neighbors. No culprits were apprehended, but Mr. Perry's troubles were ended.

The progress that has been made toward ending many other racist practices permits optimism about open housing. Not many years ago Negroes could not be served in most restaurants, often had to use "colored" public facilities, and were categorically excluded from most jobs. The virtual elimination of such blatant racist practices — which many people once thought impossible — has been accomplished in a relatively short time. In much the same way, a combination of strong enforcement of antidiscrimination laws and strong community leadership can now be effective in combating housing discrimination.

One of the best examples of successful racial integration has been the armed forces. Twenty-five years ago military units were completely segregated except for Negro personnel assigned to menial jobs with white units. In 1945 an army board headed by Lieutenant General Alvan C. Gillein, Jr., while holding integration to be a desirable goal, recommended a continuation of segregation with Negro personnel assigned exclusively to support rather than to combat units. These recommendations cited World War II experience, particularly the performance of the all-Negro 92nd Infantry Division, and the low scores of most Negroes in aptitude classification tests.

But, as a result of President Truman's 1948 executive order to desegregate the armed forces, integration of army units started in 1950 and was completed by 1956. In Korea it was consistently noted that the combat performance of Negro soldiers in integrated units differed little from whites' — in marked contrast to the blemished record of the all-Negro 24th Infantry Regiment whose performance in Korea was so poor that its divisional commander recommended that it be dissolved as quickly as possible.[3] In their performance of military duties whites and blacks have worked together with little racial tension and, although some racial incidents have occurred, they have usually involved off-duty problems. The racial friction which has received prominent press coverage recently does not appear to be caused by the failure of integration but by an extension of the black revolution to the armed forces. Blacks in and out of the armed forces are demanding more positions of responsibility and more acceptance of black culture.

An important consequence of the integration of the armed

forces is that the large number of whites who have shared a life or death association with Negroes will be unlikely to carry the same prejudiced attitudes into civilian life as the men of an earlier generation, most of whom never had contacts with Negroes of equal or higher status. Also, Negro servicemen returning to civilian life will be less willing to accept second-class citizenship after having tasted equality.

However, probably the most important reason to expect that open housing eventually will be achieved is that the level of education of our population is rising, and education generally improves attitudes towards other racial groups.[4] The young people of today clearly are more progressive on racial issues than their elders.

But ending discriminatory practices is only a first step towards racial integration. Open housing, by itself, is not enough. In fact, although discrimination is decreasing, the statistical indices all show that racial segregation is increasing — increasing to a point where racial division threatens the nation.[5] Racial polarization not only makes ending discrimination all the more urgent, but demands new programs which are aimed at creating racially integrated communities. That such action has not yet been taken reflects the failure of the nation to commit itself to a national goal of racial integration — a failure which is not the result of a decision that integration is inappropriate, but rather of the reluctance to face short-term problems inherent in the only reasonable long-term solution to the race problem.

Meanwhile the trend continues toward the formation of black cities surrounded by white suburbs. Between 1960 and 1966 the number of Negroes in large cities increased from 9.7 million to 12.1 million, of which 1.4 million was from natural growth and one million from migration from Southern rural areas. However, the total population of the cities remained about the same, because the blacks replaced white residents who moved to the suburbs. If this trend continues, by 1973 Baltimore, Gary, Jacksonville, New Orleans and Richmond will have joined Washington and Newark as cities with black majorities. By 1980 Cleveland, Detroit and St. Louis also will be over 50 percent black; Chicago, Oakland and Philadelphia will have Negro majorities by 1985.[6]

This polarization is more than racial; it also is economic. The whites leaving the cities are those with higher incomes. While some flee because of racial fears, most leave because of the better schools and municipal services in the suburbs. But when middle-income whites leave, the tax base is eroded and the capability of the city to provide services is even further decreased, causing more whites to leave.

It is unlikely that a predominantly white America will vote to furnish predominantly black cities with the enormous sums necessary to eliminate disparities in education, police protection, housing and health services. As Anthony Downs observes in his brilliant analysis "Alternative Futures for the American Ghetto," suburbanites are experiencing rapidly rising taxes because they are demanding more services, and the costs of such services are increasing. This has led to a general dissatisfaction with tax increases which further stiffens the natural resistance of most white suburbanites to providing disproportionate financial aid to a Negro minority living separately from them.

But blacks will want the same opportunities they see whites enjoying in the suburbs, and once the blacks have gained political control of major cities the result may be a series of confrontations unlike anything America has ever known, confrontations between fiscally bankrupt black cities and the comparatively wealthy white suburbs which surround them.

The enormity of the problem can be gleaned from a few

statistics. If in the period 1970 to 1975 the population of blacks in central cities is to remain constant, the number of Negroes moving to suburban areas, whether they be integrated areas or Negro enclaves, must average 380,000 per year. This is well over ten times the current rate. [7]

Although as we have seen in Chapter 9 there are many reasons why few Negroes move into white areas even in the absence of discrimination, there is much evidence that most blacks would prefer to live in integrated neighborhoods. A 1968 study showed that only 8 percent of more than five thousand Negroes interviewed in fifteen cities preferred to live in an all-Negro neighborhood, and only 5 percent preferred a neighborhood which was mostly Negro.[8] Other studies have shown similar results.[9]

The continuing desire of most of America's blacks for racial integration is badly underrated. The disproportionate forum received by the black separatists is only one reason for this. Another is that virtually all black leaders support ghetto-enrichment programs to the exclusion of those promoting integration. This emphasis by black leadership reflects the urgent need to make immediate improvements in the quality of life of disadvantaged blacks lest their frustrations lead to violence, and the reality that integration can occur only if accompanied by improvements in education, employment, and housing so that blacks can enter the mainstream as equals, not as the gratuitants of white America. But the lack of expressed interest in integration also reflects political realities. Because most Negroes will continue to live in ghettos for some time and the self-interest of black community leaders is best served by pushing programs which meet the short-term needs of most of their constituents, little is being said about integration in housing.

The continuing desire by blacks for racial integration is often underrated or ignored by white leaders because "gilding the ghetto" offers them a convenient escape, a way they can do something about the urban crisis with minimum risk. When a large corporation rehabilitates twenty houses in a black slum, the black community and white liberals applaud and nobody kicks. If a church does the same thing, some members complain that their money is being spent in the wrong way, but the protests are mild compared to the howls which would ensue if that money were used to promote integration. For government officials, ghetto-oriented programs can be used to build political support; programs aimed at integration carry risks without much potential gain.

Indeed, the overall position of blacks has shifted in the past few years only in that many are no longer willing to accept integration solely on white society's terms. Their thoughts are expressed by the words of the Reverend Channing Phillips "Integration is preferable, but it may not be feasible." Mr. Phillips, the tall, lean, articulate Democratic National Committeeman from the District of Columbia, the first Negro placed in nomination as a presidential candidate at a convention of a major political party, is cynical about whites abandoning their racism. At the same time he admits, "separatism [cannot be] a viable option for blacks — except as a tactical approach."

The choice is not between integration and viable black communities. Far from being alternatives, the two must go hand in hand. Integration requires vast transformations in the education, living standards and psychological attitudes of those caught in the "culture of poverty." Likewise, housing integration still permits a black community which is not territorial, similar to those of other ethnic groups. The real choice is whether or not the nation makes a dual thrust — building black communities and encouraging integration.

If racial integration is to be achieved — and the consequences which otherwise may occur are to be avoided — certain things must be done. An end to housing discrimination is indispensable; there must be an enormous increase in the construction of new housing for low- and moderate-income families, and much of this must be in suburban areas; and nonghetto housing must be affirmatively marketed to blacks. Superimposed on these housing programs, there must be a general upgrading of the living conditions of the people in the ghettos by providing better education, jobs, social services and housing. Finally, sufficient incentives must be provided to make integration work — incentives to blacks to get them to leave the emotional security of living in a black neighborhood, and incentives to whites to take the required affirmative steps to increase the heterogeneity of their communities.

New housing developments for low-income and moderate-income families provide a special opportunity to create integrated communities. Negro families are reluctant to pioneer all-white neighborhoods. But when a new neighborhood is affirmatively marketed to the black community, few Negro families will have reservations based on race.

Unfortunately, very little low- and moderate-income housing is being built even though it is desperately needed by whites as well as blacks. The reasons are complex:[10]

Construction costs have skyrocketed. The homebuilding industry has not achieved the same productivity gains per worker as most manufacturing industries and wage rates of construction workers have increased more than rates in other industries. High building costs can be reduced by "industrialized housing" — building the major components in factories which utilize efficient mass-production techniques and operate on a year-round basis. Such housing, which has the added advantage of preventing construction from being limited by a shortage of skilled labor, is technically feasible today and is accounting for an increasingly larger share of

261

new housing construction in many European countries.* But before industrialized housing becomes a substantial part of new home construction in the United States, a wide variety of institutional constraints must be overcome, including acceptance by organized labor and by homeseekers, modifications of building codes, and reorientation of the home-building industry.

There is no "available" land. Suburbs do not want low- and moderate-income housing developments and, as a first line of defense, have adopted restrictive zoning laws which usually make such housing impossible.

Because the costs of building, land and money are high, moderate-income housing can be built only by using government loans to nonprofit sponsors or limited-dividend private investors. Even in the cities, where a modest amount of moderate-income housing has been built, construction has been very limited because the government has failed to fund the programs it has adopted and has administered programs in such a way that obtaining government assistance is a tortuous process.

There is a close link between the solution of America's race problem and the nation's ability to provide low- and moderate-income housing for whites as well as blacks. Neither will be achieved unless such housing can be built in the suburbs, since there is insufficient land in the cities for the low- and moderate-income housing which is needed. But to build the housing the suburbs will require a variety of changes.

One required change involves tax policy. At present revenues for schools and community services are primarily de-

*According to a 1968 HUD report, industrialized housing has been most utilized in Czechoslovakia where the percentage of such units used for multi-family housing construction increased from 8 to 77 percent between 1958 and 1966.

rived from local property taxes. Thus for suburbanites to approve a housing development which consists of less expensive housing than the existing average, they must approve an increase in their own taxes to maintain equivalent services.

One solution is increased state and federal grants to school districts and local communities so that local taxes become relatively insignificant in the financing of community services. Such a step would have the additional advantage of giving the cities money consistent more with their needs than their ability to raise funds, thereby helping to check the flight of middle-income families from the city. The resistance of suburban communities to low-income residents could be further reduced if supplementary government grants were given in proportion to the percentage of low income residents in a community.

Tax reform alone, however, will not crack the "suburban barrier." People fear any change in their neighborhood; consequently, most suburban homeowners oppose the construction of any rental units nearby. For example, a survey taken in the suburbs of Rochester, New York, indicated that 11 percent would favor and 67 percent would oppose luxury apartments in their neighborhood.[11]

Building moderate- and low-income housing in the suburbs undoubtedly will arouse passions, but so has initial Negro entry. If such housing is to be built, however, there must be appropriate means. New York State's Urban Development Corporation (UDC), a state agency which can condemn property, build housing without regard to local zoning laws or political red tape, and borrow up to one billion dollars, may become a model. Among the projects on which UDC is working are a new town for five thousand families near Syracuse and one for ten thousand families in suburban Buffalo.

A powerful public development corporation such as UDC,

organized on a state or metropolitan basis, can plan and execute enormous programs that otherwise would never be accomplished. If development corporations are careful to consult with local residents, such agencies violate the rights of
suburbanites only in a parochial sense. The power and
restraints on the power of a public development agency are
similar to those of a town board considering a request for
zoning. As a political body the board cannot ignore the feelings of the people in the immediate neighborhood, but the
board also considers what is proper for the community as a
whole. If after several years the sum of its decisions is not
respected, it will be thrown out of office.

While public corporations with broad powers can be most
effective in leading the way and at times will be essential because of zoning problems in the suburbs, their work can often be supplemented by private, non-profit housing development corporations which provide skilled professional staffs
and seed money to get projects started. In 1969 the Greater
Hartford Housing Development Fund completed 230 new
units, rehabilitated 128 more, and started more than 500
new units which will be completed in 1970. This approach
has been promoted by Urban America which also supplies
staff assistance to those interested in organizing development
corporations.[12] Aided by its standing with the business community and church leaders, Urban America has helped in the
formation of over a dozen of the more than thirty private
nonprofit housing development corporations now operating.
The initial funding usually has come from local businesses,
but in some cases church groups and foundations have fur-
nished a significant part of the money needed to start operations. The Office of Economic Opportunity has also provided
funds for some housing development corporations. If the
development corporation is successful, it can continue to op-

erate without further assistance by charging reasonable fees for its services.

Church groups, labor organizations and community groups can contribute not only as nonprofit sponsors, but, more important, by supporting the efforts of others to get housing built. However, progress toward meeting the nation's housing needs will be even more dependent on private enterprise. Business firms build the housing sponsored by development corporations and profit-making corporations frequently act as "limited dividend" sponsors, in which role they put up 10 percent of the total capital and receive a limited but reasonable return. But the most important contribution that can be made by private enterprise is yet to come — to learn to build housing as efficiently as automobiles and refrigerators.

A variety of other housing programs also will be needed if the growth of black ghettos is to be halted.

An approach, effectively demonstrated in Seattle, is the so-called "221h" rehabilitation program set up by the 1966 Demonstration Cities and Metropolitan Development Act. This program provides federal financing for low-interest, long-term mortgages for poverty-level families to buy houses from nonprofit sponsors who have rehabilitated dilapidated dwellings. Like most such federal programs, 221h was too complicated to use in most communities, and only one-third of the $20 million available was committed during the first year. However, in Seattle, David Curen, the aggressive director of the Urban League's Operation Equality Program, made the program work with the help of an FHA regional director who minimized red tape.

One result was that Seattle's Operation Equality received 12 percent of the money that was spent in the entire nation. Another result was that in a relatively short time sixty units, each in a separate white neighborhood, were rehabilitated. Although Negro families often are reluctant to pioneer white areas, there was no shortage of blacks willing to take advantage of the extraordinary opportunity offered by this program. For example, one family was able to purchase a $17,000 house by paying $200 down plus $105 per month (3 percent interest, plus taxes, plus principal). The program has the additional advantage that adverse white reaction is small because houses that formerly were eyesores become assets to the area.

Public housing programs are another means to promote integration within the city. If public housing were scattered throughout entire metropolitan areas, it could be even more useful in promoting housing integration.

One component of public housing which can be particularly helpful in promoting integration is the Leased Housing Program enacted as part of the Housing and Urban Development Act of 1965. Leased housing, designed to make available public housing on scattered sites, permits the public housing agency to lease property at the market price and then rent it to a family eligible for public housing. The low-income family pays the housing agency the same rent it would pay in a project; the federal government pays the difference between this rental and the fee paid to the owner of the leased property. Since those eligible for public housing usually include a disproportionate number of Negroes, there is bound to be considerable integration if most of the leased housing is located in all-white areas.

However, a leased-housing program is often limited by tight housing supply. For example, Buffalo received funds for two hundred units, but after a year the Municipal Housing Authority had been able to lease less than fifty. The public housing agency was unable to compete successfully with families seeking housing for themselves. A partial solution to this problem, which has been used in Rochester, New York, and other cities, was a nonprofit corporation which bought dwellings for the specific purpose of making them available for leased housing.

Unfortunately, the mere availability of public housing in white areas does not promote racial integration. Regulations which forbid discrimination do not always stop it. People, not regulations, assign priorities, put applications in file folders, and allow prejudice to supersede regulations if the system does not have proper checks. In practice, public housing officials and their staffs have often reinforced patterns of segregation.

Discrimination in public housing can take subtle forms. When a Negro applicant requests a "white project" and the admissions clerk asks, "Why do you want to live way out there?" the interpretation is "Nigger, we are going to keep you out." The result: if a vacancy in a Negro project is offered, the Negro family will frequently accept it rather than wait for their first choice which now appears to be a lost cause. In fact, this capitulation often takes place without anything having been said. Negroes have come to assume that they will encounter discrimination in their efforts to secure housing and that, regardless of regulations, this will be the way the public housing agency really works.

Thus enlightened managers of public housing programs must do more than ensure that there is no discrimination in the operation of their organizations. They also must be successful in getting the black community to believe an equal opportunity policy exists.

Of the many possible programs which a committed nation might use to promote integration, the most suitable would be those which also accomplish other social objectives.

One such program would be to provide generous relocation allowances to low-income families whose principal wage earner obtained a job which required the family to move from an area with high unemployment to one where there is a labor shortage. This could, of course, be combined with government-funded job training programs. Employers could be motivated to recruit a limited number of such employees from poverty areas by incentive payments which realistically covered all employer costs associated with recruiting, training, and assisting the families adjust to their new communities. Political support for the program would be strengthened by the fact that it would apply as much to poverty-stricken whites in West Virginia as to blacks in Harlem, Hough and Watts. And, besides promoting integration, it would be effective in getting unemployed people off the rolls of public assistance.

Labor mobility projects of this type have been tried on an experimental basis by the Department of Labor since 1965.[13] However, these projects, only two out of thirty-five of which were directed at relocation from inner city Negro ghettos, have differed from what is proposed above in several important respects. The experimental projects to date have offered neither employer incentives nor adequate supporting social services and, as a result, the relocatees have had insufficient assistance in finding suitable housing or adjusting to the new community. Also, the experimental projects have been only for unemployed workers. But culturally deprived ghetto residents need to be "staged"; a worker who has already held steady employment is more likely to adjust satisfactorily to a nonghetto environment than one who has not been so employed. Thus a relocation program should allow employers to offer jobs with better opportunities to people already employed. Since a relocatee's original low-paying job requires few skills, he can then be replaced by an unemployed ghetto resident.

A very different type of program is needed for moderate-income families. Local nonprofit corporations, heavily supported by government loans, would purchase appropriately priced housing in "nonproblem" areas, designated as such on the basis of factors such as crime rates and school performance. This housing would then be rented to people living in "problem" areas. As an incentive for people to leave the emotional security of their present neighborhoods, the rentals would be on a sliding scale with payments increasing each year for about six years. In addition, there would be an option to buy and an effort would be made to eventually convert the renter into a homeowner. Families would be tempted to take advantage of this opportunity by the enormous improvement they could immediately realize in housing quality and, for those who wished, a chance to achieve home ownership without a down payment.

Monthly payments would be calculated so that during the first year the family received a subsidy of ten to twenty-five dollars per month. As shown by the table on page 290, if the family moved within the first five years the nonprofit corporation would suffer a loss, perhaps as much as $500. However, if the family stayed in the housing for five or more years, there would be no loss, and a small profit might be realized to cover losses from short-term moves. An alternative would be to cover such losses by a government subsidy.

The experience of the Robert Littleton Corporation in Hartford[14] indicates that short-term moves would probably occur less than 20 percent of the time. Fundamental studies by Peter Rossi also support the hypothesis that once families have satisfactory housing they will tend to stay.[15] Thus by an imaginative use of risk capital and administrative skills, not only will the tendency to polarize our society be counteracted, but many families, both black and white, could be aided in achieving home ownership and, in the process, motivated to raise the level of their own aspirations.

Another program might combine the need for racial integration with the need to provide a greater measure of justice to the victims of urban renewal. Urban renewal has provided cities with large federal grants, thereby enabling them to transform slums into new office buildings, fine apartment houses, commercial centers, hospitals and new homes. But the benefits to the community have not been shared with the slum dwellers who have been forcibly uprooted and, because they were poor, usually had no choice but to overcrowd into an already deteriorating area, thereby accelerating its conversion to another slum. About two-thirds of those thus uprooted have been Negro.[16] The result is that urban renewal has become synonymous with "Negro removal."

It does not seem unreasonable that when people are forced to leave their home for the convenience of the general public, the public should give them just compensation and attempt to administer the relocation program so that the same families do not have to repeat the process. This could be done by supplementing the existing compensations given relocatees with additional benefits if they relocated in a "preferred relocation area." The latter would be defined as one not scheduled for urban renewal and by other parameters (e.g. low crime rates) which would tend to exclude central city Negro neighborhoods.

If special benefits such as rent supplements or low-interest loans were offered those who relocated in a "preferred" area, some of those displaced by urban renewal — both blacks and whites — would be able to transform what is often

270

a family disaster into an opportunity.* If a sufficient number of people leave the area, others being displaced will have less difficulty obtaining housing near their present homes since there will be less competition. As a result, such a program would also benefit the general public since less opposition would arise to needed urban renewal programs.

These proposals use incentives to motivate dispersion from central city ghettos into areas which are overwhelmingly white. Such subsidies will be necessary until a better rapport is established between the races.

The use of subsidies to motivate voluntary actions required to achieve national goals has been a standard operating procedure in the United States for a long time. The land given to homesteaders to encourage settlement of the West was an early example. Today, home ownership is encouraged by federal tax deductions.[17] Ironically, subsidies to aid the growth of suburban areas — the billions of dollars spent for toll-free expressways and FHA insurance programs — indirectly fostered the ghettos by making it easier for middle-class whites not to live in the cities which provide their livelihood.

Incentives also must be provided to suburban communities, employers, and nonprofit organizations to motivate them to promote integration. Subsidies to privileged groups to encourage voluntary action in the national interest has also been a standard practice in the United States. Examples are oil-depletion allowances, tax reductions to investors and subsidy payments to farmers.

Government programs to achieve racial integration, how-

*It is more difficult for most low-income families to move to a new neighborhood than for families higher on the socioeconomic scale since low-income families tend to establish stronger roots in the neighborhood in which they live.

ever, are not enough. They need to be supplemented by the work of private organizations at the local level. Traditional fair housing organizations are effective means of ending discrimination, but to achieve integration other vehicles also are needed. New housing must be built and existing housing rehabilitated for low- and moderate-income families; management of these housing units should be in the hands of organizations geared to handle the problems of low-income residents; the people in the black community must be made aware of the housing options open to them.

These housing functions can be carried out by one organization or many. More important than the number is that each organization have specific missions which complement rather than conflict, and that the members of policy-making boards are carefully chosen to provide representation from all segments of the community and to be a source of useful contacts and expert guidance. Thus the boards of organizations dealing with construction, finance, rentals and land acquisition need a substantial number of businessmen and bankers; on the other hand, the board of a housing information program should consist primarily of blacks and people experienced in social work and community action.

But programs and plans, however sound, do not guarantee achievement. Many fail to recognize the enormity of the task. Getting different people to live together in equality has been a world problem for a long time. What has happened to the American Negro is unjust, but not unique. Those who have held power have usually discriminated against those who did not. The Japanese oppress their Korean minority; the Jews have discriminated against the Arabs who live in Israel; and black Africans have enslaved other blacks of different tribal background.

Excesses of black militancy will probably hurt efforts to achieve integration, but the inescapable truth is that only through militancy have America's blacks won the gains they have achieved and this lesson is now well understood in the ghettos. As a result, militant tactics often may be used to eliminate the remaining frustrations, particularly since it has generally been true that the closer disadvantaged groups come to their goals the harder they find it to tolerate the disparities which remain.[18] Such tactics obviously will tend to polarize whites and blacks. But an even greater danger is the effect of continuing racial confrontations on the next generation. Those who created the Black Power movement may someday find they have created a Frankenstein.

Racial integration poses a dilemma: the progress of integration depends on how black people feel about whites and how whites feel about blacks — and the best way to improve relationships is by integration in housing. Consequently, until there is more integration in housing, there is a need to promote interracial contacts by other means. Studies clearly indicate that interracial experience has been a common factor in the background of most pioneer families.[19]

Home visits between whites and blacks living in different parts of the metropolitan area are one way contacts have been achieved by church and community groups. While these may help, such programs are best scrapped in favor of ones which involve whites and blacks working together for a common objective — such as co-sponsorship by suburban and inner-city churches of a nursery school or a housing program. These programs are useful by themselves, and much more effective in promoting racial understanding than artificial social contacts. Joint action toward shared objectives is, of course, an important by-product of fair housing groups.

Racial bigotry is not the only type of bigotry which challenges our ability to achieve integration. Fair housing activists frequently practice an intellectual bigotry of their own which hurts what they are trying to accomplish.

"I cannot understand how people can be so stupid not to agree . . . " was the way one Midwestern fair housing worker demonstrated the problem. Progress toward integration is not helped when fair housing activists are completely indifferent to the fears and concerns of those who do not share their views. Too many fair housing workers have a perspective which is confined to the viewpoint of someone living in a high-priced area where blacks cannot move in great numbers. As a result, the fair housing movement usually does not relate well to the real problem: working-class whites who feel threatened by black inundation of their neighborhoods.

Another weakness in the fair housing movement was shown by a staff member of a civil rights organization when he said, "We now tend to consider white attitudes irrelevant." Battles can be won in opposition to the attitudes of a majority in the community, but to ignore the importance of changing such attitudes is to risk ultimate victory because of laziness.

Overall objectives are also hurt by fair housing activists attempting to do too much at once. Progress usually needs to be accomplished in stages; attempts at giant strides often become giant failures. For example, it is poor strategy to try to build an integrated housing project for low- and moderate-income families in a suburban area where discriminatory barriers have hardly been touched. A more realistic strategy would be to first get some pioneer families into the area so that the residents no longer equate a black neighbor with the end of the world, and then to move toward the project.

The difficulty of seeing things from the viewpoint of others, and the tendency to form relationships only with those like oneself, account for the consistent failure of those who believe in open housing to work together. A good example of how this has hurt the cause of integration in the past is the conflict between some of the fair housing activists in Chicago and John Baird, the president of Baird and Warner, a giant real estate firm which sells more used housing than any other company in the United States.

In 1962, John Baird, as president of Chicago's Metropolitan Housing and Planning Council, made front-page news when he publicly supported fair housing legislation — a position he continued to support forcefully even though it was contrary to the view of most of the other real estate people in Chicago. Yet during 1966 there were weekly open housing demonstrations at one of Baird and Warner's suburban offices, including one march in which one hundred clergymen participated. The reason: Baird's sense of justice usually was of no value to blacks going into one of his offices. While Baird had directed his staff to sell to Negroes when the seller was willing, restricted listings were also accepted. In addition, the "open housing" policy of the firm was not followed by many employees.

However, the fair housing people had little understanding of Baird's problems. If he had insisted that customers sell on an unrestricted basis, he would have driven most of those who did not wish to do so to other brokers, accomplishing little in open housing and destroying a business that had taken a century to build. Moreover, the implementation of his internal policies was extremely difficult. Every executive of a large organization has encountered the frustration of not having things done the way he wishes. In Baird's case the situation was made all the more difficult because the racial policy of the firm was in conflict with the position of local real estate boards in which Baird's employees were urged to participate for professional reasons.

Because people did not get together, the victim was progress. With little risk Baird could have done more to help black families, and probably would have done so had the fair housing movement presented ways which he could accept. As it was, Baird took greater risks and more personal abuse for his support of open housing than many of those who picketed his office.

The story of John Baird and the fair housing people in Chicago exemplifies the greatest challenge of all — the need for leadership — leadership which brings together a sufficiently powerful group of those who favor integration to support a program which accomplishes their common goal.

To provide good leadership is like finding one's way out of a complex labyrinth where there are endless opportunities to take a wrong turn. Usually those who are trying to achieve integration operate from too narrow a base. Racial integration does not depend on impressing the liberals as much as winning the moderates. At the same time, a powerful coalition is useless if the price of broad support is an inadequate program. The best approach is to limit objectives to those which can be achieved with available resources, while trying to increase support in order that the objectives can be expanded.

Challenges of leadership also are not met because of the temptation to engage in self-serving actions. Closely related is the lust some men have for power which, far more often than a desire to lead, is what causes men to fight and which, more than the improvement of society, often causes some to seek shifts in power.

A good example of a failure of leadership is the inability of the fair housing movement to provide itself with a national organization capable of giving unification and direction to the battle to achieve integration. The National Committee Against Discrimination in Housing (NCDH), whose membership consists of more than fifty national organizations, should be doing the job. And, for many years after its formation in 1950, NCDH did the best that could be done under the circumstances by using its very limited funds to promote fair housing laws and by encouraging the formation and growth of local fair housing groups. But when racial integration in housing finally took a place on the agenda of the nation, NCDH chose to concentrate more on the opportunity to be self-serving than the challenge to serve the nation.

The major priority of NCDH clearly has been to obtain funding for itself. In seeking contracts and grants the committee functions as a private consulting firm and on occasion has competed for funds with local fair housing organizations in a manner which has appalled the fair housing activists involved.[20]

NCDH is making some contributions to the fair housing effort. By just being there the committee serves to bolster local groups through a national identification. By sponsoring conferences and publishing a newsletter called *Trends*, NCDH serves as a source of information for many fair housing workers. The committee also prods federal agencies into making desirable alterations in policies and recently instituted legal suits against restrictive zoning laws.

But NCDH is doing far less than it could. *Trends* is mainly devoted to publicizing the activities of NCDH and its leaders; consequently, a pressing need continues for better communication of successful techniques and proposals for new programs. Because most of NCDH's staff have not participated directly in fair housing activities, their suggestions on tactics have been deficient in many ways: they overlook the difficulties encountered with enforcement of fair housing laws, the motivation needed for ghetto residents to pioneer white neighborhoods, and the discrepancies between federal guidelines and community practices.

But the basic failure of NCDH has been that it has not as-

277

sumed the role of true leadership: to be the means by which the job gets done by others. NCDH should have developed an overall national strategy for racial integration in such a way that most of NCDH's members and other groups which support racial integration became committed to its execution, a strategy which attempted to use effectively every available resource which could be mustered, a strategy which recognized that success depends not only on programs, but also on achieving basic changes in the values and attitudes of a large part of American society.

While the National Committee Against Discrimination in Housing represents an extreme case where organizational interests have been placed above the basic objectives of the organization, NCDH is only one of countless failures which demonstrate the importance of good leadership.

Another is shown by the irony that the groups who most vigorously oppose efforts to improve conditions for Negroes are the whites who are just above the blacks on the socio-economic totem pole. The common goals which might unite these groups with the Negro are great and, while an alliance might seem to some to be only a dream, it is the type of dream a skillful political leader could make a reality.

Probably the most costly failure of all has been that the federal government has given little more than lip service to a national goal of a racially integrated society. Within the framework of our present tax structure, only Washington can provide the necessary resources.

There are no cheap solutions. The costs of integration in housing cannot be separated from the costs of uplifting the people in the ghettos — a package which will run in the tens of billions of dollars. This is a lot of money. But we do not hesitate to spend eighty billion a year on national defense at a time when the greatest danger to our country is from within. We are an affluent society whose gross national product is increasing more than fifty billion dollars each year, yet we practice a special brand of hypocrisy which causes us to proclaim equal opportunities even though we have not mustered the national will to support with dollars the types of programs which result in equal opportunities. Unfortunately, too few Americans have seriously pondered the alternatives.

The commitment of sufficient resources, however, does not insure success; success also depends upon proper allocation of money and human talents. Unless there is careful management of programs aimed at solving America's race problems, progress will beget problems.

Ghetto enrichment programs tend to increase the black population in the cities. If benefits to poor people living in big-city ghettos are raised and little is done for poor people elsewhere, the migration of blacks to big-city ghettos will increase. Racial segregation will be worse and the ghettos will remain overpopulated, greatly complicating the problem of improving inner-city life.

However, massive programs aimed at integration also pose dangers. If those at the bottom of the black community see the enormous gap which already separates them from the rest of society widen further, they may turn to more desperate tactics. In addition, if integration is carried out too rapidly, the resulting loss of middle-income blacks would make more difficult the job of upgrading those who remained behind.

Thus programs aimed at ghetto enrichment and racial integration require close coordination and control. Indeed, success may well hinge on the ways in which the impact of programs is monitored as the nation attempts to socially engineer its way to a new kind of society. For example, it might be desirable to take a biennial census in critical cities to provide information for such decisions as whether efforts at integration should be increased or decreased, and whether there should be more or less emphasis on specific programs. The success of the Apollo mission to the moon clearly demonstrates the ability of a government agency to plan and coordinate a complex program when backed by a committed nation.

The United States has led the modern world in new concepts of democratic government and in new systems for the manufacture and distribution of goods. Now America is challenged with the task of getting different people to live together as equals.

Some believe that racial integration in housing will never be achieved. Others feel integration will take several generations. Most would say that getting whites and blacks to live together is harder than harnessing nuclear power, or landing men on the moon. But there is no real basis for comparing the challenge of our race problem with our scientific accomplishments, for we have never mustered resources toward the solution of our human problems comparable to those committed to military-scientific goals. That is why today we find "two societies, separate and unequal" — when all has been said and done, almost everything has been said and nothing done. Now the time has come for good wishes and pious platitudes to be replaced by commitments, for priorities to be reordered.

If we do not succeed, we can blame only ourselves.

Notes

Notes for Chapter 1

[1] Arnold Hane, "The Black Rebel Who 'Whitelists' the Olympics," *New York Times*, May 12, 1968.

[2] *Time*, Vol. 56 (December 4, 1950).

[3] William Shakespeare, *The Merchant of Venice*, Act 5, Sc. 1.

[4] *Newsweek*, Vol. 60 (September 3, 1962).

[5] U.S. National Advisory Commission on Civil Disorders. *Report* (Washington, D.C.: U.S. Government Printing Office, 1968).

[6] *Newsweek*, Vol. 70 (November 20, 1967).

[7] U.S. Commission on Civil Rights. *A Time to Listen and A Time to Act* (Washington, D.C.: U.S. Government Printing Office, 1967).

[8] Alvin L. Schorr, *Slums and Social Insecurity* (Washington, D.C.: U.S. Government Printing Office, 1963).

[9] Charles C. Moskos, Jr., "Racial Integration in the Armed Forces," *The American Journal of Sociology*, Vol. 72, No. 2 (September 1966), p. 143.

[10] Gordon W. Allport, *The Nature of Prejudice* (Garden City, N.Y.: Doubleday Anchor Books, 1954); Kenneth B. Clark, *Dark Ghetto* (New York: Harper and Row, 1965); Morton Deutsch and Mary Evans Collins, *Interracial Housing* (Minneapolis: University of Minnesota Press, 1951); Thomas F. Pettigrew, "Racially Separate or Together," *Journal of Social Issues*, Vol. 25, No. 1 (January 1969), pp. 43-69.

[11] Jack W. Brehm and Arthur R. Cohen, *Explorations in Cognitive Dissonance* (New York: John Wiley & Sons, 1962).

[12] Eunice and George Grier, *Privately Developed Interracial Housing* (Berkeley: University of California Press, 1960), p. 195.

[13] Robin W. Williams, Jr., *Strangers Next Door* (New York: Prentice Hall, 1963), pp. 70-71.

Notes for Chapter 2

[1] Report distributed by Pittsburgh Commission on Human Relations.

[2] Charles Abrams, *Forbidden Neighbors* (New York: Harper & Row, 1955), pp. 89, 103.

[3] *House and Home*, Vol. 10 (October 1957).

[4] *New York Times*, June 21, 1965.

[5] *New York Times*, October 7, 1966.

[6] Harry and David Rosen, *But Not Next Door* (New York: Avon Books, 1962).

[7] Davis McEntire, *Residence and Race* (Berkeley: University of California Press, 1960), p. 288.

[8] Nathan Glazer and Davis McEntire, eds., *Housing and Minority Groups* (Berkeley: University of California Press, 1960).

[9] See pages 200 and 201.

[10] Davis McEntire, *Residence and Race*, pp. 204-5.

[11] On page 203 it is pointed out that in the past five years about one tenth of one percent of the black families who moved to white areas encountered acts of terrorism.

[12] Harriette Robinet, "I'm a Mother — Not a Pioneer," *Redbook*, Vol. 130 (February 1968), p. 12.

[13] Only about five of over one hundred sellers surveyed in Buffalo experienced any harassment *after* there was a fair housing law. Fair housing workers in other areas have reported similar experiences to the author.

[14] James A. Tillman, Jr., *The Journal of Intergroup Relations*, Vol. II, No. 2 (Spring 1961).

[15] Robin W. Williams, Jr., *Strangers Next Door* (New York: Prentice-Hall, 1963), p. 326.

[16] Luigi Laurenti, *Property Values and Race* (Berkeley: University of California Press, 1960).

[17] Paul F. Cressey, "The Succession of Cultural Groups in the City of Chicago" (Ph.D. thesis, University of Chicago, 1930).

E. F. Schietinger, "Real Estate Transfers During Negro Invasion, A Case Study" (Master's thesis, University of Chicago, 1948); "Racial Succession and Changing Property Values in Residential Chicago" (Ph.D. thesis, University of Chicago, 1953); "Racial Succession and the Value of Small Residential Properties," *American Sociological Review*, Vol. XVI, No. 6 (December 1951); "Race and Residential Market Values in Chicago," *Land Economics*, Vol. XXX, No. 4 (November 1954).

Thomas L. Gillette, "Santa Fe: A Study of the Effects of Negro Invasion on Property Values" (Master's thesis, University of Kansas City, 1954).

Richard Stewart Wander, "The Influence of Negro Infiltration Upon Real Estate Values" (Master's thesis, Wayne State University, 1953).

Urban League of Portland, *Nonwhite Neighbors and Property Prices in Portland, Oregon* (1956).

[18] Erdman Palmore and John Howe, "Residential Integration and Property Values," *Social Problems*, Vol. 10, No. 1 (Summer 1962), pp. 52-55.

[19] However, note pages 124-126.

[20] Chester Rabkin and William G. Grigsby, *The Demand for Housing in Racially Mixed Areas* (Berkeley: University of California Press, 1960), p. 17.

[21] Brochure of Fair Housing Council of Delaware Valley.

[22] Project Good Neighbor, Chicago, *Fact or Fancy* (1967).

[23] Rapkin and Grigsby, *Demand for Housing*.

[24] Charles M. Barresi, "Residential Invasion and Succession: A Case Study" (Master's thesis, University of Buffalo, 1959).

[25] Gillette, "Santa Fe."

[26] Clarence Senior. *Strangers — then Neighbors* (New York: Freedom Books, 1961), p. 45.

[27] Laurenti, *Property Values and Race*, pp. 234-235.

[28] Paul H. Jacobson, *American Marriage and Divorce* (New York: Holt, Rinehart and Winston, 1959).

[29] "What the White Man Thinks of the Negro Revolt," *Newsweek*, Vol. 62 (October 21, 1963), p. 45.

[30] Albert I. Gordon, *Intermarriage* (Boston: Beacon Press, 1904).

[31] "Confessions of a Blockbuster," *Saturday Evening Post*, Vol. 235 (July 1962), pp. 15-19.

[32] Mildred A. Schwartz, "Trends in White Attitudes Towards Negroes," Report 119 (Chicago: National Opinion Research Center, 1967).

[33] Buffalo *Evening News*, June 14, 1965.

[34] *Look*, Vol. 27 (June 29, 1965).

[35] Angus Campbell and Howard Schuman, *Racial Attitudes in Fifteen American Cities* (Michigan University Institute for Social Research. Survey Research Center).

[36] Arnold M. Rose, "Inconsistencies in Attitudes toward Negro Housing," *Social Problems*, Vol. 8 (Spring 1961), pp. 286-292.

[37] Rapkin and Grigsby, *Demand for Housing*.

[38] John P. Dean and Alex Rose, *Manual of Intergroup Relations* (Chicago: University of Chicago Press, 1955).

Notes for Chapter 3

[1] C. Vann Woodward, *The Strange Career of Jim Crow* (New York: Oxford University Press, 1955), p. 68.

[2] Davis McEntire, *Residence and Race* (Berkeley: University of California Press, 1960), pp. 241-49.

[3] Charles Abrams, *Forbidden Neighbors* (New York: Harper and Bros., 1955).

[4] Nathan Glazer and Davis McEntire (eds.), *Housing and Minority Groups* (Berkeley: University of California Press, 1960), p. 140.

[5] Eunice and George Grier, *Privately Developed Interracial Housing* (Berkeley: University of California Press, 1960).

[6] Society of Friends. American Friends Service Committee, *A Report to the President; AFSC Experience and Recommendations re: Executive order 11063 on Equal Opportunity in Housing* (Philadelphia, 1967).

[7] George and Eunice Grier, *Equality and Beyond* (Chicago: Quadrangle Books, 1966), p. 35; Davis McEntire, *Residence and Race*, pp. 224-47.

[8] *Realtor's Headlines*, June 13, 1966; June 20, 1966; July 18, 1966.

[9] Davis McEntire, *Residence and Race*.

[10] e.g., see McEntire, *Residence and Race*, pp. 241-42; Luigi Laurenti, *Property Values and Race* (Berkeley: University of California Press, 1958), p. 49. Many fair housing groups also have accumulated evidence of Realtors ignoring the desire of a client that a house be sold without discrimination.

[11] "Confessions of a Blockbuster," *Saturday Evening Post*, Vol. 235 (July 1962), pp. 15-19.

[12] Margaret Price, *Neighborhoods* (Atlanta: Southern Regional Council, 1967).

[13] Douglas Connah, Jr., Baltimore *Sun*, January 26, 1969.

[14] Chicago Mayor's Commission on Human Relations, "Selling and Buying Real Estate in a Racially Changing Neighborhood" (Chicago, 1962).

[15] As of this writing the Contract Buyers League, a group of Negroes exploited by such contracts in the Lawndale section of Chicago, have brought a federal court suit against a group of speculators and the lending institutions which cooperated with the speculators. This court action seeks to void the contracts, reduce the price of the houses, and give the Negro families the equity they have paid. The U.S. Department of Justice has joined the case on behalf of the Contract Buyers League.

[16] See pages 102-104 for examples of effective blockbusting action.

[17] H. Swados, "When Black and White Live Together," *New York Times Magazine*, November 13, 1966, p. 47; George Schermer and Arthur J. Levin, *Housing Guide to Equal Opportunity* (Washington: The Potomac Institute, 1968), p. 30.

[18] George Schermer and Arthur Levin, *Housing Guide to Equal Opportunity* (Washington: The Potomac Institute, 1968).

[19] "How Eichler Sells Open Occupancy with No Fuss," *House and Home*, Vol. 25 (February 1964), pp. 132-136.

[20] See pages 276-278.

[21] During this period Sherman worked closely with Baltimore Neighborhoods (a professionally staffed fair housing group) to avoid panic in those areas where his sales were responsible for integrative moves.

[22] Harry and David Rosen, *But Not Next Door* (New York: Astor-Honor, 1962).

Notes for Chapter 4

[1]*Newsletter* of the Leadership Council for Metropolitan Open Communities (Chicago: September 1968).

[2] New York (State) Governor's Committee to Review New York Laws and Procedures in the Area of Human Rights. *Report* (March 1968). The Committee was headed by Eli Whitney Debevoise, a prominent New York City lawyer.

[3]*New York Times*, September 20, 1967.

[4]*Wall Street Journal*, July 5, 1968.

[5] H. H. Hyman and P. B. Sheatsley, "Attitudes Toward Desegregation," *Scientific American*, Vol. 195 (1956), pp. 35-39.

[6] Richard Powell in Denton (ed.), *Race and Property* (Berkeley: Diablo Press, 1964), pp. 21-27.

[7] Survey published by the Chicago Commission on Human Relations.

[8] This experience is summed up most completely by Eugene W. Feingold and Robert J. Harris in an unpublished manuscript.

[9] See pages 170 and 171.

Notes for Chapter 5

[1] While obtaining tax deductibility rules out certain types of political action, such as lobbying and the support of political candidates, the fair housing group can still support legislative goals and disseminate information to win public support for these goals. The general experience of fair housing groups is that tax deductibility improves their ability to raise funds and that the restrictions thereby imposed usually are beyond the scope of activities in which they wish to engage.

[2] See pages 117-118.

[3] TV and radio stations are required to devote a certain amount of time to public service announcements for which there is no charge.

[4] See Chapter 6.

[5] A book which deals extensively with campaigns involving fair housing legislation is Lynn W. Eley and Thomas W. Casstevens (eds.), *The Politics of Fair Housing Legislation* (San Francisco: Chandler Publishing Co., 1968).

[6] Julia Abrahamson, *A Neighborhood Finds Itself* (New York: Harper and Bros., 1959).

[7] Norman M. Bradburn et al., *Integrated Neighbors* (Chicago: Aldine Publishing Co., to be published in 1970).

[8]*New York Times*, January 24, 1965.

[9] Margaret Price, *Neighborhoods*, published by the Southern Regional Council (Atlanta, 1967) cites successful experience of this type in both the Windsor Hills and Ashburton sections of Baltimore.

Notes for Chapter 6

[1]The passages cited in the text are: Malachi 2:10, Ezekiel 47:21-3, Galatians 3:28, Luke 10:28, Matthew 5:47, Luke 10:37, and Matthew 25:40. Other examples include Exodus 23:9, Leviticus 19:33-4, Amos 9:7, Proverbs 14:21, Romans 15:2, and John 2:9.

[2]Jeffrey K. Hadden, *The Gathering Storm in the Churches* (New York: Doubleday & Co., 1969).

[3]Julia Abrahamson, *A Neighborhood Finds Itself* (New York: Harper & Bros., 1959).

[4]*New York Times*, April 10, 1966.

[5]See pages 119-121.

[6]Ernest Q. Campbell and Thomas F. Pettigrew, *Christians in Racial Crisis* (Washington: Public Affairs Press, 1959).

[7]*Detroit News*, August 26, 1967.

[8]For example, James Harvey, who was the national director of the AFSC housing program before becoming director of the Housing Opportunities Council of Metropolitan Washington in 1969, is one of the best-liked and most respected men in the fair housing movement.

[9]George and Eunice Grier, *Equality and Beyond* (Chicago: Quadrangle Books, 1966), p. 76.

[10]A survey by the National Opinion Research Center of the University of Chicago showed the following as the percentages of white interviewees who reported their clergymen had "taken a public stand in favor of more rights for Negroes."

Jewish	75%
Presbyterian, Methodist, Lutheran, United Church and Episcopalian	43-52%
Roman Catholic	38%
Baptists in North	24%
Baptists in South	5%

This work is being published as a monograph in 1970 entitled *Integrated Neighborhoods* by the Aldine Publishing Co.

[11]Harvey Cox, "Ferment in the Churches," *The Nation*, Vol. 201 (October 11, 1965), pp. 216-20, points out that clergymen who have staff jobs, and hence are more insulated from direct lay control, have participated disproportionally in civil rights demonstrations.

[12] e.g., see *New York Times*, August 10, 1969, pp. 1, 64.

Notes for Chapter 7

[1]St. Louis *Globe Democrat*, October 21-22, 1967.

[2]See pages 240 and 241.

[3]Boston *Globe*, July 9, 1969.

Notes for Chapter 8

[1] Data from U.S. Bureau of Census, *County Business Patterns*, presented in report by National Committee Against Discrimination in Housing, *The Impact of Housing Patterns on Job Opportunities* (New York, 1968).

[2] In particular, see Dorothy K. Newman, "The Decentralization of Jobs," *Monthly Labor Review*, Vol. 90 (May 1967), pp. 7-13.

[3] John F. Kain, *The Quarterly Journal of Economics*, Vol. LXXXII, No. 2 (May 1968), pp. 175-197.

[4] Jeanne R. Lowe, "Race, Jobs, and Cities," *Saturday Review*, Vol. 52 (January 1, 1969), pp. 27-30; Louisville *Courier-Journal*, June 29, 1968.

Notes for Chapter 9

[1] Nathan Glazer and Davis McEntire, *Studies in Housing and Minority Groups* (Berkeley: University of California Press, 1960), p. 46.

[2] Glazer and McEntire, *Studies in Housing*, p. 63.

[3] Thomas Fleming, "Take the Hatred Away and You Have Nothing Left," *American Heritage*, Vol. 20, No. 1 (December 1968), p. 74-80.

[4] "Letter from Birmingham Jail," reprinted in *Christian Century*, Vol. 80 (June 12, 1963), pp. 768-69, and in Martin Luther King, *Why We Can't Wait* (New York: Harper & Row, 1964).

[5] For example, see Robin M. Williams, *Strangers Next Door* (New York: Prentice Hall, 1963), pp. 250-251.

[6] Williams, *Strangers Next Door*, p. 247, and personal discussions by the author.

[7] Henry G. Stetler, *Racial Integration in Private Interracial Neighborhoods in Connecticut*, (Hartford: Commission on Civil Rights, 1957).

[8] L. K. Northwood and Ernest A. T. Barth, *Urban Desegregation: Negro Pioneers and their White Neighbors* (Seattle: University of Washington Press, 1965).

[9] Margaret Price, *Neighborhoods* (Atlanta: Southern Regional Council, 1967).

[10] Planners for Equal Opportunity, New York Chapter, *Planning for Open City* (1967).

[11] M. Watkins, "White Skins, Dark Skins, Thin Skins," *New York Times Magazine*, December 3, 1967, p. 127.

[12] Countee Cullen, "Incident," in *Color* (New York: Harper & Bros., 1925).

[13] Angus Campbell and Howard Schuman, *Racial Attitudes in Fifteen American Cities* (Ann Arbor: University of Michigan, Institute for Social Research, Survey Research Center, 1968).

[14] J. L. Hecht, "The Negro in the Suburbs," *The Challenger* (Buffalo, New York), August 1965.

[15] Norman M. Bradburn et al, *Integrated Neighbors* (Chicago: Aldine Publishing Co., to be published in 1970).

[16] William Brink and Louis Harris, *Black and White* (New York: Simon and Schuster, 1967), p. 27.

[17] Statement by Bayard Rustin in *Newsweek,* November 20, 1967, p. 40.

[18] The results of the poll by the Opinion Research Corporation for CBS in mid-1968 were very similar to the University of Michigan study. A 1969 study published in *Newsweek,* June 30, 1969, indicated those with separatist leanings were about 10 percent.

Notes for Chapter 10

[1] George and Eunice Grier, *Equality and Beyond* (Chicago: Quadrangle Books, 1966), p. 77.

[2] See pages 170 and 171.

[3] See page 221.

[4] Nathan Glazer and Davis McEntire (eds.) *Housing and Minority Groups* (Berkeley: University of California Press, 1960), p. 34.

[5] *New South*, Spring 1967.

[6] George Schermer and Arthur J. Levin, *Housing Guide to Equal Opportunity* (Washington: Potomac Institute, 1968), pp. 55-56.

[7] For a discussion of preferential marketing see pages 64 to 66 and 69.

[8] See pages 250 and 251.

[9] See pages 191 and 192.

Notes for Chapter 11

[1] Morton Deutsch and Mary E. Collins, *Interracial Housing* (New York: Russell and Russell, 1968), pp. 97, 98.

[2] See pages 17-20. Also, see Thomas F. Pettigrew, "Racially Separate or Together," *Journal of Social Issues,* Vol. 25, No. 1 (January 1969), pp. 43-69. This article has been reprinted as a pamphlet by the Anti-Defamation League of B'nai B'rith.

[3] Charles C. Moskos, Jr., "Racial Integration in the Armed Forces," *The American Journal of Sociology*, Vol. 72, No. 2 (September 1966), pp. 132-144.

[4] Robin M. Williams, Jr., *Strangers Next Door* (New York: Prentice-Hall, 1963), p. 55.

[5] For example, see the NACCD Report. Also, while some have the illusion that the Negro is following the pattern of other ethnic groups, this is contrary to evidence that the segregation of Negros has increased with time while segregation of immigrants has generally declined. See Stanley Lieberson, *Ethnic Patterns in American Cities* (New York: The Free Press, 1963), pp. 120-132.

[6]U.S. National Advisory Committee on Civil Disorders, *Report* (Washington: U.S. Government Printing Office, 1968).

[7]Anthony Downs, "Alternative Futures for the American Ghetto," *Daedalus*, Fall 1968, pp. 1331-78.

[8]Angus Campbell and Howard Schuman, *Racial Attitudes in Fifteen American Cities* (University of Michigan Institute for Social Research, Survey Research Center, 1968.

[9]For example, see William Brink and Louis Harris, *Black and White* (New York: Simon and Schuster, 1967), p. 43; James Gallagher, "How to Sell Negro Home Buyers," *House and Home*, Vol. 35 (March 1969), p. 28; and summary on page 24 of Pettigrew.

[10]Anthony Downs, "Moving Toward Realistic Housing Goals," *Agenda for the Nation* (Washington: The Brookings Institution, 1968), pp. 141-178.

[11]Survey conducted for the Metropolitan Housing Committe, Rochester, New York by Slade Research Associates, Inc. 1968.

[12]Urban America, with headquarters in Washington, is a nonprofit national-al organization dedicated to the improvement of the American city and includes many large U.S. corporations among its members. The nonprofit housing division of Urban America receives most of its funding from the Ford Foundation and four major Protestant denominations.

[13]Audrey Freedman, "Labor Mobility Projects for the Unemployed," *Monthly Labor Review*, Vol. 91 (June 1968), pp. 56-62.

[14]See pages 219-221.

[15]Peter Rossi, *Why People Move* (New York: The Free Press, 1955).

[16]Nathan Glazer, "The Renewal of Cities," *Scientific American*, Vol. 213 September 1965), pp. 195-203.

[17]According to one calculation, this subsidy for homeowners was 1.7 billion dollars in 1962 just for those whose incomes were in the top 20 percent of the population. See Alvin L. Schorr, "National Community and Housing Policy," *Social Service Review*, Vol. 39 (December 1965), pp. 433-443.

[18]Charles E. Silberman, *Crisis in Black and White* (New York: Random House, 1964).

[19]L. K. Northwood and A. T. Barth, *Urban Desegregation* (Seattle: University of Washington Press, 1965); Study by Kenneth Kaufman, University of Chicago, June 1967, reprinted by the American Friends Service Committee.

[20]For example, in Los Angeles NCDH offered to help Curt Moody, the Executive Director of the Community Relations Conference of Southern California, obtain funds for a proposal for a housing opportunities center. NCDH advised Moody against contacting Michael Mazer, an O.E.O. housing official who was described as unfriendly to this type of program, but Moody, on the basis of other advice, submitted a proposal through Mazer and obtained a $258,000 grant. During this period, NCDH was itself seeking a contract from O.E.O. which it did not get.

289

SLIDING RENT SCALE for PROPOSAL
on pages 269 and 270

Year	Rent charged to tenant $ per month*	Rent for nonprofit corporation to break even, $ per month**	Cumulative loss at end of year in $
1st	100	115	180
2nd	110	118	276
3rd	120	122	300
4th	132	126	228
5th	140	131	120
6th	146	136	0

*Families would have to be financially qualified on the basis of present and projected earnings to meet the increasing payments. Only families who appeared to be permanent residents of the area would be considered.
**This is the amount needed to pay market-rate interest, taxes, maintenance and all administrative costs. The yearly increase represents a forecast of rising taxes and labor costs.